LOST
IN A
ROOM FULL OF DINOSAURS

LOST
IN A
ROOM FULL OF
DINOSAURS

P. J. CHRISTMAN

Highgate Lane Press

Highgate Lane Press

Santa Fe, NM 87501

FIRST PAPERBACK EDITION – December30, 2022

ISBN-13: 979-1-0880-7906-6

WHERE/WHEN WRITTEN: in Tesuque, New Mexico, in 2018

COVER: iStock

PHOTO LAYOUT: by Author

CONTACT: runstats@aol.com

~ THE SETTING ~

It has been called 'The City Different.'

Early in the third millennium there was at least one identifiable unique difference: the USA's highest State Capital repeatedly challenged for the lowest State Capital school system test scores.

Once titled *Ogha Po'oge* (White Shell Water Place) or *La Villa Real de la Santa Fe de San Francisco de Asis* (The Royal City of the Holy Faith of St. Francis of Assisi) the high-elevation metropolis founded in 1610 is now simply Santa Fe. It's plaza rests at 7,000 feet in a State having more than 20 Pueblo, Navajo and Apache, and other tribes with as many glittering casinos as tribal beads and feathers. Probably more residents of *Nuevo* Mexico's capital city speak *Español* than English. The metropolis has few sandstone-colored buildings taller than certain imported deciduous trees; intermittent dehydrating droughts that can last 30 years; arroyos and creek beds so dusty residents and visitors alike can walk or run in them with impunity; a plethora of thirsty plants such as prickly pear cactus and *cholla* offering skillfully protruding spines to avoid being eaten; and enough intermittent solar energy—if its storage can be miniaturized—reigning down upon the mythical high desert destination to power the Earth for geologic eternity. Nearly unlimited sunlight illuminates adobe and stucco during most days. Cold December nights mean supermarket bags with candles in them called *farolitos*. Ten miles outside of town it is dark enough to see almost our entire Milky Way Galaxy.

Not really that different than those from say, Chicago, have been government scandals far more prevalent than water. Maybe a crafty sheriff selling paraphernalia online; a secretary of state gambling with public funds at Native American casinos; a city council-man paving his church's parking lot with government equipment; a departing mayor bequeathing bonuses to city employees without approval of the city council; a Governor respectively offering 'pay-to-play;' or another telling the front desk of the city's tallest hotel to ignore the State leader's entourage's enthusiastic party participants throwing snowballs and beer cans off a late-night balcony. After all, it is still the Wild West.

Another difference has been the Southwestern State's lack of industry and surfeit of poverty. New Mexico usually alternates with Mississippi for citizenry with the lowest per-capita average annual income. For instance, poverty gradually becomes more evident if you drive south down Santa Fe's Agua Fria Boulevard. Culinary celebrations and truck purchases seem cultural imperatives among those whose incomes hover around a minimum wage affording little else.

In this enormous, sunbaked, under-populated realm, schools are not exempt from being different. Most Santa Fe institutions of learning, except those few housing the privileged affluent, find their students unusually bereft of adequate test scores. Tests and national standards often originate from northeastern locales with great edu-cational history, as well as possessing schools attended by far fewer English-as-a-second-language speakers. Santa Fe schools have barely been able to keep the 'Holy Faith' when literacy and math pro-ficiency, by national standards, have been perennially attained by perhaps one in four students. Most enrollees get free breakfasts with lots of sugar retarding concentration, while provided free nutrition-ally balanced lunches including savory cultural offerings of nachos, Frito pie, and enchiladas. Vitamin-and-fiber-packed salads more-often-than-not are ignored, however, while alternating canned with natural fruits offers another potential soporific choice and barrier to attention spans.

Frustration can rear its ugly head among both students and faculty in such underperforming institutions, and not surprisingly, often does. The City Different consistently tries to come up with at-tainable answers. More financial resources, better-educated talented staff, smaller class sizes, and a thirst for knowledge and learning are all part of the equation for success. Yet as everyone knows, education starts with lofty aspirations, goals, and a persistent curiosity more potent than a magic wand...

~ ONE ~

Santa Fe's Coronado Elementary School was a microcosm of a Great Desert State's effort to improve education for those from apartments, *casas* and *casitas* hosting families of limited means. Several third- through fifth-grade classrooms held 26-28, while others between Kindergarten and second grade's even more important formative years contained a more manageable 15-17. Ninety-five percent of the students were Hispanic, with Anglos, Native Americans, Asian- and African Americans, comprising the remaining five percent minorities.

Coronado's Library was high-ceilinged and spacious. Its contents represented paper dinosaurs populating one of the last physical reliquaries of knowledge, sanctuaries providing books that could be felt and touched rather than scrolled through on electronic devices increasingly precluding verbal conversations once considered the mainstay of educated existence.

On that a mid-August day, the Librarian, an aging enthusiast attempting perhaps a seventh career, was energetically delivering his introductory speech to Ms. Sevilla's fifth-grade class. They were unusually quiet. The previous year's boy who disruptively struck plastic bookmarkers against the shelves, and others mentally or behaviorally challenged, had been passed on through graduation to the nearby Cortez Middle School.

When he began speaking, Mr. C scanned mid-August eyes to signal the usual chattering during boisterous arrival could cease.

"You've all heard this before," he said, quieting two giggling girls by focusing upon them, "but think of this Library as two worlds. You are all sitting at tables surrounded by shelves of books. Posters depicting some of those more famous books hover above you. This is the real world," Mr. C gesticulated with his hands. "And what is holding you real citizens in your chairs here?"

A boy with black-rimmed glasses raised his hand and the Librarian motioned to proceed. "Gravity," he replied.

"Gravity," Mr. C nodded. "All part of our real world at the moment."

He paused for effect to survey how many in front of him seemed engaged.

"Yet there are different worlds," he said, pointing to his brain, and then toward the contents throughout the Library, "that can be created through these books, their stories, and your imaginations. Through their pictures, letters and words, these books offer the world of the vicarious. In them you can't see anything but letters, words, photos, and illustrations. But each of us can differently and infinitely further visualize all those abstract markings and photographic contents through a wealth of imaginations."

Antonio Lopez was listening. He was unusually short for a boy of 10 yet was devouring Mr. C's inspiration. A buzzcut of a Denver Bronco was carved into his short hair. His Aeropostale hooded medium sweatshirt enveloped a body that was truly configured for a small. That night Antonio's father, Juan Lopez, diligently would confine himself to emptying wastebaskets, vacuuming carpets, and polishing Argenta High School's linoleum hallways. With his dad working his nocturnal maintenance job, and his mother, Valeria, softly making beds and placing new toiletries and towels in the renovated La Fonda Hotel, Antonio's home life was fleeting. Even though her son's interactions with his father were mainly confined to weekends, Valeria, often while still in uniform, read aloud to Antonio when she returned home from long days and early evenings near the city's plaza. On weekends father and son would shoot baskets at the Genoveva Chàvez Recreation Center. Antonio Lopez was lucky. He had two parents under the same humble apartment's roof, and though both lacked formal educations, each knew its value.

"You can't go to Mexico today," Mr. C continued. "Yet you can visit Mexico using your imagination and books in this *biblioteca*. Or Junie B. Jones is a fictional character," he said, gesturing at a hanging poster illustrated by two (one in Spanish) JBJ book covers as well as text regarding one of Coronado Library's **Authors and Famous People**.

Kids' attention spans were difficult to engage and maintain. *This was the tricky bit*, thought Mr. C. You knew when you had them and when you didn't. Telltale signs that you were losing your student audience were swinging legs, furtive openings of books within reach on tables, surreptitious whispering, and back table listeners reaching for books on nearby shelves. Mr. C knew that information and learning had to be dispensed in limited doses. You needed to create occasional dialogue through questions and answers. Mr. C had never really been good at such interchanges, however. He had a special command of language but found less enjoyable creating dialogue with those who didn't yet possess such expressive capabilities.

"Close that book and put it in the center of the table," he admonished a girl in glasses who quickly complied. Mr. C scanned his audience. "I hope I don't have to go over the rules with fifth graders," he said. "You people only have nine months until you move on to Cortez. And that means you, Carlos: put that book back on the shelf."

Discipline issues were never-ending. Kids were kids, skin colors having little to do with it. While the few Native American Pueblo or Navajo students at Coronado almost invariably were quiet well beyond any stereotyping, the Hispanics and Anglos offered a broad range of behavior from educational complicity to outrageous defiance.

Take Odysseus Ray, for instance. His blond locks flopped down from various points above hatband level. His un-tucked golf shirts and khaki pants further differentiated him from most Latinos. A variety of smirks and aloofness could be expected. And the lad's elbowing and whispering in the Library simply incited others at his table to misbehave. Odysseus leaned across a table, the tops of his shoes defiantly placed upon his chair's back.

"Odysseus," said Mr. C, having stopped his commentary midsentence. "Everyone in the class is paying attention, but your fellow students and I can see that the behavior you were warned about in fourth grade seems to be annoyingly resistant to change. If you would remove your feet from the back of the chair, sit properly with your feet under the table, and further desist from attempting to pass off Kindergarten behavior as entertainment to others, I think all of us would appreciate it."

"Not everyone," Ray muttered under his breath.

"You're right," Mr. C nodded, using his cane to pace in perpendicular across the front of the class. "Not everyone. Certainly, every country, State, city, and class has its school clowns. Those who have difficulty adjusting his or her behavior from beyond that of a five-year-old." Mr. C stopped and looked down at Ray.

"ATTENTION, PLEASE," Principal Penelope Guadalajara's voice suddenly interrupted over the P. A. system. "This is a Shelter in Place. I repeat, you are now to Shelter in Place."

There were several grades of alarm in the Santa Fe Public School system. The loud beeping noise of a fire alarm meant everyone lined up and quickly filed outside. Teachers grabbed emergency red backpacks filled with green and red cards, class rosters, a bottle of water, first aid kit, and a snack bar, and everyone filed out the nearest door and across a parking lot where they were assembled, identified, and counted. Fifteen-minute disruption. Minimal distraction. And almost inevitably, simply a drill.

A Shelter in Place meant a dangerous situation or person of danger could be in the area. The Teachers and students went on with what they were doing. It was merely a warning to be vigilant. In Mr. C's case, he used the interruption to return to his commentary refreshing memories on a few rules and to deliver some first-semester announcements.

"So, at the end of the hour, I shouldn't find any books on top," he said, demonstrating with one hand as a plane above his head and parallel to the floor, "on the floor and tables, or put in the wrong place. As always, remember to use these plastic markers. I'm going to pass them out now to the quietest table."

Oddly enough, even fifth graders still quieted down and held still at their tables. Those called first got their choice of bookmark colors, as important to many as being first in line, climbing on a school bus first, or being called upon to answer a Teacher's question. Status remained important in all facets of life.

Table number two of the four round tables in front was selected. Farther back, shelves and tables between them purposefully were situated like spokes of a wheel for maximum viewing by the Librarian. The fewer places invisible to the Librarian in the room, the fewer opportunities remained for rascals to hide or perform shenanigans.

Four kids began to file toward Mr. C, who sat on the front of his long, round green desk with an array of markers spread out in his hands. Calling one table at a time for markers dramatically helped eliminate mass grabbing, confusion, and eruptions of chatter, the latter noisy behavior a bad way to begin the quiet portion of any class' 'special' in Library.

"Attention, please," Mrs. Guadalajara's voice began again on the intercom. "This is a Lockdown. I repeat, this is now a Lockdown."

A series of white charts hanging near the door detailed what was to transpire during a Shelter in Place or a Lockdown. The latter was considered far more serious. Its invocation meant some dangerous person(s), or situation might be in the school area or even building. A heightened sense of security had arisen.

Mr. C always wondered what he would do should such a real situation unfold. Would the perpetrator or perps be students with automatic weapons? Or more like what once happened while he was substituting at an elementary school closer to the center of Santa Fe? Then a man who shot his wife had begun wandering in the neighborhood adjacent to the school. Everyone had hovered under tables for two hours before being released back to a 'normal' school day.

"O. K. kids, I want you all to sit quietly in front of the book-shelves or under the rectangular tables in the back of the Library. Ab-so-lute-ly no talking!"

Mr. C grabbed some previously cut black paper from under his desk. Using his cane to enable smooth walking with his weak left leg, he stumped to the front door, reached outside, and locked it with his key. Then he closed it again. "Iván, can you bring me the scotch tape dispenser from off my desk?"

Blacked-out windows on the front and emergency doors, drawn Venetian blinds in the window nooks and floor-to-ceiling windows in the back reading corner, as well as turned-off lights, were intended to prevent intruders from knowing who, if anyone, was inside a school room. Yet Mr. C wondered why anyone in a rage wouldn't just break the front door window, reach in, turn the handle inside, and begin his (hadn't it always been enraged or despondent males?) spree. There was a sense of inevitability about such an incident. Throughout the USA countless school shootings made it apparent that going to school was somewhat like playing Russian roulette. A bullet could be in any chamber. It wasn't so much *if* it would happen, but rather when and where. School shootings now seemed almost as commonplace as school playground injuries. Police, ambulances, hospitalizations, sobbing students and relatives, all now were considered part of educational reality and a part of contemplations and expectations. No school could claim exemption.

"I hear voices," said Mr. C as he was taping black paper covering the window of the emergency exit door at the back of the Library. Just 20 feet away in the corner and from under certain rectangular tables he could hear giggling or whispering. "NO TALKING OR NOISE! I don't want to hear another voice."

Suddenly the cavern became as silent as a tomb.

Mr. C quietly walked through the room, contemplating whether this was the usual periodic drill, or the more potentially unfolding lethal disaster. Each interruption was a mystery. Much like every time you got behind the wheel of a car, the possibility loomed that either you or a fellow vehicle operator would make a mistake leading to accident, injury, or death. In elementary schools the likelihood that a 5- to 10-year-old would obtain a gun or automatic weapon to bring to school was remote. Most incidents involved high school students. But then there were Sandy Hook, Columbine, *et al*, to dispel any thoughts of elementary exemption.

A fusillade of knocking suddenly came from one of the two oak-and-glass-paneled front doors.

"Help, help," came a desperate tiny voice from outside the entrance.

The repeated jerking of the door handle could be heard.

"Shhhh," whispered Mr. C, "nobody move!"

"Let me in! Let me in!" the youthful voice pleaded along with more desperate knocking.

Total silence.

Later it would become evident that one Teacher had relented and admitted a student thought to be returning from the restroom. But Mr. C was aware that *under no circumstances or pleading* was anyone to be readmitted during Lockdown. It could be a ruse. A device used by the perp forcing a student to help him or her gain admission.

The chances were very high that this was merely a drill. But what if it weren't? Could Mr. C hide around the corner from the door and then disarm anyone breaking the glass to begin spraying his Library kids with bullets? Would he be shot? How many kids would die? It was his opinion that any town or city fielding a police department mandate gun owners to secure their weapons in gun clubs, to be withdrawn outside the city for hunting or skeet shooting. Strict gun control. No weapons in town. Definitely no automatic weapons. If citizens were legally denied tanks, flamethrowers, bazookas, and other weaponry normally possessed by the military, why not automatic weapons? He knew there was a restaurant owner in Pie Town, New Mexico, wearing a holster and pistol while serving patrons. But that small village had no police, and his pistol might be argued to be a deterrent to those contemplating doing 'a runner' with their bill. Then there was the often-overlooked factoid in the Manchester book on the killing of President Kennedy. In the year of his assassination, there were more murders in Dallas than in all of England, the latter at that time having strict gun control.

Minutes later the kids in the Library were getting restless. Sitting quietly when you have boundless energy is a short-lived discipline.

"You are released from Lockdown," unexpectedly came Principal Guadalajara's voice from the intercom. "Thank you for your cooperation."

Mr. C flipped all the lights back on and began removing black paper from one of the front door windows. He felt a feeling of relief, while most of his students felt the end of an exciting diversion. Within minutes he had his fifth graders back in their chairs.

"Why do we have these drills?" he asked generically while surveying faces slowly refocusing on the return to safe reality.

"Carolina?" Mr. C pointed at a student with a raised hand.

"Because someone might come in the school with a gun."

"Indeed," nodded Mr. C. "But whether an alarm has been raised due to a gun, automatic weapons, knife, suspicious package, or any other potential danger and violence, we all need to know what our best alternatives are to remain safe."

This time no one was harmed, and no violence occurred. But the minds of many Coronado students and Teachers alike at the time and later that evening while lying in bed, reading, texting, or cruising the internet, would wonder if a seemingly innocuous drill could ever suddenly devolve into the far more volatile fear, countless injuries, and needless deaths.

~ TWO ~

"Papa lay down on his stomach and looked up at her, patting the ground next to him," fifth grade Teacher Amanda Sevilla read aloud to her class from Pam Muñoz Ryan's *Esperanza Rising*. "Esperanza smoothed her dress and knelt down, their faces looking at each other.

"She giggled.

"'Shhh,' he said. 'You can only feel the Earth's heartbeat when you are still and quiet.'"

Ms. Sevilla looked up into her students' faces, surprised that all, as in the book, were being still and quiet.

"She swallowed her laughter and after a moment said, 'I can't hear it, Papi.'

"'*Aguántate tantito y la fruta caerá en tu mano,*' he said. 'Wait a little while and the fruit will fall into your hand.'"

Like Mr. C in the Library, Amanda Sevilla believed in the value of reading aloud to her students. In her 25 years of teaching, she had long ago learned the lesson that although you couldn't inspire or rescue every student, you could help to enlighten those willing to attempt the journey. Waiting well beyond a little while ensured that more would be inspired, encouraged, incited, excited, enthused and even rescued. The imperfection of being unable to educate every student to level or to becoming exceptional did make teaching difficult. A secret was accepting incomplete success. Having twenty-eight 10-year-old's with various energies, learning capabilities, and behavioral tendencies meant almost an infinite number of challenges, successes, and failures. Yet fifth-grade Teacher Amanda was up to it, year after year dealing with the endless variety of humanity in her charge.

Ms. Sevilla certainly exuded confidence. She was a big woman, but wore her clothing and carried herself with style, conviction, and moderate flair. Sometimes her long wavy hair fell below her shoulders and other times it remained bound up, further conveying an unpredictable variety of appearances to a woman of great depth of knowledge and expertise.

Yet there was an ongoing balancing act to be maintained, one requiring continuous combinations of enforcing discipline with constantly conjuring creativity to keep students engaged. These efforts involved serious limitations of how much stress each Teacher, administrator and student could take. And since alcohol and drugs often had long-term health effects and were generally not a factor for elementary school students, many Teachers and administrators, as well as students, turned to eating as a lesser evil in providing some relief. In Coronado Elementary School, which students were 95 percent Hispanic and almost all coming from homes considered below the poverty level, cultural prerogatives often involved celebratory bouts of eating. Weekly and sometimes daily celebrations included cupcakes for birthdays, pizzas for fund-raising contest winners, and potlucks provided by parents and students with limited means to put food on their own tables.

As Ms. Sevilla continued her reading, toward the back of the room one of many daily distractions or disruptions was beginning. Odysseus, the Anglo student needing merely the slightest provocation to become disruptive, grabbed a paper flower Christian De Leon had been making and threw it at him.

"Hey, Piñata Brain," Ray taunted the undersized De Leon.

De Leon's face had despondency written all over it. Not only had he been identified by an IEP (Individualized Education Program) as being a Special Education student of limited mental capabilities, his compact stature and quiet nature made him a natural target for bullying. He said nothing in return, his eyes looking downward.

"Hey, *stupido*, I'm talking to you," Ray further hectored.

Sitting in front by the Smart Board, Ms. Sevilla had become aware of the altercation.

"Odysseus," she began, making eye contact with him, "the class is finding it difficult to pay attention to our reading while rude insinuations are erupting from the back of the room. Christian is one of many trying to listen attentively. Do you think you are making a good decision in disturbing all those interested in learning?"

Many faces turned around to see Ray leaning back with his arms crossed. He quickly leaned forward and then back, sweeping a long lock of blond hair out of his face while trying to regain his habitually arrogant composure. "I wasn't doing anything!" he whined, re-crossing his arms.

"Mr. Ray, adding a lie to unacceptable behavior is a further poor decision." Ms. Sevilla looked away from Christian's tormentor and surveyed the class. "Please pardon Mr. Ray. Eventually he will learn that being the class clown not only is disruptive, but also leads to the loss of class privileges, as well as his fellow students' respect. Odysseus hasn't recognized this shortcoming yet, but we are all hopeful he will come to his senses. Mr. Ray," she paused for effect while again raising *Esperanza Rising* to signal a return to reading, "see me outside after I'm finished reading."

Christian De Leon repeatedly folded and unfolded his paper flower, gazing down upon it as if it were a bottle into which a genie had disappeared. There was a bruise upon his chin, caused the previous evening at his grandmother's house where he lived. His father,

Cisco, just released from prison, came for a visit to his son. *Abuela*, as Christian called her since she lacked fluency in English, was in the kitchen, purposefully avoiding any more contact with her son in law. Cisco had been drinking. Christian's father intermittently berated his undersized son as being weak and afraid to stand up for himself. De Leon had learned much earlier that responding in any way to his father's derogatory remarks simply invited further verbal abuse or even occasional beatings. Just then backing away from a torrent of being belittled, the timid Special Ed student slid upon a beer can, fell, and clipped his chin on the arm of his grandmother's wooden rocking chair.

Now back in class, while Ms. Sevilla resumed her reading aloud, Christian still feared further trouble from Odysseus. Maybe the reprisal wouldn't come in class, but most certainly would during lunch or on the playground. The Special Ed student wondered if he would ever grow big enough, or gain enough confidence, to defend himself.

Sitting beside De Leon, Odysseus was doing his best to appear immune to the coming confrontation with Ms. Sevilla. His cockiness partially derived from a brother at Argenta High School. His older brother was nearly six feet and under 140 pounds. Where some would play basketball, Ray's brother Courtney chose to smoke pot to try and be accepted by several influential gangbangers in his neighborhood. The two brothers lived with their parents in a relatively new two-story stucco house off tree-lined Meadows Boulevard. The houses each sat on minimal property in a neighborhood unusually affluent for the south side. Ms. Sevilla and others were mystified by Odysseus' erratic behavior. His father, who worked at Cottonwood Mesa National Laboratories as a physicist, intentionally located his family in a heavily Hispanic district. He wanted his children to grow up with less prejudice about skin color than he had in Lake Forest, Illinois. The boys' mother had graduated *summa cum laude* in English from Lake Forest College. The pedigree was there. Yet both the offspring were growing up recalcitrant, perhaps wishing to project a different image, one from which few might detect their family's affluent and educated background.

Later in that second hour, Ms. Sevilla asked her students to write a page on the major focus of *Esperanza Rising* and to draw a picture to illustrate their thoughts. Quietly she walked among them, encouraging as she went. When she reached Odysseus, she discreetly pointed to the classroom door. "Outside," she said in a soft but firm voice.

"Look at me," she commanded to the blond boy still posturing and fidgeting outside the classroom door. "What is it that prevents you from using that gifted intelligence of yours in a positive way?"

Odysseus shifted from one foot to the other. He put his hands in his pockets, still not making eye contact.

"Look at me. And take your hands out of pockets and answer my question."

Ray was like many bullies and clowns. When confronted by someone of authority and confidence, he could be intimidated. "I...I don't know."

"Well, I'm rapidly tiring of your lack of respect for me, your fellow students, and for the work you should be doing," said Ms. Sevilla. Although Odysseus was one of her taller students, she was still able to look down a couple of inches at his eyes, both of which were still trying to remain evasive. "Mr. C and I have already written conduct reports on you; Principal Guadalajara has spoken to you in her office; and I have talked at length with your mother. Your home life is far better than that of most of our students. What, exactly is your problem?"

"No excuse, ma'am," he answered in calm fashion. Ms. Sevilla knew that one of his favorite tricks was acceding to almost anything requested, the young impetuous lad having no plans whatsoever to implement any such behavioral improvement or change for the better.

"You will join my Tutorial group after school today until 4:30," said Ms. Sevilla, arms akimbo.

"But my mom's picking me up after school," he protested.

"Call her from the office during lunch. You will not be leaving school today until 4:30."

~ THREE ~

Lunchtime in Santa Fe elementary schools generally was chaotic, noise levels coming close to reaching that of a moderate prison riot. Educational assistants stood with arms folded to call tables one by one to go through the nearby food lines. Others passed out utensils or squirted catsup on potatoes or mustard on sandwiches. The early-lunch Kindergarteners, first and second graders behaved somewhat like a hungry flock of sheep: while they were supposed to remain in lines or at tables, two or three students might take up gamboling throughout the gymnasium serving as a cafeteria. Pieces of rolls or chicken occasionally served as missiles to liven up the somewhat deafening cacophony. Raised supervisory voices did little to calm the excitable diners.

"Ms. Katarina, Diego threw a piece of chicken at Maribel," informed a quiet girl wearing glasses.

Educational assistant Katarina Española was tall and convincing when she so chose. She quickly walked over to Diego, who was enjoying his recent novelty with a group of second-grade boys.

"Diego, why are you throwing food in the cafeteria?"

Another girl began pulling on Katarina's hand. "Emmanuel threw his roll, too,"

"Alright, alright," Ms. Española said, still looking reprovingly at Diego. "Should another bit of food find its way somewhere besides your mouth, you will be missing recess." She turned and began using a more moderate voice. "And let's have no more bad behavior, or tattling."

A table of Kinders were going through one of two food lines, the little ones' arms reaching not much higher than their trays sliding along metal guides. Surgical-gloved hands placed chicken nuggets into one groove of a tray, while mashed potatoes and gravy were plopped and ladled into another. Most of the tikes skipped the self-serve salad and carrot sticks but used tongs to pick up one or more orange quarters. Chocolate or plain milk made up the remainder of calories necessary for sustaining growth as well as energy to bound round the playground for 15 to 20 minutes.

"No running!" the EA passing out forks yelled at a careening first grader. "And if I see you kicking Cornelia again, you can say good-bye to playground time," she admonished a young boy thinking he had successfully gotten away with one.

Mr. C came stumping into the makeshift cafeteria, soon reaching in his wallet to cough up the $3.75. Sometimes you got substantial value for it, and sometimes not. But chicken, mashed potatoes and gravy, along with the salad and fruit, was better for him than two burgers and fries from McD's or a $5-6 submarine sandwich from a dispensary a half mile down Airport Road.

"Hi, Mr. C...Hi, Mr. C!" rang out tiny voices looking up at him from expectant faces waiting for the Teacher to get served ahead of them.

"How 're you doing?" he smiled as he waited for a tray. Mr. C had a special place for Kindergarteners. The five-year-old's were malleable and held so much enthusiasm when first able to go to school. They felt grown up being away from home for the first time. Being recognized by a Teacher or adult made their day, just as their smiles and energy gave Mr. C a similar feeling of belonging.

Ms. Española and a couple more EA's led lines of first- and second-grade classes onto the playground. Once kids cleared the two doors, however, they spread out, streaking and yelling as if in a mid-nineteenth century gold rush. An array of dervishes raced for their favorite mode of movement, swings, hanging tire, slides, overhead bars, playhouse, or basketball courts. A soccer ball bounced off one boy's head, the contact only temporarily distracting him. Four more kids leaped and skirmished for three sitting positions on the hanging tire. A boy hung from one of the parallel bars while another tugged on his pants.

Kids need to play, there's no doubt about it. The thinking process for Teachers was that the more they tired themselves running round the playground and kicking and throwing balls, the less restive their charges would be for the classroom. Sitting in one place for any considerable time was anathema to most children. Movements with no patterns and with impetuous whimsicality were the perpetual gods and goddesses of the unleashed.

The swings were always unpredictable. Kids kicked their legs and leaned back to gain height. They were no longer permitted to go 'round the world' like kids did in the twentieth century. But nearby adult supervisors, particularly substitute Teachers and volunteers, mentally bridled as their kids swung higher and higher. Kids were also climbers, seeing almost any towering slide, bars, or suspended moving walkways as simple challenges for the fearless. Falls were inevitable and the EAs and Teachers constantly hoped for a session with no serious injury. Cuts and bruises were as much a part of the playground as dirt and wood chips. Band-aids and ice were repeated antidotes. Crying was also part of the playground, kids spontaneously pushing, shoving, hitting, and tripping each other. There were age, agility, speed, strength, and other considerations. Social hierarchies also developed among classes and genders as students skirmished for attention, power, and domination.

The Kinders had their own fenced playground, with falls, escapes, bathroom visits and other possibilities requiring stricter supervision. Kinders pushed each other and fell more, hit each other more, said 'bad words' to each other without even knowing the meaning of such expletives, and often began crying with the slightest provocation. Yet they often held hands while gamboling, helped each other up off the wood chips, shared utensils in the sandbox and displayed other impromptu acts of kindness. And while there was some bullying, they partially remained protected by isolation for their introductory year in school.

Back on the main playground a group of second-grade boys was attempting to play basketball. Shooting was difficult. Their small hands had trouble gripping the large, rubberized balls, and tossing them high enough to even reach the rim was beyond the capabilities of some. Still, they tried, hoping eventually to play with fourth and fifth graders on vaunted school teams.

Suddenly a girl dropped from the overheard bars. She landed in the wood chips, and a nearby substitute Teacher ran over to her, worried that the girl had seriously injured herself. The child looked herself over, brushed some chips off her blouse and jeans, and jumped to her feet. Where an adult might have sprained an ankle or bruised a hip, the girl was pliant enough simply to begin climbing the stairs back to the bars.

"Are you alright?" the substitute Teacher nervously inquired.

The girl nodded as she went, her black patent ballet shoes taking one rung at a time.

It was somewhat like Doc's dispensary in the movie Mr. Roberts. After a couple of questions, the slackers were told to take two aspirin and get back to duty. For kids, their eyes often searched those of the supervisor to determine how much they were hurt or should be crying. "You'll be alright," was usually the response permitting them to save face without tears. "Go inside and wash your hand off in the bathroom sink. If it still hurts later, you can get some ice from the nurse."

Katarina Española had seen it all. Only in her mid 30s, the Kindergarten educational assistant was married to a cable television installer and had raised two girls, now in Argenta High School. Katarina was bilingual yet her daughters year by year were losing some of their Spanish fluency. It was the way of all immigrants. Successive generations eagerly wanted to speak English and be a part of the land of the free. Many of their parents or grandparents would speak to them in Spanish at home. In elementary school the recent student arrivals from Mexico and other Spanish-speaking countries addressed each other in Spanish, as well, particularly when being overheard by a nearby Teacher. Still, there remained the constant desire to adapt to their English-language surroundings. Even Spanish-speaking Kinders gravitated toward the English non-fiction corner of the Library, where picture books with dinosaurs, insects and ocean mammals including whales were sought out with enthusiasm. Even surprisingly docile kids felt a unique attraction to sharks. There seemed to be a natural thrill in gazing into the mouth of a creature with perhaps 50 teeth and hundreds behind to replace them should they break. Photos of open mouths sent terror into the hearts of some. It didn't matter that they could read little if any of the text. Even five-year-old's wished to be enveloped by books of the country their parents or other relatives had adopted.

"Do *not* push her!" Española admonished a first-grade boy with a bowl haircut. "Come over here!"

The boy, perhaps lucky to reach his supervisor's waist in height, diffidently came over to the tall EA.

"Eduardo, *que paso*! What are you doing pushing Esmeralda?" She put her hand on the child's shoulder and bent over to make eye contact. "I want you to go over and sit against the wall for the rest of recess! It's time you learned to behave."

Some might call an elementary school survival of the fittest. The tall, the big, the strong, and the heavy usually prevailed over the smart, quiet, thin, short, and little. That would all change slowly in the progression toward and into adult life. Yet confidence and safety were won or lost on such playground battlefields. Just like small puppies, kids physically grabbed or hit each other playfully. Yet often they overdid it, differing from adults in not knowing when enough was enough. Esmeralda was brushing tears from her eyes.

"Don't worry, Esme," said Katarina. "Eduardo didn't mean to push you down. He just made a bad decision. I want you to go back with your friends climbing through the playhouse."

"Ms. Katarina, Ms. Katarina!" another boy gasped as he tripped and fell while running toward her. "Carmela took our soccer ball and won't give it back!"

Carmela was unusually large for a first grader. Somebody was feeding her too well at home, and her food-stained sweatshirt came up short in reaching her torn pleated skirt. This shortcoming defied clothing regulations, but so did logoed sweatshirts, stylistically torn jeans, sleeveless shirts, sequined toreador pants, shoes with rings of flashing lights illuminated by foot movement, or any other novel attention getters. Dress codes were mere guidelines rarely enforced. Kids could be sent to the nurse's office to get alternative dress. This was especially necessary for five- and six-year-olds too timid to ask to go to the bathroom and wetting their pants. Yet dress was an evolutionary process inspired by celebrities, athletes, and trend-setting kids. Some kids wore sneakers and torn jeans. Others broke conformity with logoed sweatshirts. Lipstick and makeup were no-no's, but little girls felt grown up when defying any such restrictions.

~ FOUR ~

Antonio Lopez sat quietly at one end of a burgundy couch purchased used at Savers. At the other end, his mother held a book in her hand. It was a Saturday morning in September when Valeria Corazon Lopez had the day off from her chambermaid duties. Whenever she got the chance, Valeria read aloud to her son. Several of his friends had telephoned to ask him to join them skateboarding. Toni said he would have to see them in the mall parking lot later. He didn't elaborate as to why: they would have scoffed had he told them the reason. Their perception of his mother reading aloud to her son was no better than his having to clean his room on Saturday morning. Several of them had older brothers either cruising in high-strut monster trucks or low-rider, skinny-windowed sedans with small wheels. His friends' parents often began weekend backyard parties around noon, their kids, after token efforts at some chores, scattering from home as quickly as possible.

"Can you read *La Llorona* again?" Toni asked his mom.

"Of course," she replied, crossing a jeans-covered leg and turning back to the beginning of the story. "I'll read in English and Spanish," she said. "English is our second language and Juan and I are both working hard to improve our English so we can eventually get U.S. citizenship." She was turning pages as she talked, pausing briefly to push her reading glasses higher on the bridge of her nose. "Since you are in a bi-lingual class, you want to be proficient in both languages. *Hablamos Ingles y Español."*

Toni looked at the royal blue watch his mom had purchased for him for $15 at Walmart. The band displayed a high-tech robotic appearance with mottled blue-and-black camouflage. Very few kids wore watches, but Toni felt wearing the device as important to his fifth-grade image as spinning through phone pictures or possessing a Dallas Cowboys sweatshirt was to certain classmates.

Juan walked in as Valeria was reading aloud. Below his jeans could be glimpsed purple Doc Martens, an expense he had justified to his wife after skipping two Isotopes games with his friends in Albuquerque the previous summer. Juan and Valeria both took pride in their appearances, their clothing consuming more of their two monthly wages than their incomings justified. Valeria regularly had guests leave generous tips upon their bed or dresser, while Juan often picked up overtime at Argenta when other maintenance people took sick or comp days. Toni's father had been washing the truck outside their Meadows apartment but was careful to avoid getting soaked by the hose.

"Toni, what say we take Pancho (the name of his truck) up to the Bradbury Museum after your mamá finishes reading aloud to you?"

"Sure," answered Antonio. "A kid whose father works at Cottonwood Mesa was telling us about Little Boy and Fat Man at lunch. He said they have life-size models of the two bombs in the Bradbury Science Museum."

Coming down the long descent of Opera Hill, people in cars, on bikes, or running could see a hundred miles across yellow and red mesas to San Antonio Mountain. Juan Lopez had done the drive many times when he had worked in maintenance at Cottonwood Mesa National Laboratories. The job paid a lot better than his current job at Argenta, but then there had been the WIPP barrel incident in the underground storage of hazardous waste 26 miles from Carlsbad. No one really knew how the mishap occurred. Yet it was rumored that two or three managers of waste disposal were dismissed over the incident, the mistake acting as a catalyst for improved safety at the labs. When anyone worked with plutonium or other highly fissile uranium offshoots, there was always the problem of disposing of the materials. It wasn't like just throwing trash in a dumpster. Substances remained highly radioactive and dangerous for many years. The rare storage mistake proved a difficult dilemma. Yet someone or several upon whose watch the oversight occurred had to take the fall. Juan didn't directly lose his job, but he felt too many at different levels of the Labs had been blamed tacitly if not directly, and that eventually many more would be transferred or let go. He quit after securing his Argenta High School maintenance job.

Even with the mishap in mind, and although the town's population and the Labs' main physicists, engineers and managers primarily were Anglo, Juan Lopez knew and loved the Cottonwood Mesa town and laboratories. The town was said to include among the highest per capita income averages of any city in the United States. Most of the Hispanics working there, often in maintenance, food service and laundry, lived in Española, south Santa Fe, or other affordable areas. Still, Lopez loved the wide streets, Ashley Pond, and being left alone to do his work with minimal micromanaging and periodic direction. Racism reared its ugly head almost everywhere. Yet he felt CMNL's population did a pretty good job of sublimating skin colors and racial stereotyping to the ability to perform in any job. You either did the job or not, whether Hispanic, Hungarian, African American, Jewish, or any other category sometimes unwittingly inviting prejudice.

He wanted his son to be exposed to the town and laboratories deriving their existences and fame from weaponry design. The controversy remained as to whether nuking two Japanese cities and several hundred thousand people shortened the war and saved many more lives. Yet Lopez knew few of the residents below and beyond the Cottonwood Mesa community were aware of the many projects such as the likes of cable drag reduction research, Accelerating Low-Cost Plasma Heating and Assembly (ALPHA), coreboot, and systems biology modeling (q-bio), ultimately having civilian applications affecting the futures of millions in positive ways. Weaponry design still remained a central focus, yet so were hundreds of other civilian research and development projects.

They drove up the alternate truck route to the Pajarito Plateau and town. This avoided some two-lane hairpin turns on the original, now paved but once dirt, road having led to the mid-20th century's Cottonwood Mesa Ranch School. In 1943 the U.S. government had taken over most of the School's buildings and cabins to create the National Laboratories. After cruising by Ashley Pond (also the name of the man having founded the Ranch School), the pair stopped at the Blue Window for lunch, each of them ordering a burger with fries or coleslaw and iced tea.

A half hour later the pair entered the Bradbury Science Museum, a vivid two- and three-dimensional experience highlighting the focus of CMNL in World War II, as well as other projects. Lopez felt it important his son was taught the history of the laboratories and the town, as well. The ethics of bomb making certainly remained in question. Yet Cottonwood Mesa was a unique town and set of laboratories still largely possessing their own destinies.

Antonio stood looking up at mockups of the world's first two atomic bomb prototypes. It was hard for him to imagine the power that derived from nuclear fission and fusion. It seemed impossible a metal container could hold a small amount of plutonium that could then be bombarded simultaneously by particles causing an implosion and explosion of immense destructive powers. Either on-line or in the *Santa Fe New Mexican* or *Reporter*, Antonio sometimes read parts of news stories speculating on what North Korea might do with its missiles and nuclear weapons. Among the speculations on potential targets were Boulder's front-range, high-tech concentration; Silicon Valley; a Metropolitan Seattle area containing Amazon, Apple, Boeing, Microsoft, Starbucks, and other cutting-edge U.S. high-tech, industrial, or other companies; and the Cottonwood Mesa National Laboratories. Antonio couldn't read all the words in the articles, but he could understand the thrust of the stories meant his father and he were climbing into a town housing research and development laboratories in which innovative scientific experimentation evolved in unique creative atmospheres.

"Pop, how could such small metal devices create such huge explosions?" Antonio asked.

"The atom is a strange component of everything on this planet," his father answered in a room full of devices developed during the twentieth century. "Once complex atoms like those of uranium are converted into more fissile forms like U235 and plutonium, bombarding atoms with even small particles releases a disproportionate amount of energy." As he related this to his son, Juan was proud his readings and discussions when working at the labs had given him the English vocabulary to explain such phenomena. If he could explain things like this, he knew, eventually passing his citizenship test should be a mere formality as easy as making Frito pie.

"Dad," Toni asked while looking back and forth at the large replicas, "did you have to serve in the U.S. military?"

Juan felt his son's question was freighted with larger questions, but he replied as if he had been asked if he finished high school. "No, son, I didn't have to. Your mom and I arrived from Chihuahua as visitors. Later we obtained green cards. I never had the obligations of a citizen, plus we were both 30 when we got here."

Juan believed strongly in the freedoms and opportunities offered by his adopted country. Had he been able, he would have liked to serve in Iraq or to help out any arm of the U. S. military however he could. Juan Lopez felt a worldwide ban on all nuclear weapons would be best. Yet as the two of them studied three-dimensional real devices, exhibits, photos, and text passages mounted on the walls of the museum, the complexity of war weaponry as well as civilian scientific developments became evermore apparent.

"Do you think our dropping atomic bombs on Japan was the right thing to do?" Antonio asked his father.

"Shortening the war against either the Japanese or the Germans certainly remains an argument in favor of the bombs. To me, chemical weapons, flamethrowers, grenades, artillery shells and even bullets still kill people. I think we would be better off further exploring diplomatic solutions rather than bombing or killing people with differing economic, religious, military, geographic or other beliefs. It would be great if democracy and fairness thrived in all parts of the world. But we're a long way from any such peaceful conditions everywhere. I think the U. S. would be better served using trillions of dollars on infrastructure such as highways and high-speed rails rather than military devices and lives going up in smoke in places like Iraq and Afghanistan."

On a Saturday the two had to share the science museum with quite a few others. Still, Antonio remained in his own cloud, totally absorbed in the exhibits and video documentaries on display or available in the theater, defense, history, research, and tech lab rooms.

"The bombs seem like bigger versions of school shootings," Toni commented to his father after a short documentary on the development of the labs and Manhattan Project. "Kids fight with their fists, throw things at each other, pull each other's hair, and kick each other. Some kids can't control their tempers. When I get mad, I just use my voice. I never feel like hitting anyone. And it's hard to understand why certain students get mad enough to shoot other kids. Why do countries attack each other with bombs and bullets?"

Antonio's father felt the question too broad to answer in a short form. But he also believed it important to respond to his son in a way that identified violence as a last resort. "Lots of reasons, son, almost all of them unreasonable. When one country takes some of another's land is one reason. Another might be one country wanting other countries' resources, like petroleum or natural gas. Greed often fuels economic and political decisions. Poverty, jealousy, and the desire for more power incite others. But you're right. Words are the most powerful tool we have to avoid violence."

As they turned into the Research Gallery, Antonio gravitated toward the description of a project converting algae to energy.

"The non-defense and civilian projects are pretty much anonymous to the general public," Juan told his son. "This room and its contents are much like what goes on in many of the laboratories here. Quiet surroundings, people with glasses examining test results, computer animations, chemical reactions, and many other research projects having nothing to do with defense or weaponry, but rather having civilian applications. You know how you have 'aps' on your cell phone. Well, these projects are far more intricate applications involving improvements to conditions on our planet."

"Yo, Toni," a voice suddenly came from nearby.

Antonio and his father both looked at what appeared to be a boy about Toni's age and perhaps his father.

"Oh, hi, Odysseus," Toni said in a manner conveying to his father a certain uncharacteristic diffidence.

Juan Lopez's son recognized the cocky Anglo kid with a contemporary haircut sporting shaved sides and hanging blond forelocks. He was standing with one leg cocked, his father in a navy-blue sports jacket, white shirt, and striped tie above pressed khaki pants.

The pair couldn't appear more different to either Lopez. Odysseus Ray was an intermittently angry kid in Toni's fifth-grade class known for his bragging and arrogance; the man with him, a stingy-brim straw hat cocked to one side like Robert Oppenheimer wore in some of the Bradbury photos and books Toni had seen, appeared conservative enough to be unrelated. The Hispanic classmate knew the taller Anglo kid's father was an engineer or physicist at CMNL, but somehow figured the father might wear Hawaiian shirts or tattered jeans to work. How could such a wild kid like Odysseus come from a family with a father wearing a striped tie?

Odysseus touched knuckles with Toni.

"Hi, I'm Penn Ray," Odysseus' father said, extending a hand toward Juan Lopez.

It was one of those awkward moments where two people unlikely to see each other again feel compelled to feign interest in their encounter, all because their sons are acquainted with one another.

"Dad works at the labs," Odysseus said to Antonio as if confiding in him. "He's a physicist working on secret stuff—"

"Oh, come on, Odie, don't start bragging about me again," Penn said, nervously looking at both Juan and Toni. "I'm just a man doing a job at the Labs."

"Yah, but it's secret stuff," Odysseus said.

His father ignored him. "Do you work at the Labs?" he asked Juan.

Toni's father smiled. "Used to," he replied. "I'm now working in maintenance at Argenta High School."

Juan was one of the few people in what had formerly been known as janitorial services who not only took pride in his work, but also felt no shame or inferiority in working with his hands far more than with his brain.

Penn Ray was of a similar mind. Although having a doctorate in nuclear engineering from Cal Tech and an undergraduate degree in physics from Harvard, he didn't suffer from a superiority complex.

The CMNL physicist knew a quick innocuous comment of some sort was necessary to avoid appearing condescending.

"I painted houses for a year after four years of college and almost made it a career," he smiled, hoping his reply was appropriate to dismiss any awkwardness.

"Come on, dad," Antonio said, lightly poking his dad's arm with an elbow. "Mom will kill you if you don't help her with the yard work some this afternoon."

Penn Ray was relieved his son's friend had cut any trading of banalities short. Juan Lopez seemed to be a confident, levelheaded guy, but in New Mexico the physicist had repeatedly encountered some sort of undeserved humility from Hispanics. He felt the whole racial tension thing to be difficult to overcome. Physicist Ray tried to avoid any sort of preconceptions based on skin colors or formal education. He had met brilliant scientists with little college, or from institutions of lesser repute. And he had also met amazingly articulate tradesmen and high school graduates, informed from self-motivated reading, travel and life experience. Pre-judging someone based on lack of formal education, skin color or religion was a behavioral intolerance Penn Ray had long ago learned to avoid.

"Sorry dad," Antonio said after they had cruised the art shop now occupying some of the Fuller Lodge a couple blocks up Central Street.

It was a short walk to the Cottonwood Mesa History Museum, another building once an integral part of the Ranch School. The city seemed a quiet town, with wide streets, no trash or homeless lying about, and few people on the sidewalks. Toni tried to imagine what it had been like in 1942, with kids in scout uniforms, dirt roads, eventually replaced by ramshackle buildings and highly secret activities carried on nearby.

"Did you ever know about Odysseus' father when you worked at the Laboratories, dad?"

"*Mi hijo*, the buildings I cleaned mainly housed civilian projects. I didn't have the security clearance necessary to go into some of the weaponry development buildings. Plus, to physicists such as Mr. Ray, we were invisible. Everyone in weaponry knew keeping his or her mouth shut was more important than being friendly to anyone you didn't know. Talking about almost any job at the Labs is a good way to lose it."

Inside the History Museum, the former Ranch School's Guest House, Toni stopped to peruse the many books depicting the WW II era as well as contemporary related topics. The museum stood at the top of Bathtub Row, so named because of containing bathtubs other 1940s housing lacked. Oppenheimer, Bethe, and other physicists once called the log cottages home.

Just across the street Odysseus and his dad were awkwardly strolling around Ashley Pond. Penn was doing his best to encourage interest from his son, both in the work he felt to be important at the Labs, and in their relationship, which he perceived to be anything but intimate. Penn felt even his most persistent efforts did nothing to make the two closer. Odysseus seemed to idolize his older brother Courtney, both sons currently doing their best to be different from their father. They seemed ashamed rather than pleased with his scientific as well as financial success.

Odysseus' mind kept drifting to skateboarding with his friends. His father desperately wanted the pair to become close. He knew that. Yet there was no way Odysseus was going to follow in the footsteps of a father he always felt to be nothing more than a suburban bread winner. He felt his father had a limited meaning of the word 'fun.' He loved golf and football; Odysseus had no talent for any sport, wishing he could spend more time snowboarding up at Ski Santa Fe. And then there was his mother: all she could talk about were her book and bridge clubs.

"Some really bright minds have lived upon this mesa," Penn said, hoping to encourage some interest.

"I know, dad," Odysseus answered with a hint of annoyance. "You told me before." He threw a stone into the pond. "This town is so white bread and predictable. Everyone's a physicist, engineer, or highly trained college grad of one thing or another. There's nothing to do here, unless you want to read books or listen to someone drone on about the history. I'd go nuts if we had to live up here."

"I know, son, I know. That's why we live in Santa Fe. And I agree about the town's population. It's pretty conservative. I just wish you could develop a little more interest in what I do up here." Penn nervously adjusted his hat, understanding how little his son cared about his work.

Odysseus threw another stone he had picked up in the pond. "It's not your job, dad. I know it's challenging and you love it. It's the whole life that our family has to be a part of. I don't want to play golf. I don't want to belong to the country club. I don't want to go to church. I'm surprised we even live on the south side of Santa Fe rather than in the northeast quadrant."

The pair walked on in silence before completing a circuit of the pond.

As a contrast, Antonio Lopez idolized J. Robert Oppenheimer, hoping that someday his own mind and analytical skills would further develop into those as inquisitive as physicist Richard Feynman's had been. While browsing the History Museum's bookshelves Toni came across a book by Meloy called *The Last Cheater's Waltz*. It was one of many encounters too difficult for a fifth grader. But the Coronado student hoped, again, that eventually devouring such books would simply become infusions of enjoyment.

Juan and his son strolled down Bathtub Row to what once had been Hans Bethe's house. Toni was disappointed while being toured through the cottage by an informative volunteer. Apparently one recent winter the pipes had frozen and broken, new wood flooring now giving the residence a contemporary rather than 40s look. It was also disappointing that Oppenheimer's house next door was not yet open to the public. An elderly woman had lived there for many years and understandably was accorded permanent residency until she chose to leave or died.

"I've got a lot of work to do if I want to be able to be able to read all these books on the history of Cottonwood Mesa," Toni said quietly. "I mean, during that one documentary, I felt like I was right there."

"There's no substitute for the real world, Toni," his father said. "*Pero*, books, magazines, online news services, films and videos help us to experience and rethink the past."

~ FIVE ~

The stream of Kindergarteners was steady. They had hands behind their backs, educational assistant Katarina Española acting as a shepherdess. Each one looked up at the tall Librarian attired in a parti-colored red-and-black lumberjack shirt and jeans. His black leather belt's silver buckle, end tip, and belt loops glistened under the florescent lighting.

"Sit crisscross on the carpet in the corner," Mr. C told the somewhat awestruck five-year-old's.

Minutes later he carried his hammered metal container of plastic bookmarks and several books to the group sitting quietly in the Library's far reading corner. The carpeted area was nestled between various bookshelves and closed venetian blinds, the windows only occasionally admitting the light of day and glimpses of the distant Jemez Mountains. Mr. C felt creating a magic environment of books imperative for students and adults of all ages. Sunlight made reading easier; but artificial light illuminated a different unique environment of the vicarious.

He set down his can of markers and squeezed his books beside him on the antique armchair. He scanned the rows of kids to make eye contact, each of the apprehensive children now quieting down and stopping their fidgeting.

"Welcome to the Library," he began, knowing many of the

Kindergarteners in front of him were only recent arrivals from Chihuahua and other points south. "*Hay estan muchos libros magnificos en la biblioteca.*" Mr. C knew only some rudimentary Spanish yet felt it important for his new charges to hear at least a little of their first language. He signaled to Katarina, who had drawn up a chair behind the kids, and in English requested she translate his instructions in Spanish to them. He knew five-year-old's were sponges, absorbing quickly almost anything in terms of behavioral nuance and language. Some had been to pre-school. Within the year most of them would be able to comprehend an increasing vocabulary of their second language.

"First, why are we here?" he asked the expectant faces gazing up at him.

"Reading," said a boy without being recognized.

"You are right," Mr. C nodded, "but just like in your class, when you want to say something, you have to raise your hand." The Librarian raised his hand above his head. "You are here to learn to find books that interest you, and to make all kinds of fun discoveries in them. Right now, most of you won't be able to read much of the texts in these books. You can only look at the pictures. But with the help of your Teachers, by next year you will be reading."

"Excuse me," Mr. C. interrupted himself, gazing at a boy with some of his breakfast chocolate milk staining the front of his shirt. "What is your name?"

The boy quit giggling and poking the boy next to him also stifling giggles. "Javier," he answered with the J pronounced as an H.

"Well, Javier, do you think it's a good idea to be poking your friend and laughing while I'm talking to your class?"

The boy shook his head.

"*Mira,*" Mr. C said quietly but firmly, duplicating the request or command, 'Look,' used in English. He gazed at the boy, who now realized he was the center of 13 others' attentions. "One of the first things everyone needs to learn in school is to make good decisions. Paying attention is always a smart decision to make. Do you understand me?"

The boy nodded, looking down at the floor.

"Who can tell me what two of the most important rules are?"

A girl with blond bangs waved her hand wildly. Mr. C. pointed at her and nodded.

"No talking."

"That's definitely one." He then lowered his voice to a whisper. "In the Library we always have to be quiet." he said, putting a finger up in front of his lips. "If you have to say something to your friend or neighbor, *use your whisper voice.*"

Another boy with a bowl haircut and black-rimmed glasses raised his hand.

"No running," he said, after being recognized, "and no fighting."

Mr. C nodded. "Those definitely are two more important rules. You are here to read quietly," he continued softly. He then lifted the markers container and pulled one out.

"Now, what's this," he asked, holding up a long red plastic marker. "Who can tell me what it's used for?"

Several hands shot up and Mr. C pointed at a girl in the first row. She had flowered barrettes holding back freshly shampooed locks, and her miniature crisscrossed legs and navy-blue dress looked too small for the head smiling up at Mr. C.

"It's a marker," she replied.

Next Mr. C showed the kids how a plastic bookmark is inserted in place of a book they remove to take to a table to read. They were instructed to take no more than one book at a time, to search for books alone rather than in groups (difficult for Kinders, he knew), and to be careful to put the books back correctly, not upside down or backwards, and with the spine out. He asked for volunteers to pretend to be taking books to tables and then putting them back. He also showed them colored dots on the books to signal various reading levels. "Your colors are orange or *naranja* for Kinder, or some of you might also want to look at yellow or *amarillo*, for first graders."

He was aware that using the Library properly, as well as the ability to sit still for substantial periods of time, were long processes, requiring patience on both the Librarian's and the students' parts. Books were like disguised treasures. Some you could judge by their covers, but most contained remarkable hidden contents to be discovered by persistent sleuths. Five-year-old's could examine the photos. But only with time and effort could most Kindergarteners comprehend their abstract offerings challenging reading skills and imaginations.

"O.K. now I'm going to look for the quietist kids to pass out the markers," he said. "No squirming," he warned several boys scooching up. "You two," he pointed, "move back to where you were."

"One, two, three," he said, pointing sequentially to each of three kids in the first row. He spread the bookmarks out in front of each one in turn, one of them ruminating on which color she wanted.

Fifteen minutes later there was a certain din in the room. Five-year-old's not only had boundless energy, but also could for the most part only talk about books rather than read them. Paging through picture books meant one exciting discovery after the next, enthusiasm to be shared, particularly with Disney books showing princesses, animals, and evil sorts. Many of the kids moved immediately to the alternate far back corner, the entire wall shelves filled with English non-fiction books in numerical order by Dewey Decimal System topic. It mattered little that the colored dots on the books were mainly third-grade light green, fourth-grade red, or fifth-grade dark blue: the books in the back corner offered a cornucopia of exotic animal photos, from land and ocean mammals to insects and dinosaurs, and their favorites, sharks.

"Mr. C, where do I find dinosaurs?" a child only as tall as his thigh asked.

The younger the children, the more questions Teachers and Librarians had to answer. Sometimes three and four asked all at once, the trick being to point out the error to those interrupting another child's question because of one thought to be more important.

"I'll show you," he answered, several other kids having overheard joining in the search party. Mr. C pointed out picture books on a middle shelf they could reach. "Remember to use the stools and step ladders to reach the higher shelves," he told them.

"Mr. C," a little girl said after tugging on his sleeve, "Roberto was running."

"Which one is Roberto?" he asked, looking around at kids examining books at tables, on the window seats, or pulling books off shelves randomly.

"He's hiding behind that shelf," she pointed.

Mr. C peeked round one side, just glimpsing the sleeve of a boy disappearing at the other end of a rolling two-sided set of shelves. "Excuse me!" he said loudly, making eye contact with the child trying to avoid contact. "No running in the Library!" He walked up to the boy, disappointed to have his location discovered, and squatted down. "Now Roberto," he began quietly, "what did we just talk about? This is school now and there are rules. Do we run in the Library?"

Roberto shook his head 'no.'

"O.K. then. You've got two minutes to find a book and take it to a table." He hadn't told the Kindergarteners of his policy of students sitting every other seat, two to a round table with four chairs, and three at a rectangular table with six chairs. It was hard enough just to keep them seated, let alone by themselves and without talking. Generally, Kindergarteners were always moving and/or chattering. They were one step up from whirling dervishes. Running was the fastest way to get between two points. By first grade they had to settle in and obey the rules. Meanwhile Kindergarteners were granted a year's pardon, a nine-month introductory period during which all but one English-speaking class were not able to check out books. Five-year-old's lose things easily, and even the class that was able to check books out had to put them in a transportable plastic bin. They could only read them in class and could not take them home.

Fortunately, this was Mr. C's sixth year as the school Librarian. He had initially obtained the job as a long-term substitute. The offer had come in the central office, from a University of Michigan graduate after the two had bonded over a discussion on college football. Later when he started in the Library it became patently obvious that an imposing fifty-something-year-old woman from central office had been placed at a computer near him for covert observation. Even though he had a four-year history of substitute teaching, including nine weeks as the head of special education at another school, there were always apprehensions about a single male in his 60s being around little children. Mr. C didn't mind, as he felt he had nothing to hide. He found only adult women sexually attractive. Fortunately, his gray-haired female monitor, ostensibly over several weeks working on a school project of some sort, discerned that the aging bibliophile could be trusted in the Library. Over time in every school, however, there were altercations.

Mr. C had just completed the reading aloud of *La Llorona* (the Weeping Woman), considered a classic Hispanic fairy tale about a married woman who drowns her children in a river when she discovers her husband's unfaithfulness.

"I found that story you read aloud to that third-grade class inappropriate," she chided.

"How so?" asked Mr. C.

"Well, there's womanizing, drinking and violence, and I don't think those are appropriate subjects for kids eight years old."

Mr. C knitted his brows for a moment. He restrained himself from denoting that many of his kids witnessed violence, drinking, and even unexpected guests in their homes. "Well, what about Little Red Riding Hood, in which the wolf eats a grandmother?"

The woman shuffled some papers on her desk before responding, a clear signal to Mr. C that certainly many violent fairy tales in English made her points difficult to defend.

"That's different. It's a wolf rather than a woman who's violent. And there's no sexual innuendo."

"Not even by the wolf in the forest or bedroom?" He felt he had additional ammunition, should he need it, in Hansel and Gretel. How would she respond regarding two children who are lured into a house by a cannibalistic witch, who wants to burn them alive?

Anyway, the conversation went downhill from there, and Mr. C agreed she should discuss the matter with the Principal. The music Teacher who sometimes acted as assistant Principal at that time commented, "I don't think she understands our culture."

Meanwhile in the Library during the Kinder class a month earlier, Mr. C had just guided another two students to find picture books on fairy princesses. He was cutting across between shelves to check on some running kids in the K-2 bookshelves area, when he heard crying.

"What happened?" he asked a sobbing boy with his hands in front of his eyes.

Several girls began to converge upon them.

"Javier pushed Christopher down," a girl told him.

Alright, alright, I'll talk to Javier in a minute," he said, motioning for Christopher to follow him to a nearby rectangular table. The two sat down.

"Are you alright?" Mr. C asked Christopher.

Kinders seemed to find humiliation worse than any other negative occurrence. Christopher put his head down on his arms spread out on the table. He was still crying, probably less hurt than humiliated.

"He hit his head," said another girl having seen him fall.

Mr. C glanced down at the boy's hair and could see nothing unusual.

"Christopher, are you O.K.?" Mr. C repeated. "Do you need some ice for your head?"

Still nothing.

Mr. C glanced at Katarina, and she rolled her eyes.

"Alright, let's let him rest for a while," Mr. C said to the others clustering around. "And where's Javier?" The Culprit appeared from behind the stacks and diffidently approached.

"Why did you push Christopher?" Mr. C asked, standing up and looking down at the small, disruptive boy.

Javier shrugged his shoulders.

"I want you to go sit in the chair by my desk and stay there until your Teacher arrives at the end of the hour."

Later that night Mr. C contemplated his handling of the whole scenario. Kinders pushed, shoved, and hit one another, fell down, and careened round the Library with regularity. Such disruptive behavior occasionally spilled over into later grades, as well, but over time most learned the various consequences of being sequestered at the front desk, sitting with their heads down, skipping recess, conduct reports, and other consequences. Socially behaving in a quiet manner was an acquired taste for most. Mr. C likened the process to horses getting used to harnesses and saddles. Many young students had to be weaned from violent and or disruptive behavior. It was clear Javier might take longer than most to learn how to behave in an acceptable manner. There was no telling what his home life was like. He wasn't designated as a special education student. Still, it was amazing how defiant certain children three feet tall and under-50 pounds could be. With a history of observing many such incidents from previous years' Kindergarteners, Mr. C hadn't bothered to report the incident to Javier's Teacher. The assistant, Katarina Española, seemed to take the incident in stride, as well. However, the contretemps would prove to be one of many career-disturbing oversights Teachers and their assistants make.

Two days later Mr. C was summoned to Principal Penelope Guadalajara's office.

When he arrived, she waved him in. Mr. C knew her as one of those rare individuals in a position of power who neither micromanaged nor lorded her superiority over her Teachers and students. Kindness was an attribute, and even her morning announcements had a ring of enthusiasm and encouragement to all.

She was tapping the keys of her computer as if finishing off an e-mail. Mr. C's previous discussions with her, over potential book purchases, suggested overhanging Library posters, behavioral issues, and other topics, had always been amicable. It had been rare when Mrs. Guadalajara denied any of his requests, and even rarer that she received his book purchase requests with other than unbridled encouragement.

She turned from her computer and placed her hands one on top of the other upon her desk. To Mr. C the gesture connoted a seriousness he hoped to avoid.

"Mr. Connelly, I wanted to talk about what happened in the Library between Christopher and Javier," she said.

Mr. C waited patiently, having noticed that the usual salutation of 'Mr. C' or 'Christopher' (his first name) was formalized into Mr. Connelly. This did not augur well.

"I understand Javier pushed Christopher down," she continued. "Can you tell me what happened?"

This was crucial, Mr. C felt. The fact that the Principal had summoned him to her office signaled the gravity of the matter. Yet his conscience was clear on how the matter had been handled.

"Well, as you probably know, Javier apparently pushed Christopher down and Chris hit his head. I didn't see the incident. He was crying but didn't seem to be hurt badly to either Ms. Española or myself. As a consequence, I had Javier sit in a chair at my desk for the rest of the hour. I told the other kids to let Christopher rest for a while. He then seemed to be O. K."

"This morning his parents came to see me," she said, glancing up from what looked like some notes she had made. "They said Christopher had a substantial lump on his head, and that you had done nothing about his condition."

Mr. C gathered himself, still feeling he had done the right thing.

"I didn't actually see him hit his head and I didn't notice any swelling. However, I did talk to Javier and others to get his and their renditions of the incident. And I repeatedly asked Christopher if he needed to see the nurse or to apply some ice to his head. He didn't respond."

It was only then, that Mr. C recalled what could be a redeeming factor. "Do you have the video from that day?" he asked, gaining some assurance that a camera in the Library might have recorded at least parts of the incident.

Many might feel that the obtrusive Library camera, placed high on the wall opposite his desk, might constitute an invasion of privacy. There were only two classroom locations in the school having cameras: the small gym and the Library. Both had male instructors. Yet Mr. C welcomed the recording device, installed after he had begun his first year as a long-term substitute paraprofessional Librarian. He felt he had nothing to hide and that there might possibly come a time when the camera could exonerate him, providing contrary evidence, should there be any questionable report of incorrect behavior.

Mrs. Guadalajara nodded, turning to her computer screen. "Yes, I do," she replied, beginning to use the cursor to select the correct period. "It was the 10-11 period, right?"

"Right," Mr. C replied. "If you can advance the video about 20 minutes in, I think the incident would have happened right about then."

The Principal turned the Apple screen so they both could see it and Mr. C leaned in.

"I sat Javier down and talked to him," Mr. C said. "I think the camera angle and the shelves will have prevented recording the actual push and fall—there it is!" he interrupted himself, pointing to the screen.

Mrs. Guadalajara had been high speeding the video, when suddenly in the distance Mr. C had been seen taking a seat along the side of a rectangular table. She backed up the video and let it roll at normal speed. Mr. C felt a sigh of relief as he noticed Christopher take the end seat near him, put his head down, and to begin crying. Javier could already be seen sitting on a chair in the foreground near the Librarian's desk.

"You can see me talking to Christopher and his lack of response. I try to avoid touching any student, so I didn't try to push his hair aside to check if there was any swelling or blood. But I did ask him if he was O. K. I thought it a good idea if we waited awhile to see if he recovered, before determining he might need a visit to the nurse. You will see in several minutes, and after several kids talked to him, that he got up and went back to looking at books."

Principal Guadalajara was greatly relieved. Over time Mr. C had proven reliable, trustworthy, respected, imaginative, inventive, and an inspirational reader. She knew Mr. C could have retired by now. But he hadn't. And he had shown himself and his Library to be an inspiration, without any formal Library science degree. As she gazed across the desk, she was also glad that the video demonstrated that he had made a substantial effort to check on Christopher's wellbeing. Sometimes explaining Teachers' behaviors to parents and relatives proved to be one of the most difficult parts of her job.

She looked at his lumberjack shirt and a few always slightly askew locks of hair. He wore it long and several years ago she had told him the style suited him. He now looked a bit apprehensive, as anyone would be in his situation.

"I'm glad to say you did all the right things," she said, smiling slightly for the first time. "Fortunately, I can report to the parents that our Librarian made the correct responses, given the situation and outcome. I wouldn't worry about it any further."

As Mr. C caned his way back down the linoleum halls to his Library, he was relieved. Yet there was still some apprehension. In contemporary litigious American society, parents in the Santa Fe school district periodically sued over poignant and occasionally flimsy provocations. He could only hope there wouldn't be a lawsuit. During his ten years in Santa Fe, the district had avoided legal imbroglios when a Teacher was almost killed by a flying car door after a parent floored his vehicle through a pickup zone, and another possible financial dilemma when a third grader broke his arm while playing basketball. Minor to serious disasters, far more prevalent than school shootings, could occur at almost any time. This time Mr. C had been saved from possible suspension, termination, and becoming an unwitting victim of a potential lawsuit. Some would have decried the Big Brother Watching in the Library. But Mr. C had been saved by one of several omnipresent cameras.

~ SIX ~

One of the fifth graders from another class threw a lump of play dough that hit Christian De Leon on the head. There were about 30 kids on the after-school bus ferrying them to an area known as The Elms Gardens. Christian was aware that kids took advantage of his lack of confidence regularly. Christian the Dimwit. Christian the Simpleton. Christian who never fights back.

The inequities of life found throughout the world, in like fashion affected many adults and children living on the south side of Santa Fe. For most elementary and middle school students there was to be no Desert Academy or Santa Fe Prep, no Harvard law school, and no vacation in Europe. Many would be lucky to finish Argenta High School, fortunate to move up from common laborer to trades-man, from maid to house-cleaning supervisor, and happy to make an annual car trip to Mexico during the Christmas (now Winter) holidays. In a vast democratic country that allowed perhaps one-tenth of one percent of its population to amass forty percent of its wealth, poverty remained commonplace throughout both rural and urban areas. This meant school children's parents and relatives often working two or three jobs, paying minimum wages or less, to make ends meet. There was little time for disciplining and inspiring their children. There was little money to buy the food, clothing, and amusements of the wealthy. Survival became the primary focus.

Earlier that week Christian's father had been released from the Penitentiary of New Mexico south of Santa Fe. Several years earlier the student's mother had died of alcoholism, while Christian's *abuela*, Maria, was doing her best to instill some sort of purpose and enthusiasm in her grandson. His grandmother did what she could. Yet many times Christian had taken several steps backwards emotionally and intellectually after enduring verbal and physical abuse by his father. Chris had learned to become deferential, hesitant, slow to react, patient, quiet and circumspect. What once had been a vibrant child, over his formative years had become an almost speechless hermit, beaten down mentally and physically.

On the bus Christian De Leon didn't even allow himself to turn around. Doing anything in response to the missile-strike humiliation would merely invite further abuse. The meek fifth grader pretended nothing at all had happened.

"Hey Dolt De Leon," a kid well behind him yelled.

Many tried to ignore any such insults, aware of the differences in ages, strength, power, size, and mental acuity leaving some kids weak targets by the older, more imposing bullies, braggarts, show-offs, and posers. Several girls in front of the row of boys taunting Christian looked down at the colorful backpacks on their laps. Even though two of them were taller than the boys, none wished to provoke a change of target from the three behind them. Of that trio, only one was a true bully. As in many school situations, the other two felt they needed to join in to avoid becoming targets themselves, or to be considered wimps. In school as in life, pecking orders developed and were often desperately maintained.

Christian could only hope his stop came soon. If he could just get off the bus, relief would come when he escaped the disparaging remarks hurled from the departing bus windows. Unfortunately, Airport Road was long enough to almost replicate a feeling of trying to survive the Bataan march.

"Hey, fat boy," the kid with a backwards baseball cap said even louder as he poked a girl's shoulder in front of him for emphasis. "Iguana got your tongue?"

Once again Christian ignored the taunt. He could see out the front window of the bus that his turnoff was coming. He prayed he'd be able to jump off and escape this latest torture.

"Hey, you two back there," the bus driver said while glancing in the rearview mirror at the guilty parties. "Knock it off, or you'll be getting off the bus early." The driver with the porkpie hat was normally a gentle soul. Kids knew the usually soft-spoken man with arms like cottonwood trunks, however, could be incited to transform into a no-nonsense type of guy to be avoided.

This time Christian was lucky. The big yellow-and-black student delivery service vehicle rolled to a stop at his corner without further incident. He bounded off the bus, the usual taunts from the windows not forthcoming.

His grandmother's house was not far around the corner, set in a neighborhood with barking dogs, torn chain link fences, cracked stucco, and in some back yards, dead vehicles without wheels. Christian anticipated the sanctuary of *abuela*'s modest stucco house. The front door had scuffmarks on it, and slightly bent wrought-iron trellises supported a sagging front *portale*. Inside, a faded armchair with one arm's stuffing chewed loose by a dog sat uninvitingly. Yet it was home, and as Christian turned the loose brass doorknob, he felt a sensation of relief.

As he walked through the door, however, the first thing he saw was a man slumped on the low sofa against one wall. The man had a Dos Equis lager in his hand, held aloft between sips as he watched an ESPN show on the upcoming World Cup soccer in Russia. Mentally, Chris bridled as he dropped his Batman backpack on the floor near the door. It was his father.

"Thought I'd make one more quick visit, kid," the scarred-faced man said, smiling like someone receiving an unwanted Christmas gift from a great aunt. "Don't worry. I'm leaving for El Paso tomorrow. Got a deal cooking down there." His father took a swig of Mexican beer, then turned back to his son. "Learn anything today at Coronado?" he asked with an inflection signaling disparagement.

Christian nodded, knowing his father would scoff at any positive response.

"What kind of answer is that? You must have learned something today."

"I did," answered his son, unsure how he should respond.

"Well?"

Chris paused as he considered his answer. He now regretted having left his backpack by the door. Somehow, he might have retrieved some books to divert the incipient attack. "Well, Ms. Sevilla read aloud to us from a biography of Frida Kahlo."

His father popped breath through his lips in disdain. "Frida Kahlo," he scoffed. "Wasn't she that Mexican painter who looked like a guy in drag? And married to that muralist 20 years older than her?"

These were treacherous waters for Christian. His father could be easily provoked, and when he was drinking almost any type of response might annoy him. There was no telling how many beers he had had.

"She did have a mustache," Chris offered in what he thought might placate his father, "but she was an amazing painter." As soon as he had added the positive element of his answer, he regretted it.

"Amazingly self-indulgent!" his dad roared. "She painted herself over and over again, and how is that going to help you on your testing, anyway?"

Chris realized the futility of continuing, but no response at all would undoubtedly further cast him as a wimp in his father's eyes.

"Are you going to live here?" the son meekly asked to try and divert his father's building animosity.

"No way! Your grandmother drives me crazy," he said, jumping to his feet. "I'm going to El Paso today."

Christian was afraid of saying almost anything further. Adding encouragement to his father's trip to El Paso might annoy him; trying to get him to stay in Santa Fe might infuriate him even more. The boy kept his head down as he went to retrieve his backpack.

"See, that's typical of you, kid," his father said, rising to his feet. "You're afraid of the kids at school, you don't play sports, and your grandmother says you've been put into a special category for the weak and stupid."

Chris tried to avoid any further confrontation by walking toward his room.

"Where're you going!" his father yelled. "I'm talking to you!" His father grabbed him roughly by the shoulder. "Act like a man, not like a wimp!" he added, whacking him across the top of his head.

Cisco De Leon bore no resemblance to the eponymous surnamed explorer of Florida. His head had been shaved during incarceration and his arms displayed a panoply of tattoos ranging from a snake winding around a cross, to his name in script, to photographic imagery of the devil with a halo. Years of drugs and alcohol not only had deteriorated his mental capacity for rational thinking but had also reduced his demeanor to that of a temperamental bull with several *varas* in his *morrillo*. The parolee's life had gone downhill after he had long ago dropped out of high school and fallen in with a motley crew of gangbangers.

"Alright," his father said, slamming his beer can down on a stained coffee table. "I'm outta here. I'm tired of my kid being a wimp, I'm tired of this town, and I'm headed south to do the only thing I can do for a reasonable amount of cash: a drug delivery."

Two hours later Christian could barely eat his dinner. His grandmother had made his favorite green chili enchiladas with *calabacitas*, but he had lost his appetite. At first, he had been relieved to see his father take off in the old beat-up Ford truck. But as mean-spirited as his *papá* was, he was still somewhat of a protector when he was around. Cisco inevitably belittled his son, yet he could also strike fear into any of the boys in the neighborhood bothering his weak offspring.

Christian ate a few bites of each dish, the fragrance of the Hatch green chilis one of the *casa's* most delectable distractions. Food provided pleasures even people with few means could enjoy. Christian had never known a home with new furniture or appliances. They had moved a lot before and after his father had gone to jail. His mom's drinking twice got them evicted when she yelled at his father for his constant torrent of complaints and abuse.

At least the 10-year-old had his own room. On the walls were a poster of Harry Potter and another of a famous Diego Rivera painting. Christian took sustenance in the ever-present workers in Rivera's works. They never had it easy and neither did most of the kids he knew. He wondered if he would ever amount to anything in life. His lack of reading and mathematics skills seemed insurmountable. Yet maybe there could be something he could achieve creatively.

There was a knocking at the front door. Because his *abuela* had retired to her room to watch television, he yelled: "I'll get it."

Twice in the past the knocking had brought ICE or prison officials. And they usually came around the dinner hour when they felt there would be a better chance of an adult being at home. The last time he had been out to dinner was when his mother was still alive. Then they had entered through the metal door leading to the bar in the back of P.C.'s, a south side Mexican restaurant. Because his grandmother was a citizen and got some money for her arthritic disability and limp, she treated that last night. Six months later his mother was dead, and father was in prison.

When Christian opened the door, he was startled. Standing before him appeared what resembled a fairy queen in a Disney book or movie. Her long, jet-black hair was held in place by a sparkling tiara. Chris wasn't sure, but the green stones in the glistening crown catching the last light of sunset looked like emeralds he had glimpsed in one of his favorite Library books on gems and precious stones. He could barely divert his gaze from the sparkling tiara to smooth teak-colored skin framed by her glistening dark locks. He had never seen dark hair with that dazzling sheen. Ivory teeth bore a smile between lips of emerald color as well. A wonderful fragrance of flowers drifted by him. Chris was wondering if he had fallen asleep and was dreaming.

"Hi," was all he could say.

"Hello, she replied, gently holding up a wand with a diamond-covered star tip in a friendly gesture. "My name is Emerald Star."

The first thought to cross Chris' mind was that she was canvassing the neighborhood for some charity. They both stood there without speaking further. Then suddenly the sunset was gone, and a thousand stars sparkled above them on an all-black canvas. It was if any light from surrounding homes had evaporated.

"It's magic," Christian blurted, not knowing how to respond to the dramatic sky above them.

"Yes," she answered with an even brighter smile. "It is."

Chris glanced down at her glittering purple amethyst-covered ballet slippers, reminding him of Dorothy's ruby shoes in the Wizard of Oz. The Santa Fe Fairy Princess' smile conveyed a genuine enthusiasm as she gazed intently at him. It was as he was the male equivalent of Cinderella and the Princess had come to take him to the ball in the magic castle.

"Would you like to come in," he said, ashamed of his humble surroundings. Yet he pulled the door back and gestured for the Fairy Queen to enter. As he pointed toward the tattered couch, everything about his home and his life felt inadequate. She sat down, her back very straight and her knees and shoes placed gently together in front of her. Emerald Star's radiance still overwhelmed him.

"You are probably wondering just who I am and why I am visiting you," she said, smoothing her sparkling emerald green dress further down below her knees.

Chris was entranced yet wondered if this was some strange macabre costume party spoof. She had a regal elegance he had only seen in films, her voice enchanting and melodic. Emerald Star's legs seemed perfectly formed in white nylon stockings, and her purple gemstone slippers without even a direct light upon them seemed to radiate their own magnetic attraction.

"Twice during each Santa Fe school year, I select a student whose lack of confidence (*and dormant mental faculties, awkward social abilities, and inability to speak and write in an engaging manner,* she thought to herself) has left him or her with a feeling of hopelessness." She punctuated her remarks with another smile to launch a thousand skateboards. "How do you feel about your life in Coronado Elementary?"

"Aa...um..." he began, unsure of how to respond. "I feel my life is weird."

"Exactly," she smiled, before pointing her wand at him. "Yet the life you consider weird, and I consider temporarily overwhelming, is about to be transformed if you will allow me to help you."

Chris wondered what Fairy Queen Emerald Star could do to help. He had trouble concentrating in class; he could answer very few questions posed by Ms. Sevilla; his classmates considered him to be slow-witted and weak-minded; and all in all, he was certain school was not an arena in which he'd ever succeed.

"I've tried Tutoring," he shook his head while looking down at his Walmart brown leather shoes. "But I still only read at a second-grade level. My dad says I'm weak and unable to do anything right."

"Ahh, yes," she nodded. "I can't tell you how many students I've encountered like yourself. Most of them had lost the will to proceed. Many found their lives without a pathway to even a modicum of success." She smiled and used her wand to create an imaginary circle around him. "Yet when they were able to spend time with me, and to put all their troubles and sufferings aside for even a few minutes here and there, suddenly progress in reading and mathematics was very similar to a toddler's learning to walk." She then straightened up and winked at Christian.

"All this hinting at magic seems merely another impossibility, I know," she continued. "Yet Hope is on the magic horizon. Soon you will discover that with almost unimaginable patience, persistence, and my help, you will reach heights never thought possible. Know that I am the one person in your world right now that cares about you with enough energy to ensure amazing future accomplishments."

And with that, there remained only an oval of fairy dust resembling the halo surrounding the Santa Fe Santuario's statue of Our Lady of Guadalupe. It was as if Emerald Star had disappeared into the vapors of the Milky Way above. She was gone.

It is at such times that mortals wonder if fraternizing with a goddess merely becomes an ephemeral experience soon lost to reality. Christian shook his head, then walked back inside his real world.

~ SEVEN ~

It was quiet time in Ms. Sevilla's fifth-grade class. The Teacher sat in front of her computer, occasionally tapping keys, or using the mouse to move the cursor. She was checking her e-mails, and all was temporarily quiet among her normally hyper-animated band of 28 students. For a half hour after lunch and recess Sevilla had them reading at their desks. The interval provided a slow transition back to the reality of orchestrated learning. Some of her best students could quickly unwind from careening round the playground back into the afternoon's science projects. Yet the silent reading interval didn't enable that transition for everyone. Others needed more time, or a heavy dose of tranquil evolution unknown in their behavioral makeup. Certain of these eruptive sorts could then better reacquaint themselves with slightly uncomfortable wooden chairs and a zipping of the lips. Fortunately, Odysseus and other kinetic and vocal souls had worn themselves out during a competitive basketball game with some fourth-grade school team members.

There were only a few African Americans in a school predominantly Hispanic, yet the two in Ms. Sevilla's class were exceptionally bright. To look at the pair, the only thing they had in common with each other was skin color and hair consistency slightly different than most of their contemporaries. One had shot up like a cornstalk to become the tallest of either gender in the class. Her hair sometimes appeared as if she were satirizing a Little Rascals black caricature. The other's mane had enough kinkiness and body to float out to her shoulders. The taller one, Matilda Blackstone, had a demeanor rarely allowing her voice and projection to equate to her size. She could usually be found engaged in a book, giving her the rare confidence of a fifth grader, whose voracious reading resulted in a cornucopia of knowledge. Her reading propensity was belied by her early history. Matilda's father had disappeared in a southern breeze; her original mother had given up Matilda when the former had been confined to a wheelchair after an automobile accident. Matilda Blackstone's surrogate mother, Daniela, however, did everything in her power to encourage a love of books.

Matilda's pal Carolina Montoya's Hispanic father had married an African American professor of biology at Sangre de Cristo Community College. Both of her parents did their utmost to further each of their children's educations.

Carolina was nearly as bright as Matilda, and well-liked by classmates for her unpretentious kindness and sincere interest in others. While Matilda nearly always dressed in torn jeans and sweatshirts, Carolina sometimes sported flared skirts instead of her more prevalent faded jeans and sequined tops. Even though Carolina was shorter than Matilda, both were taller and bigger than most of the boys in all three fifth-grade classes. This left both girls free of any male attempts at intimidation. None of the opposite gender hectored them over their love of books, either. Yet schoolboys in packs of three or four tended to jape, and even Matilda and Carolina were not always immune to the occasional unpleasant dig.

"Yo, Matilda, you may read a lot," Odysseus whispered from nearby to the amusement of sidekicks Manuel and Carlito, "but you're still stupid."

Totally used to the brazen yet predictable attempts of her male adversaries, Matilda replied without looking up from her book: "Of course, Odysseus," she nodded in agreement for effect, "That's why we communicate so well."

Ms. Sevilla had briefly turned from her computer during this minor conflict, but upon seeing it was Matilda dealing with Odysseus & Cie, simply went back to her e-mails. The 30-year veteran knew to pick her battles. She also well knew the internecine quarrels that sometimes erupted between various students. And over time she had learned which ones required her attention, and the many who resolved issues without intervention.

"Remember," she said while tapping her keys and facing away from her students, "this half hour is to be devoted to silent reading. I should hear no whispering or talking. Otherwise, I am forced to put names and checkmarks on the white board, and I doubt if any of you would like to miss the field trip to the Lensic."

Over her many years teaching at Coronado, Amanda Sevilla had heard every kind of excuse, listened to recreations of a vast array of disputes, defused numerous types of anger, cited a variety of consequences, handed down effectual and ineffectual punishments, and joined with the Principal in meeting with parents or meting out suspensions. Generally, Ms. Sevilla found the best methodology for enforcing discipline to be the tried and true from past educational experiences. Still, different students required different warnings, corrections, antidotes, direction, and quite often, diversions.

Odysseus was a given. He was an excitable boy. The fact that his parents were highly educated, for some reason, was having the opposite effect upon him. His behavior could be merely a stage before an eventual maturation process; his outbursts might be explained by an emulation of an older brother's behavior; or his disruptive nature might simply be an attention getter. Years of teaching taught many things, but among the most important deductions were: that any given Teacher would prove incapable of rescuing every child desperately needing attention or un-endowed with the tools to run with the pack; and that preparation, patience and persistence trumped almost all other virtues. Kids could drive you nuts very quickly if you let them. On the other hand, giving them direction and learning sometimes occurred at the strangest moments and when least expected. You had to stay with it, and Ms. Sevilla was staying the course.

"O.K., please gather your science projects," Ms. Sevilla said after walking in front of the Smart Screen to post the vital points they should be including in their projects. "Four of you have twenty minutes to do classroom computer research on Mr. C's research sites listed on the Library Destiny home site; four of you will go to the Library and do book research at separate tables for those twenty minutes; and the rest of you while awaiting your twenty-minute sessions here or in the Library will either do paste-ups on your storyboards or discuss layout and presentations for your projects. Your group assignments and times are posted below the project vital points on the Smart Board."

Christian De Leon was working by himself on his project focusing on gravity. While others had chosen friends as partners, the special education student had been too timid to try and cooperate with anyone else. And no one else had solicited his help, either. For the entire morning thoughts of Emerald Star intermittently had interfered with his concentration on matters at hand. He kept trying to avoid his daydreaming, yet beneath all these attempts was the hope that the Fairy Princess would help him be reborn, both emotionally and academically. Chris felt convinced that God and genetics had not bestowed adequate intelligence upon him. He usually scored near the bottom of his grade level in both literacy and mathematics. Yet Emerald Star's enthusiasm had given him new hope.

"De Leon, why's that guy sitting in a chair?" Carlito asked while walking behind him. The reference was to a photo of a student sitting in a chair with a book. Christian had downloaded the photo from a free online illustrations site. It was just one example of the effect of gravity, soon to be joined by a text box, that De Leon had pasted upon his science project board.

"Um...well..." Christian stuttered, intimidated by the implied condescension in the question, "he's held there."

"What do you mean, he's held there?'" Carlito asked, implying he could see no one holding any part of the boy's body.

"...Aaa...gravity."

"You mean, he's held in his chair by gravity?" Carlito asked, as if any numbskull could deduce his reason for sitting.

Chris nodded. "Th-throw your pencil in the air," he added.

Carlito, wearing a Dallas Cowboys polo shirt, crossed his arms. "Why?" he asked the object of his intimidation.

"S-s-since the Earth has a mass larger than either your pencil or the boy in the ch-chair," Chris stuttered. Yet suddenly the image of Ms. Star and her wand appeared in his mind, and he gained courage: "your pencil will come back to you, and the boy will be held in his chair by the force of gravity." Christian was amazed. He had not only given a correct answer, he also had given it with force and conviction.

Carlito just shook his head as if the object of his scorn had simply accidentally come up with a correct answer. He uncrossed his arms, opened his mouth to say something more, but thought better of it.

Christian's self-esteem soared, even if just for a few moments. Maybe there was something to the help of the beautiful Princess. Then his thoughts returned to his project on gravity, and how he needed to focus upon it, with or without any outside help. Carlito and others could make fun of him. Yet the twinkling stars on the black velvet sky of a previous evening returned as a vision to eclipse his heckler's intrusion. Even though working alone on his project, Christian De Leon felt an inexplicable sense his destiny could alter.

~ EIGHT ~

Mr. C was sitting on one of the Library's wooden chairs, placed in front of the Smart Screen. He was reading aloud from a book of stories from *Wayside School* by Louis Sachar:

"Mrs. Jewls said, 'John, you can't go on reading like this. You can't spend the rest of your life turning your books upside down.'

"'Why not?' asked John.

"'Because I said so,' said Mrs. Jewls. 'Besides, what happens when I write something on the blackboard? You can't turn the blackboard upside down.'

"'No, I guess you're right,' said John.

"'I know I'm right,' said Mrs. Jewls. 'You are going to have to learn to stand on your head.'"

Mr. C was reading from author Sachar's introduction out of an actual paperback book to Ms. Cristina Cortez's fourth-grade class. The group of students listening was challenging, not because of the story, but because four of the boys in the class made it a practice constantly to make faces at one another during their Library period. The Librarian had seated each of the four at separate tables, but the effect only occasionally achieved the desired outcome.

Luis was undersized but constituted the quartet's *de facto* leader. Basically, the boy had a good spirit, and was one of the more competent readers. Yet he had a habit of saying what he wanted, when he wanted, and in a loud voice. Discipline and punishments seem to have little effect on his outré behavior. Luis would have fit right into the type of offbeat story Mr. Sachar had created from his imagination.

While Mr. C continued reading aloud, it was evident to him that most of the students spread out at the tables in front of him were engaged. Even the fulsome foursome enjoyed the voices he assumed as Mrs. Jewls, John, *et al.* Yet attention spans were limited, even for fourth graders. Most of the third through fifth graders who were capable of reading 'text only' books additionally had poor grade-level reading abilities due to having so many visual alternatives. Television and motion pictures were almost passé. With the advent of the internet, video games, and a plethora of devices on which Facebook, Twitter, YouTube, and many other visual sites were available, most preferred graphic novels where the illustrations far exceeded the written word. Texting the written word had devolved into a shortcut language further reducing reading skills.

Luis and Marcus were playing a form of as-ridiculous-as-possible faces. One would make a face by holding his mouth open with both hands. The other would roll his eyes and attempt to stifle a plethora of giggles. At two other tables Manuel and Francisco were making a token effort to pay attention. But one glance apiece in the direction of their cohorts' clowning and they, too, were being disruptive.

Mr. C was multi-tasking. While slipping in and out of Mr. Sachar's characters and descriptions, he caught the carnival act within his peripheral vision. The Librarian put his book down on his lap and made eye contact with the diminutive leader.

"Luis, the circus left town earlier in the summer," he said, also gazing at Marcus. "As far as I know most of the clowns wore costumes rather than jeans and sweatshirts, and they were paid for their efforts. The purpose of my reading aloud, as a contrast, is designed to provoke an interest in at least one book some of you might wish to read on your own, particularly if you find the characters and writing of interest." Mr. C looked back and forth between the two jesters. "It's hard to concentrate on what I'm reading, however—even when most of the class are paying attention—while out of the corner of my eye I can see two students making faces a Kindergartener could make more amusing." The Librarian pursed his lips. "Now," he continued, "I could report you two, as well as your assistants in disruption, Manuel, and Francisco, to Mrs. Cortez. She mentioned something about letting her know who would skip recess and join her during lunch break in the classroom. Then again," Mr. C paused for effect, "you could decide to sit quietly, without facial expression, for the remainder of both the story and your time spent in the Library. Do I make myself clear?"

Minutes later Mr. C found himself facing no fewer than four students across the front of his desk. The first one, a quiet girl with black-rimmed glasses named Karen, held two books out to the Librarian to scan.

"Number?" he asked, requesting the five-digit identification number used in the cafeteria, Library, and elsewhere.

"9-7-5-3..." she said, trailing off in audio level to the point only attuned animals could hear.

"Mr. C, can I go to the bathroom?" a girl to her side asked.

"Somebody has the stick and is there. When she comes back you can go." He was referring to one of two 'girls' and 'boys' sticks that must accompany a student to the bathroom. This helped to prevent more than one student of a gender in the bathroom at a time, to avoid opportunities for remote frivolity.

"Where do I find Spanish biographies," a boy named Francisco interrupted.

Mr. C stopped his scanning process. "Do you see that I'm in

the middle of a transaction with Karen?" he asked in consternation. "Did you ever hear of waiting your turn instead of interrupting?"

In a news organization like NBC years ago they called such a madhouse location the 'traffic' desk, one at which someone used the phone, fax, lists of names and numbers and now other accessible information such as internet sites. This multi-tasking enabled setting the coverage of news stories in motion, the assigning of camera crews, making travel reservations, fielding of phone inquiries, etc. To man the desk you had to be able to do a minimum of four things at once, with dispatch, and in the right order.

Mr. C's Library desk somewhat resembled a news traffic desk. Often several students at one time would be putting books to be scanned in front of him, asking to be permitted to go to the bathroom, saying they had a stomachache and could they get a nurse pass, complaining about another student's behavior, and an almost limitless variation of questions, requests, complaints, and interruptions. This all happened with intermittent pushing, shoving, and chatter. Mr. C had to prioritize, had to answer or redirect with alacrity, and he had to maintain his cool. Lose you temper, which he sometimes did, and a Librarian or Teacher often lost control of his or her Library or classroom. The most effective desk behavior often became an erratic blend of book scannings, explanations of why check-outs or renewals were refused, book location directions, washroom permissions, phone calls, nurse pass issuances, and correctional responses. Periodic inappropriate behavior, visible or audible from somewhere in the rest of the Library, also had to be addressed.

"Alright, I want to see one line in front of my desk," he said while scanning their faces. "One line, no talking, and one at a time." Briefly he recalled which request was current.

"I'm sorry, Karen, what was that number again," he asked, seeing her books in hand.

"9-7-5-3-1" she answered, emphasizing the last digit more clearly this time.

Mr. C looked at his screen. "Sorry, Karen, you still have two books outstanding."

There was a quizzical look upon her face.

"*Double Fudge*," by Judy Blume, and a chapter book entitled *Maggie*," he added, turning his Apple computer screen so she could see the photo of the books' covers.

"Oh, yeah," she said after suddenly recalling her outstanding books. She nodded. "I've got them in my backpack," and she darted to where all the students place their jackets and other belongings as the last class of the day before dismissal.

Soon Karen was back with the two outstanding books, Mr. C scanned them back in, and he was then able to scan the new books she wished to check out.

As the line thinned in front of his desk, he could see three of the fulsome foursome wandering aimlessly throughout the Library. The Librarian cared about all his students, even the most disruptive ones. He never blamed the children themselves, aware of the lack of discipline and inspiration missing from many homes with one or no parents, parents working two or three jobs and seldom home, and even homelessness. Yet Mr. C believed in semi-strict discipline, and most infractions needed to be addressed.

"Luis, Marcus, and Manuel, you need to look for books separately," Mr. C. said, rising from his chair and grabbing his cane. "I'll be right back," he quietly told two students still hovering to have their books scanned. "And Francisco, crawling is for toddlers, not in the Library," he said more loudly as he legged it toward the escaping three boys. "You three have two minutes to find a book and sit at separate tables," he continued upon reaching them in the back corner just as Francisco was standing up. The Librarian then angled off toward one of four window seats. Three girls in jeans were talking while holding books in their laps. "Dulce," he said upon arriving in front of them. "How many people are allowed to sit on a large window seat?"

"Two," she answered, as if an amusing revelation.

"O.K. then, which of you arrived last?" The other two girls stopped chewing gum and pointed at the same time to Dulce, sitting between them. "Alright, Dulce, find a seat at a table in the middle aisle—no, not there," he said as the girl with a long ponytail tried to sit at a table still close to her friends in the window— "at a table in the middle aisle."

She shook her head in mild disgust but lifted a large book on Cinderella off the table and began shuffling dejectedly toward the center aisle.

"And you two, spit your gum into the wastebasket and then I want you sitting in the two corners of your window seat, reading not talking."

That was the worst part of being an instructor in a school, Mr. C thought to himself. Much of any Teacher or instructor's time was wasted with discipline issues, many of them in broken-record repetition. Even though Library shelves and tables were arranged in lines to afford the smallest areas to hide, and to enable the Librarian at his desk maximum viewing of the room, kids still were difficult to control. Sitting out-of-sight at the end of a rolling set of shelves, on footstools tucked in the corner, or on the floor in the back corner were favorite hiding places. Most kids knew the rules and obeyed them, but even the best students found occasional amusement at throwing paper wads, crawling under a table, making and flying paper airplanes, throwing books or pencils, deliberately returning books to the wrong shelf, or putting them in backwards, and hiding books under shelves or in a shelf of books rarely removed, to horde their prize for a future hour in Library. While re-shelving books, eagle-eyed Librarians often found these deliberately misplaced hidden gems, and replaced them in their correct shelf positions.

Mr. C looked at his chronograph and realized they were approaching the end of another hour of the siren-like mix of turbulence and book learning. For certain of the students, the healthy ingestion of language necessary to assimilate pearls of wisdom or to find amusement, was one of the wonderful tangents of an hour in Library. Often students with the least reading skills perused *Guinness Book of Records* massive volumes to look at bizarre photos accompanied by text they couldn't read. "Five minutes," the Librarian chimed loudly on the way back to his desk.

Now came another interesting interval.

"Line up," he said, relieved that another day had drawn to a close. "Time to line up."

It was as if the California gold rush had begun. From all corners of the Library kids either quickly put books back in the correct places, tossed them on shelves anywhere, or left them on tables, window alcoves, or on the floor. Yet most took the trouble to return their plastic bookmarks to the container on the front desk. It was amazing the sprint speed some could demonstrate on their way to their backpacks and jackets, and to get a good position for the bell releasing them to freedom.

"No running," Mr. C yelled to try to stem the tide. "And I shouldn't find any books lying on top of the shelves, tables, other books, or on the floor!"

A rule of thumb is that with each year students gradually become capable of books with fewer pictures and more text. Yet the rate of such change can be dramatically different from child to child. Gigantic photos and illustrations and just a few words a page work best for most Kindergarteners. As a contrast, certain fifth graders may wade through Harry Potter tomes in two weeks or less. One of the pitfalls of determining just what books kids ages four to ten like is that for certain kids the Librarian in doing so can often make or break the propensity to read.

Some kids hide books until the next Library period; others slip them into jackets or backpacks for greater permanence. Certain popular books, like the four *Minecraft*, are stolen so often the Librarian may choose to keep them behind the front desk and demand checkout even to simply read them during Library hour. Yet these mysterious phenomena often occurred at the end of the last period. It wasn't the careering and return of books to the shelves. It wasn't the eagerness or speed with which students arrived in a motley line of pushing and shoving. It was the mystery of the missing books. If books with attractive covers and interesting contents are combined with students whose parents either do not value books or can afford to buy many for their kids, you've got an equation for theft. And when it is the last period of the day and kids have backpacks, coats or jackets that can act as secret containers, a critical solution for some of the missing books is often explained. Kids steal books because they want them, because they can't afford to buy them, because the few Library copies are almost continuously checked out, and because some students achieve status among friends for the simple derring-do of getting away with stealing a prized book.

Mr. C blew a soft note on his PAX harmonica, signaling the students to quiet down. He caned over to the motley line looking like a group of 20 trying for the last 10 free tickets to a Shrek film.

"Luis, did you check that book out?" the Librarian asked, having observed the student grab a Batman book off a tall carousel on his way to standing in line.

"I was just looking at it," Luis disdainfully replied, putting the book back in its carousel cage.

Light-fingered children, particularly in the last period, had to be watched. Every year for every $500 paid for lost books, probably

$200 more of the popular gems were stolen. The large amount of specific book-type losses signaled the Librarian what books were valued most. It also often put books into the hands of those who could least afford to buy them. It was all part of doing business in schools and libraries. Win a few; lose a few.

~ NINE ~

Three of the four yellow buses were lined up along the curb near the front door of the school. Nearby kids chased each other on the extensive concrete apron while parents and relatives greeted students pouring out the front doors after the dismissal bell. Teachers in orange vests acted like sheepdogs corralling kids into a line for the number 14 bus, one that somehow usually arrived late. Kids streaked across the concrete, risking contusions, abrasions, broken bones, and missing teeth, to secure a better place in line and seat on the bus. Making them go back and retrace the same distance while walking did little to slow them down in future.

Mr. C had bus duty that day. Part of the job consisted of ensuring students got on their buses in orderly fashion. Orderly, of course, is relative, as kids pushed as well as joined others trying to save them places in lines. All the while an afternoon breeze whipped long hair around faces and reminded certain children they had somehow, somewhere left behind jackets worn for the high-desert morning chill.

Another facet of the job was to keep an eye out for 'cutting.' Bigger and older kids often shot up to the front of the line and tried to board the bus. It was the Teacher on duty's obligation to prevent such deceptive efforts.

Mr. C's arm shot up and grabbed the opposite edge of the bus door. "Odysseus," the Librarian shook his head, pointing toward the back of the line.

"I was in line here," Odysseus complained, trying to push under Mr. C's arm.

"No, you weren't Odysseus," Mr. C replied, moving his arm lower to stop the fifth grader pushing in front of younger and smaller students.

"I was in line!" Odysseus whined, at the same time ducking and diving his head to try and push by Mr. C.

Mr. C looked at a third-grade girl patiently waiting. "Was he in line?"

The girl shook her head. No.

"Go to the back of the line, now!" Mr. C said loudly and with a deeper voice.

"But I was here," Odysseus said defiantly, still trying to wiggle by the Librarian.

Mr. C felt he had gone as far as he could go without putting hands on the defiant student. He dropped his arm and Odysseus bounded up the stairs.

"O.K., said Mr. C as he was bounding, "That's earned you a conduct report!"

Nearby Odysseus' Teacher, Ms. Sevilla, was making sure the last of a line of kids was safely boarding the final bus of four that had arrived late. Mr. C walked over to her and waited until the last child was aboard.

"Amanda, I had a real problem again with Odysseus."

"Oh, really," she replied, the smile evaporating from her face.

"Yah, he kept trying to cut in the bus line and when I tried to block him by putting an arm up, he kept trying to duck under my arm refused to go to the back of the line. He seems to have a defiant attitude, and he lied about being in line while cutting, as well. I told him he's earned a conduct report."

She shook her head. "Write him up. I had an issue with him today in class, and I've already written him up before. But do it," she said, looking over at the other buses. "Where is he?"

Mr. C. walked Amanda Sevilla over to his bus, the fifth-grade Teacher climbing aboard and standing with her hands on her hips next to the bus driver.

"Odysseus," she said curling a finger to summon her student.

The two stepped down to a lower step of the bus as Mr. C stood on the curb right below them.

"Odysseus, Mr. C tells me you defied his instructions."

"I was in li—"

"Never mind. Listen to me. You owe Mr. C an apology."

"But I—"

"No buts. I talked to your mother this week, and it looks like I'm going to have to talk to her again," she said, staring intently into his eyes. "When Mr. C or any other Teacher tells you to go to the end of a bus line, you do what he tells you. Do you hear?"

The now contrite and intimidated boy nodded.

"Now go and sit down."

It was one more example of how discipline issues could rear their ugly heads at almost any time. Not a great way to release students to afternoon freedom for either Ms. Sevilla or Mr. C. Yet in the grand scheme of education, discipline was as critical as learning from Teachers, books, videos, and other educational aids. Spare the mental rod: spoil the child.

Ten minutes later approximately 40 Teachers, assistants, Counselors, and administrators sat in chairs with wheels in the computer lab. Lining the walls stood perhaps 30 Apple computers in each of the two rooms in which kids were introduced to other than video games.

With their password during their computer lab session each student might learn typing, or key in internet sites to learn student news, read books online, research science or other projects, take literacy or math Tutorials in the form of games, and discover other wonders of the third or previous millennia. The world of electronic information had exploded with the advent of the internet. While the school district recognized the present and future necessity of student familiarization of computers, Smart Boards, Chrome Books, iPads, and other electronic devices furthering educational availability and dissemination, district administrators also constantly were forced to reassess which hardware and software purchases to make. Decisions were determined by facility of usage, cost per hardware and software, length of use, ease or difficulty of learning curve, *et al.* This seems simpler than it actually is. The ever-accelerating rate of change often meant a computer could easily morph into a fossil in 5-6 years. Illustrations, drawings, and photographs might fall from fashion in a matter of less than a year. Electronic information not only might appear with immediacy and little or no fact-checking but could also be found out-of-date within as little as a year, several months, weeks or days, or even be found erroneous in a matter of minutes.

"I hope to make this short," Principal Guadalajara said, looking down at her computer-printed agenda and waiting for the talking to die down. Each person at the bi-weekly staff meeting had a copy of the agenda, some of which items would take time, and others perhaps one to three minutes each.

Nearby the lab's front desk, from which the lab's Teacher could electronically patch things onto the Smart Board, stood a tall woman with the posture and bearing of a flamenco dancer. This Literacy Coach's whole demeanor projected confidence. Not only was she from Spain, but Martina Madrid employed a true Spanish accent different from those emanating from Central or South America. She had her master's degree in education, had taught several grades in both Spain and the USA, and in previous years had been in public relations for a large Spanish corporation. Her floral dress fit much like a bespoke suit fit a Savile Row man about town in London, yet demurely fell just below the tops of black boots the Three Musketeers might have dashed about in.

"Martina wants to discuss initial testing for a few minutes," Ms. Guadalajara said by way of introduction. "Her talk and Smart Board presentation shouldn't take long; and once our staff meeting ends, we would like all Teachers to stay after for a few more minutes so that she might discuss some particulars with you."

The small computer laboratory room with a low ceiling could get quite hot with 40 bodies exhaling in it. Yet Ms. Guadalajara had switched meetings from the high-ceiling and far more spacious Library to the lab because she felt the Library shelves made it hard for her to see everyone at one time, difficult for them to see her all at one time, and for them to see each other during comments.

Seven hours in many sedentary jobs seem to pass quickly and with little emotional drain. However, for Teachers and most school personnel, time on their feet as well as at desk meant a dizzying schedule of duties. Posters and other educational aids needed constant creative placements upon walls. Grades consistently had to be tabulated and posted online. New material for presentation had to be chosen and adapted, photocopying had to be done, attendance records had to be maintained. Yet all these duties merely set the stage for a six-hour set of performances.

Most kids had the attention spans and movements of a squirrel. Students held still when engaged. Being engaged meant being captivated by interesting subject matter, intermittent eye contact, as well as energetic delivery with varied emphasis, confident voice, and projection. The best Teachers simply held more attention spans longer. Deliver any learning without confidence, in a monotone, or with an inability to make eye contact, and any instructor's classroom could become chaotic. Control and engagement were serious classroom techniques. Any parent complaining of so much holiday time for Teachers has not ever sat in a classroom for an entire day.

Staff meetings were only slightly different. Teachers, many of them further enervated by after-school duties and additional time on their feet, arrived tired well beyond serious fatigue levels. Very few were ever seen falling asleep in their eighth hour of a school day. Yet in the moderately stifling containment of a computer lab most heads could still be held on high intermittently. Ms. Guadalajara was more adept than most Principals at engaging her staff. Yet somewhere between 3:30 and 4:00 many of the staff found themselves surreptitiously checking their watches, scrolling through their devices for e-mails or urgent scenarios needing attention, or pencil-checking their agenda sheet to see how many additional items were yet to be bandied about.

"O.K.," Ms. Guadalajara smiled, "please don't forget to check with the office if you don't have an updated set of rosters. We will have several fire drills soon; make sure your red emergency bags have all their required contents. If not, see Genoveva for any missing items. Also, check with Amanda if you want your duties changed. All right," she enthused, pumping a fist in the air, "we made it in under 45 minutes. Teachers, please all stay for just a few extra minutes more so that Martina can clarify several critical testing details and duties. Have a great evening."

As she left the laboratory, Ms. Guadalajara internally breathed a sigh of relief. Possible retirement was only nine months away, the latest prescriptions she had received had greatly reduced the pain she still suffered from a rare form of early arthritis, and her husband on the security team at Argenta High School had learned his intestinal problems were not cancerous. Her niece was doing brilliantly at another elementary school, her daughter had her diabetes under control and had found what looked to be a kind partner, and there could be a post-retirement administrative job, doubling her pay, on the horizon.

There was, however, her 4:15 meeting. One of the most challenging of the Principal's array of obligations was dealing with hirings, firings, and the myriad problems stemming from a broad range of staff member complaints, requests, and sometimes demands.

At 4:15 a man in a rumpled corduroy jacket, khaki pants and a shuffling, avuncular bearing came into her cluttered office. Principal Guadalajara signaled the special education instructor to a nearby round table. Assistant Principal Victoria Sandoval was already seated, turning the pages of what obviously was a written report. School Counselor Genoveva Juarez, a large woman with a stern appearance belying a kind and generous soul, sat with her arms crossed, a hard-bound blue binder closed in front of her on the table. It was the end of a long day for all three women, and it was about to get longer.

Ms. Guadalajara moved a stack of folders from the table to a nearby cabinet countertop. She took the last of three modern silver tube and black Naugahyde chairs. Ms. Sandoval crossed one tan leg over another under a stylish print skirt, yet avoided looking up from her turning of pages. The Principal's immediate task was made even more difficult because for years Mr. Coffee had been found by special education students, fellow Teachers, and administrators alike to be focused on any task at hand, as well as soft-spoken, quiet, and in most cases, deferential. He was also considerably older than both administrators. Penelope Guadalajara shifted the report in front of her slightly to the left and then the right. It was difficult for her to know how to begin.

"Mr. Coffee, I requested you to come to my office because of several reports we hope you will be able to clarify." She looked up from holding the report in front of her. An attempt at a smile was stifled.

"Several of our female Teachers have reported that you have made inappropriate remarks to them. Would you care to comment?"

"Well, I..." Mr. Coffee said without looking up at either administrator. "I can't think of...anything I've said..."

"Let me refresh your memory," Ms. Guadalajara said, turning to the page below the cover page of the report. "On August 23rd a report has you telling one of our female Teachers that 'you don't know what satisfaction is until you've been with me.' On August 25th another report indicates you made the comment of one of our younger female Teachers that 'Have you ever had sex with an older man?' Both administrators now looked at Winston Coffee.

"I don't remember saying anything like that...Just joking maybe..."

"The two Teachers in question felt your remarks to be serious. Two others gave similar verbal reports involving innuendo of a sexual nature." Mrs. Montoya gripped the arms of her chair and leaned back. Ms. Juarez leaned forward on her elbows and clasped her hands. Mrs. Guadalajara waited for Mr. Coffee to make eye contact. "Do you have any explanation for what was said?"

The Teacher in his late 70s reached up and scratched behind his ear as if the answer might somehow appear from there. There were tan leather patches visible on the elbows of his jacket, and he shifted uncomfortably in his chair. "I don't recall saying anything like that." He picked a nit off his jacket sleeve. "I must have thought...I was...I mean..." His normally moderately pale face was now suffused with the red of a filtered sunset.

Principal Guadalajara suddenly perceived the same pity one felt when kids from single-parent, impoverished homes were called to her office for disruptive behavior. There were always explanations for inappropriate incidents, both from adults and children. Yet it was her job to prevent, alter, and bring consequences for any such aberrations. Consequences were the most difficult element of her duties. Being diplomatic in the face of difficult or dire infractions never got easy, particularly when a Teacher having spent years giving good service somehow strayed from the path of correctness.

"Assistant Principal Montoya, Counselor Juarez, and I have discussed the matter with the Teachers in question and their allegations. All of us agree that your behavior has put both you and Coronado Elementary School in a difficult situation. The consensus is that your inappropriate behavior demands more than a suspension with or without pay. The safety and mental security of our Teachers in the future could easily be considered in jeopardy, as well. It is probable you could be fired for cause due to your inexplicable behavior. Any such outcome would particularly be unfortunate and sad after the years of good service you have given Santa Fe City Schools."

Principal Guadalajara turned to the last page of the stapled report in front of her. "At this point in your lengthy career in our school system, and in consideration of your post-retirement age, it might be best if you resigned effective immediately."

"You mean I couldn't even finish out the semester?"

"Under the circumstances, that isn't considered an option."

"Two week's notice?"

"Not even that," said Mrs. Juarez.

"However," Mrs. Guadalajara continued her summary, "you may wish to challenge our advice encouraging you to retire. The matter would be brought before a hearing where you would face probable harassment charges and allegations of inappropriate behavior, possibly leading to a loss of your license to teach as well as possible civil damages by specific individuals. Eligibility for your retirement benefits could be jeopardized if you were to be fired with cause. But again, on option would be to take your chances through legal channels. The outcome of these allegations would seem to come down, however—if I may give an opinion—to your testimony on what occurred versus the testimony of the four female Teachers."

Winston Coffee had been looking down at the table for some

time. His predicament might have been mitigated by the conundrum of longstanding positive behavior balancing short-term negative. Yet in current times, with the advent of the 'MeToo' Movement and women throughout the world asserting their rights to gain justice when mistreated or inhibited through sexual innuendo, he was aware that his chances of being exonerated were slim. Perhaps some of the drugs he was taking due to several ongoing medical conditions had provoked his behavior. In each instance during the blurting out of regrettable remarks, his libido won out over forbearance. As he was making those outlandish suggestions, each time a little voice inside his brain warned him of his effrontery. He was then also faced with consistent negative reactions from the four women. The consequences of his perceived-to-be adventuresome behavior suddenly became apparent.

"Mr. Coffee?" Mrs. Guadalajara asked, all three women awaiting his reaction.

"Under the circumstances, I think it best I resign and retire."

~ TEN ~

Matilda Blackstone enjoyed the challenge of being one of several African American students at Coronado Elementary. She and another, Carolina Montoya, were classroom *amigas*, yet more than the friendships she had made with Anglos and Hispanics, as well, was the confidence Matilda held from her voracious reading and commanding stature. Being tall and literate, even though soft-spoken, gave her an ability to vacillate between conversation, with those of varying intellectual abilities, and the silent solitude required by her devotion to reading. At times there were moments when comments were made without comprehending certain racial undertones. Yet Matilda was well thought of by almost everyone. Those who didn't feel up to her conversational levels and acute analytical skills simply gave her a wide berth, and that included Odysseus and his friends. Rarely did she encounter anyone attempting to condescend due to racial stereotyping. Seldom did she hear any denigrating slang or derogatory comments that occur in other neighborhoods, cities, or parts of the country. Santa Fe wasn't a perfect melting pot, but the Hispanic, Anglo, African American, Asian, and other cultural or religious populations seemed to mingle with minimal prejudice far better than relatives or acquaintances in other urban areas.

"How do you spell 'mistletoe?'" her mother Daniela asked her as they drank a cup of tea together before school.

"Mm," Matilda said before a sip of tea, "M-I-S-T-L-E-T-O-E."

"Good," her mom nodded. "How about 'peninsula?'"

With little hesitation, her daughter spelled the word correctly. It was a game they had played throughout Matilda's progression through the grades. Daniela repeatedly encouraged her daughter to look up words in one of the Webster's dictionaries they kept on a nearby shelf, or to find the meaning online. Whenever Matilda wrote a paper on Microsoft Word, she used the program's spelling and grammar pull-down to make corrections, as well.

Over the years, as Matilda gained the ability to read more and more complex material, spelling became easier and easier. Phonics were all well and good, but English had a lot of idiomatic words, phrases, and spellings, the most often used probably 'would, should, and could.' Students of the language had to memorize a lot of variations from what would be typical phonetic spelling. Each year Matilda had developed a broader and broader vocabulary, far greater than most of her fellow students. She hadn't won the school spelling bee while in fourth grade, but she had finished third. Her mom felt her growth in reading capabilities had now made a quantum leap during the summer between fourth and fifth, making her one of the front runners for school spelling champion.

Lately, like all kids with the options of texting, twittering, action and superhero movies, and the reinvention of comics as graphic novels, Matilda sometimes checked out a graphic novel from the Library when text-only books continued to be her focus. Her digestion of non-illustrated novels had enabled the fifth grader to distance herself light years from most other students when it came to spelling abilities.

On the bus to school Matilda ignored the other fifth graders around her and concentrated on reviewing grade-appropriate spelling lists. Today was the day the fifth-grade standout would learn if anyone else in the school had done more work during the summer and first few weeks of school, or had a better memory. Her confidence was soaring, yet at the same time if she lost, it would merely spur her to work harder.

The small gym's four rows of metal bleachers were packed with fourth and fifth graders. Some parents sat in special folding chairs placed along the wall at the other end of the gym. About 20 students sat erect or slumped in more folding chairs on one side of an aisle in front of the podium. A camera on a tripod had been placed below the top of the dais at which students were to discover how much they knew. The music Teacher, doubling as a surrogate sound person, stood at the podium and checked her image on the screen. Her upper torso was on camera, assuring that the typical fourth or fifth grader's face would be framed on screen properly. Judges were checking their red and green cards, to be used to signal correct or incorrect spellings.

In the stands kids were elbowing one another, or quietly pointing at candidates nervously sitting in chairs awaiting their destinies.

"Alright," said Ms. Sevilla, "we ask all those in the stands to remain quiet before a contestant is given a word to spell, during his or her spelling of that word, and until the point at which our judges indicate whether that word has been spelled correctly or incorrectly. Contestants will have up to one minute to begin spelling a word. Each contestant has the right to ask the moderator, which might be any of our judges, to repeat a word. A green card held up by judges indicates a correct spelling, while a red card means a word has been spelled incorrectly. Contestants misspelling a word will take a seat on the opposite side of the aisle. When just two contestants remain in the contest, we will ask each of them to spell a word. If both either misspell or correctly spell their final word, they will both be given another final word, until one misses a word but the other one spells his or her word correctly." Ms. Sevilla paused to look up at the contestants. "Does anyone have a question?"

"Are all these words taken from the lists we received to study?" asked a fourth-grade contestant.

"Yes," answered Ms. Sevilla. "Any other questions?"

When it was apparent none was forthcoming, Ms. Sevilla added: "Alright then, let the Spelling Bee begin.

An enthusiastic roar erupted from the stands.

Ms. Sevilla waited while a few last-minute shouts of encouragement went out, the fans hoping their yells would act as catalysts to competitor friends or classmates. "Remember, we ask you to remain quiet throughout until the green or red cards are raised."

One by one, contestants stepped to the podium, almost all of them successfully spelling their first round of words. 'Ache, Trouble, and Built,' were among a round designed to eliminate only a few contestants. Polite applause occurred after each set of green cards was displayed. Only three did not survive the first round. The words Flight, Wealthy and Graph were among those that eliminated all but 10 in the second round.

Waiting for the third round was a member of Ms. Sevilla's fifth-grade class, Guadalupe De Vargas, an identical twin to Maria De Vargas, the latter having chosen not to enter the contest. The girls were very slender, small, quiet, modest, and of sweet and helpful disposition. Yet both were acutely bright. Guadalupe was minutes older than Maria, and often did the speaking for the pair. Maria sang in the choir, while Guadalupe was a member of the Wizards, an after-school club for enthusiastic book lovers. Both were avid readers, but Maria had chosen to be a member of the chess club after consistently scoring higher than her sister in nearly every mathematics test. Each day their mother dropped them off at school, and each day she walked the pair from the school's front door to her SUV. Their parents were divorced, yet their mother worked part-time doing research for a New Mexican Congresswoman. This meant that with additional support from their father now living in

Seattle, the twins came from a home with rare adequate financial support.

Maria, one slender jeans-clad leg crossed over the other, sat in the first row of the bleachers to support her twin sister.

Guadalupe was the second of ten to step to the podium. Her word was 'Industrial.'

Literacy Coach, Martina Madrid, who spoke Spanish with a dialect appropriate to her former home in Barcelona, Spain, repeated the word 'Industrial.' It wasn't that Guadalupe was unfamiliar with the word, but rather that she was reframing in her mind just what the penultimate letter was: 'a, or e.' Having grown up in a bilingual household, to which her parents migrated from Ciudad de Mexico when they were children, meant the twins periodically were forced to recollect words that might have the same partial or identical spellings in Spanish.

"I-N-D-U-S," she began, hesitating to make sure she delivered the image of the word hovering in her mind, "T-R-I," she continued, "A-L."

Three green cards were held in the air. Groups of fifth graders, and particularly the twins' classmates, erupted. The noise was louder than a school victory in basketball, the popularity of the mild-mannered girls emphasized by loud yelling, stamping, and clapping.

Two contestants later came Antonio Lopez, a red-and-white cowboy bandanna tied loosely around his neck.

Ms. Madrid held another card in her hand, waiting for the crowd to quiet down.

"Peninsula," she said, placing the card face down in front of her.

The crowd gazed both at Antonio and his face on the Smart Board. Antonio was another well-liked fifth grader from Ms. Sevilla's class. In the bleachers, a fourth grader who was his cousin sat with her fingers crossed and eyes closed.

"Could you use it in a sentence?" he requested.

"Most of the State of Florida is a peninsula," replied Ms. Madrid.

Antonio paused. He remembered the word from a list he had studied, but its usage in a sentence failed to clarify his confusion over the second-to-last vowel. He knew the word had an 'a' rather than a Spanish 'e' on the end, but... "P-E-N," he began hesitantly. "I-N-S," he continued before looking up at the ceiling briefly in hopes of divine intervention, "U-E-L-A."

Red cards went up and whispering came from the crowd.

"P-E-N-I-N-S-U-L-A," enunciated fourth-grade Teacher Christina Cortez, a judge.

Antonio looked down at the podium, then quietly walked to a seat near the back of the other side of the aisle, the area designated for those no longer in the contest. The change of chairs was humiliating for most missing their word, but Antonio remembered his father's comment: 'If you do your best, win, lose or draw, you have succeeded."

Finally, the contest came down to just two students, both from Ms. Sevilla's fifth-grade class. Matilda Blackstone sat with her back straight, projecting a confidence that the girl in front of her, Guadalupe De Vargas, could not witness. De Vargas glanced at the Smart Board, and then down at the ground, her nervousness of having climbed this far suddenly overwhelming.

"Matilda," since in the first round you went after Guadalupe, you will go first," said Ms. Madrid, using a motion with her left arm to signal the crowd to quiet down.

"Go, Matilda," yelled two boys.

"Go, Guadalupe, shouted her twin sister and two friends in unison.

This time Ms. Madrid lowered her left arm to ask the crowd's forbearance.

If Matilda lacked any element of confidence, it was to do with having grown so much in fifth grade. Yet height had its own reward. Being the tallest student, not just girl, in her class gave her one of the calmer dispositions in the school. Her size was imposing enough. She didn't lack assertiveness when it came to offering an answer, comment, or opinion. Rather she always did so in a soft voice and with a look of distant assuredness. However, she walked to the podium slowly, keeping her eyes on the wall behind the judges. She diffidently looked up from the podium to Literary Coach and moderator Martina Madrid.

"Necessary," said Ms. Madrid.

There was little hesitation on Matilda's part. "N-E-C-E-S-S-A-R-Y."

Green cards were held in the air and a loud cheer went up. Matilda smiled meekly and returned to her seat.

Without her twin sister by her side, but in the metal stands, Guadalupe De Vargas was apprehensive of failure. Her diminutive stature and mild personality suited conversations with classmates, friends, and her parents. Yet facing the panel in front of her, as well as one-third of the school gazing at her now profiled on the Smart Screen, the twin was silently terrified. This was it, and she knew Matilda Blackstone read more books in a month than she did in two.

"Afterthought" said Ms. Madrid, placing the file card upside down upon the table.

Many kids in the audience whispered to each other, not knowing the correct spelling of the word.

"Silence, please," said judge Sevilla, knowing her large class of fifth graders had both representatives remaining.

"A-F-T-E-R," began Guadalupe, hesitating on each letter to make sure she delivered the image of the word in her mind correctly, "T-H-O-U," she continued, "G-H-T."

Three green cards were held aloft, and another thunderous ovation occurred from the admirers of the quiet twin. Guadalupe studied the gym floor planking as she returned to her seat.

"Actually," the moderator said amidst the loud approval, "Guadalupe, could you please stay at the podium. Since you and Matilda both have spelled your word correctly, you remain tied. However, Matilda went first last time, so you will go first this time. We will continue until one of you, in either order, misses a word, and the other spells her word correctly."

Another judge, fifth-grade Teacher Mr. Penumbra, held up a sign QUIET, turning the placard so everyone could see it.

The students in the stands quit whispering and fidgeting. No shout-outs were forthcoming: most were in a quandary on whom to support. Matilda and Guadalupe were equally popular among their classmates.

As she stood behind it, Guadalupe De Vargas was barely taller than the podium. Her head was down, as if the answer to her dreams lay on the wooden platform in front of her.

"Impatient," Mr. Penumbra read aloud before glancing at one of two remaining spellers.

"Could you use that in a sentence," Guadalupe softly asked.

"The girl with a headache remained impatient while she waited for the bus."

The twin's eyes looked upward as if beseeching heaven to supply the answer. She began her word slowly.

"I-M-P," she said almost inaudibly and barely picked up by the microphone on the edge of the podium.

"A..." she hesitated... "C-I-E-N-T."

Three red cards were held in the air. "I-M-P-A-T-I-E-N-T," is the correct spelling, said Mr. Penumbra. "However, you may take your original seat, Guadalupe. If Matilda misspells her word, the two of you will each receive another word."

"Go for it, Mattie!" shouted her friend Carolina. Most of the students in the stands were quiet, sharing Guadalupe's disappointment at having incorrectly spelled her word.

Matilda Blackstone reached the podium, clasping her hands together on its surface. She looked up at Ms. Madrid, who held the finalist's fate on a card in her hands.

"Fluorescent," Ms. Madrid read aloud, placing the card upside down and gazing at Matilda.

"That's not fair!" yelled someone from the stands.

Everyone gazed at the boy whose hair was completely shaved on the sides, while a ponytail stood up from the bowl of long hair atop his head. Caliban Chimayo was in Ms. Sevilla's class and was known for disrupting almost any classroom session when he felt compelled to make himself heard. Several conduct reports had been written by Ms. Sevilla, Mr. C, and several other 'specials' Teachers. He had been threatened with suspension after at least three trips to Principal Guadalajara's office. Numerous sessions with Counselor Genoveva Juarez had produced few positive results.

Moderator Madrid looked over at the boy. The rest of the room fell silent.

"Why is that? Caliban."

"Because there are two different spellings," the boy answered as if everyone in the room were aware of this discrepancy.

Ms. Madrid opened a Webster's dictionary on her desk.

"He's right, Ms. Madrid," Matilda said from the podium. 'Fluorescent can mean 'luminous' or 'bright,' while florescent, with a different spelling, can mean 'in bloom.'

The judges looked back and forth at one another, two of the four nodding in agreement. After looking down at her dictionary, Ms. Madrid replied:

"We are asking you to spell the word meaning 'luminous,' or the word describing the overhead lights in the Coronado Library."

"F-L-U-O-R-E-S-C-E-N-T," Matilda enunciated without hesitation. She briefly looked over at the Smart Screen to check out if she were conveying her nervous relief. Four green cards were held in the air and more cheers and applause resounded.

"We have a winner," said Ms. Madrid. "Matilda Blackstone is our 2017 Spelling Bee champion, Guadalupe De Vargas finishes second, and Antonio Lopez third." Madrid awaited the three trophies being brought to her. "Will the three winners approach the stage to collect their trophies and for photo opportunities. Let's give them a huge round of applause."

As the ovation continued, fifth-grade Teacher Amanda Sevilla smiled. She knew the possibility of turning every student into a budding genius was nil. Yet over the years, little by little she refined her teaching techniques, and during each nine-month interval felt the satisfaction of watching a few comprehend the importance of the written and spoken word. Unfortunately, the Spelling Bee could only have one champion. Yet those who did spell well enjoyed the satisfaction of accomplishment, mirroring life itself, when either mental or physical conditioning resulted in more and more acquired knowledge and capabilities. Mental acuity as well as analytical and communication skills didn't guarantee success. Yet often these abstract qualities helped meteor both children and adults into unforeseen opportunities and a fabled world of real and vicarious experiences.

~ ELEVEN ~

Courtney Ray might have been mistaken for a version of the Headless Horseman on a bike. Not that he lacked a head and helmet, but rather that for a high school sophomore, his lanky frame more resembled an aspen trunk rather than a hundred-year-old cottonwood. His bike was an aging, battered Specialized Hard Rock mountain bike he had picked up at a garage sale. The frame was undersized for his still-growing six feet of height. The seat pole was maxed out in elevation, black masking tape covering myriad seat cover cracks caused by the New Mexican sun. Courtney was wearing a Golden State Warriors baseball cap backwards and a torn blue-gray T-shirt with the logo KIND OF BLUE on it. Miles Davis was his favorite musician, and even though Courtney couldn't dribble a basketball with anywhere near the dexterity of Stephen Curry, he still dreamed of someday developing the discipline needed for success.

His after-school job of bicycle messenger for *Secret Messages* gave him spending money. His parents didn't believe in spoiling their two boys, so avoided giving them more than a nominal allowance. Courtney's younger brother, Odysseus, made a little money off skateboard betting. Yet neither of the exceptionally bright boys had pursued the straight and narrow. Odysseus idolized older brother

Courtney, and the latter craved acceptance of several gangbangers at Argenta High School.

After Courtney made his last delivery at 5:00 p.m. to a cable installation company, he did a couple of wheelies on the way over to his friend Cruzito Diaz's place. Cruzito had paid a lot of dues during his mere 17 years on the planet. The small gang he had formed didn't have the tats of MS 13. Yet each of the four members had a rose stuck on a Saguaro cactus tattoo on his shoulder. Their funds for partying and travel came from growing weed that was legal in Colorado but not yet in New Mexico. Cruzito had dropped out of Argenta after his second year. He lived in an Agua Fria village house paid for by his recently deceased grandmother, and he intended to live there as long as he could pay the taxes and upkeep, and no one ratted him out for being a minor.

The house and property differed little from an automobile junk-yard. The front room's flotsam and jetsam randomly included: his ancient BMW motorcycle, older than he was and featuring an aero-dynamically sleek white and blue streamlined body and an engine capable of 160 mph; motorcycle parts; posters depicting motor-cycle racing, WAR, rap singers, soccer stars; various faded piñatas; a standing tarnished brass lamp with a shade illuminating Latina cowgirls in chaps; and empty Dos Equis lager bottles. Cruzito felt at home in crowded surroundings; tidying up, even for aging relatives, was out of the question. When they asked to see the second bed-room, he told them it was just a storage room. Inside that secret, white-walled makeshift farm perhaps a hundred cannabis plants stood above trays and decorative pots of fertilized soil. Grow lamps hanging from chains created a vaporous illumination as if from a different planet. Black paper covered the windows, an oversight on Cruzito's part. Utility men recognized the purpose of such obfus-cation and, depending upon his or her mindset and/or friendships, might choose to let the *policia* or D.E.A. know of their discovery.

Still, unless legalization of the substance occurred in New Mexico much like it had in its northern neighbor, enormous amounts of money could be made from harvesting just one crop.

Cruzito and several others had chosen not to have a meth lab, opium/opioid cultivation and production, or to sell other highly lucrative drugs. Local officers and DEA officials generally concentrated on the more exotic substances, particularly since many New Mexicans simply drove to Colorado to get their supplies of weed.

"You want to see the latest crop?" Cruzito asked, dropping the hood of his logo-less black sweatshirt from off his shaved head. Cruzito knew the Anglo kid with the rich parents wanted to be a part of the Coldwater Carnívores, and even though non-gangstas were almost never admitted from the outside, Cruzito felt like Courtney could be useful in terms of potential sales.

Courtney nodded and the pair walked to the locked bedroom door. The Carnívore produced a key for an early twentieth-century painted door lock plate and keyhole that probably could be fiddled in less than two minutes.

Inside Courtney shaded his eyes and peered through the bluish haze at the green effusion of plants. The private viewing made him nervous, as if he not only shouldn't be seeing what he was seeing, but also because he realized these guys were serious dudes. For a moment he questioned his sanity in wanting to be a member of an organization engaged in illegal activities. Yet at the same time, both sons had little in common with their CMNL physicist father; his brother was too young to spend much time with; and the high school sophomore felt a limited kinship with either those of the same or different skin colors. The only time he really felt free and happy was on his bike. School seemed a slog. Other students were predisposed to stereotypes he didn't like. When at home he watched a lot of videos with western gunfights to escape the monotony of suburban home life.

"How much will this crop bring in?" he asked the stocky kid proud of his crop.

"Oh," Cruzito hesitated, "Not exactly sure. Depends on the market when we cut it. A lot of people say they want an ounce or a kilo, but when it comes to producing the cash, they don't have it."

"Well, I can get a small baggie, can't I?" asked Courtney, reaching for his wallet.

"'Course," replied Cruzito, reaching in a box under a growing table and grabbing a zip-lock sandwich bag with an ounce in it. "You can pay me later, C-man. I know you're good for it."

"So, dude," the substance salesman said, "the other three in the Carnívores are brothers. You bein' an Anglo and all, plus the son of wealthy parents may not be all that cool with *mis amigos*. Then again, you've got the right attitude about that high school-for-losers scene. Maybe—"

Just then there were three knocks on the door.

"That can't be Benito or anyone else I know. They don't knock that way."

"Well, who is it then," Courtney asked nervously.

"Don't know. Could be someone wanting signatures to get a friend on the November ballot."

As he held his finger up to his lips to signal Courtney should stay quiet, Cruzito went and closed and locked the bedroom door. There were two lighter knocks, this time on the screen door the caller had let close.

Cruzito walked to the door and opened it.

Two uniformed Santa Fe policemen stood side by side. Both had hats on, and one was wearing aviator sunglasses. One of the officers had his hand on the butt of his sidearm holster.

"Can I help you?" Cruzito asked, feigning nonchalance.

"We're looking for a Cruz Diaz.

"He's not here, right now," Cruzito replied, not bothering to open the door wider or invite the officers in.

"Who are *you*?" asked the officer in the sunglasses.

"I'm his cousin, Eduardo. My friend and I have a key, and we're waiting for him. He should be home in about an hour."

The officer, Nestor Ortiz, asking the questions, recognized visual and verbal behavior that tipped him something wasn't right. The kid was obviously Hispanic, though a banger, yet the cop made it a point to try to treat anyone respectfully. "Can we come in?" Officer Ortiz inquired in a deadpan voice.

"Uh...It's not my place," Cruzito answered. "Maybe you should come back when he's here."

The kid's nervousness and refusal signaled Ortiz his next question would lead to the playing of a trump card. "Mind if we come in and look around?"

"Aa... I don't think so," answered Cruzito, backing up and opening the door up just a little more. "It's a private residence and I'm not the owner. Might not be a good idea."

Ortiz reached inside his pocket and unfolded a piece of paper. "It may or may not be a good idea, but this search warrant permits Officer Mendoza and I to enter and make a reasonable search," he said, punctuating his remark by pulling the screen door open.

Cruzito backed up some more and pulled the main door open so that Ortiz and Mendoza could enter. He didn't bother to ask to see the warrant. *This is unbelievable!* the resident thought. *How could these dudes have a search warrant? Someone must have ratted out our grow lab. Now what do I do?*

Mendoza and Ortiz walked calmly through the house, looking under the sink, checking in some kitchen cabinets and bedroom drawers, and perusing the bathroom medicine cabinet. On the way back from the bathroom, Ortiz tried to turn the doorknob to the locked bedroom. When he pushed on the door it became apparent the door was locked. The officer ignored the door and walked into the living room where Courtney and Cruzito both sat with their arms crossed. Ortiz held up an orange plastic pill container with a white lid. "What's in here?" he asked.

"Levosomething," like the label says. "My cousin has a thyroid condition." Cruzito was banking on the two officers believing he was the owner's cousin, although sure they had glimpsed his name on the prescription label. Inwardly Cruzito sighed in relief. They had forgotten about the door.

Ortiz opened the large white bottle and looked at one of the oblong red pills. "These are too big and the wrong color to be levo-thyroxin. My wife takes the pills for hypo-thyroidism, and they're usually 50 or 100 milligrams, not 200."

"Oh, sorry," said Cruzito. "I thought you had the prescription bottle. "Maybe it's a different prescription."

Officer Ortiz shook his head. "Nope. It's ibuprofen." He didn't open it.

"Oh, by the way," he began as if it had been an oversight. "What's in the locked bedroom?"

"I think Cruz's got some stuff stored in there," he said. The kid now avoiding identification stood waiting, as if his answer had satisfied the cop's curiosity.

Ortiz began walking back to the door. "Mind if we see what's in there?"

Man, this guy is persistent. Now what do I do? "Um...I think it's locked, and I don't have a key."

Ortiz looked back at Mendoza and then at the kid, Diaz. "You sure you don't know where a key is?"

"Nah, man. I have no idea." Courtney was shaking his head negatively, as well.

"Officer Mendoza, do you have those lock-picking tools we got off that kid from Albuquerque?"

Mendoza nodded, reaching in his pocket while he walked back to the bedroom door. In less than a couple of minutes the lock was open.

"Eduardo, would you mind opening the door to this room now?" Ortiz asked the imposter shifting from one foot to the other. "It's open."

Cruzito now had no choice. He decided feigning surprise was his best shot. He opened the door. The three entered the plant-packed room under fluorescent illumination.

"Mm, interesting, *no*, Mendoza?"

"Certainly is," he replied.

Cruzito held both arms up with palms up. "Man..." Diaz exhaled. "I had no idea."

Officer Mendoza stepped out the bedroom door and beckoned with his finger that Courtney Ray should join them.

Ortiz turned to a now distraught Cruzito.

"Can I see some identification, please?"

~ TWELVE ~

The Library's last class of the day had just noisily exited with their Teacher. It was Wednesday, the afternoon when the Wizards Society for members by-invitation-only met. Students not only had to be fourth or fifth graders, but also had to be recommended by their Teachers as bibliophiles. Last year one fourth-grade class provided the bulk of the members. Those same members were now fifth graders, with only two new fourth-grade additions.

Doubtless some of the members joined because after-care was too predictable and boring. Kids whose parent or relatives worked and couldn't pick them up until 4:30 to 6:00, not only wished to escape the endless cycle of movies, coloring, writing and other activities to pass the after-school time, but also gained an opportunity to have a more imaginative snack. For each bi-monthly meeting the Wizards Society and Mr. C came up with cookies, fruit, or other edible and drinkable novelties slightly different from the yoghurt, health bars and fruit drinks provided by After Care.

Mr. C got out all his Wizards Society materials and placed them on his desk: the lantern with a candle in it, the large tome, and the Library hand bell. The idea was Bell, Book & Candle, based upon the Broadway play and movie. There was also the brown leather sign-in log, Mr. C. often wondering if any of his signatories would someday make their mark in the world or even become famous.

His eight to twelve avid readers forming the after-school Society hopefully were not going to cast any witch's spell on anyone. In fact, Mr. C stressed that one of the essentials of the club was to employ kindness, as well as knowledge gleaned from reading, in all their activities. Wizards could be evil or kind, and his kids, at least in principle, knew they would be better served casting helpful rather than hurtful spells upon others.

As if party boats arriving in harbor, they streamed in from a day of digesting pearls of literacy, equations in math, and from romping and wreaking havoc round the playground during recess. Each picked up a conical Wizards hat made either the previous year or just recently by following a page of instructions from an obscure Wizards book Mr. C had picked up at a cluttered Las Vegas antiques emporium. With an average age of almost 10, gender interaction often consisted of boys heckling the taller girls. Fifth graders had acute minds and a cornucopia of limited knowledge. Yet restraining them into focus was usually any Teacher's most challenging task. And an after-school club was no different. Wizards Society members were physically tired but still mischievous. Throwing pencils or paper wads at girls, stealing things from them, or spouting demeaning comments, often began the after-school hour in front of the Smart Screen. There Mr. C had placed distilled versions of a pair of biographies of two prominent characters featured in the Library's offerings.

During each club meeting the agenda included the reading aloud by Mr. C or other Society monitors, and a video mini-biography of each of the subjects. Members then underwent a series of questions asking them to contrast important behavioral facets or quirks of each character's life.

Today the two were Frida Kahlo and Diego Rivera. The bizarre self-portrait artist who limped due to a streetcar accident, and her much older muralist amour, flouted conventions, choosing to live in two houses connected by an aloft passageway. In reexamining Kahlo and Rivera, discovering unusual anomalies, ardent passions, and fiery disputes was easy. Passion was something the pair carried to rarified excess during their tempestuous relationship.

Kahlo's eyebrows nearly grew together, she had an unshaven start of a mustache, and her clothing resembled something out of 40s movie in which Dolores del Rio or Carmen Miranda wore a hat with lots of fruit and flowers sprouting from it. She bore almost constant pain in the leg nearly amputated from the accident. Kahlo also seemed to thrive on living the life of a libertine, taking lovers as she saw fit, yet always in awe of the man who painted the complex murals of Mexican, and later, American workers, their work clothing and atmosphere. Rivera was a philanderer, as well. His other passions included alcohol and food, with the stomach to match them. Long periods of his life, much like Michelangelo, were spent on scaffolding to complete his many intricate displays of art on walls. The pair's relationship vacillated between adoration and disputation.

When his eight Wizards had all finally subsided into chairs at two front roundtables, they began to listen attentively to Mr. C's biographical readings distilled from Wikipedia, the History Channel and other sources discovered on the seemingly infinite internet. The Librarian was proud of his reading skills, particularly when utilizing various voices to depict witches, bullies, stern school Principals, and other fictional characters. Non-fiction, however, was a little trickier, particularly condensed biographical material. Then student involvement was more predicated upon healthy adjacent photography, illustrations, charts, etc. supplementing the narrator's one voice.

"Alright," began Mr. C after both video and print biographies had been presented to the Society members, "so now we know a little about each of these colorful Mexican characters. Who can tell me," he inquired, scanning their faces, "the answer to this first question?" Mr. C used a yardstick as a pointer so that his people could follow his reading of the question on the Smart Screen: "What are one or more significant differences between the pair?"

Caliban Chimayo slouched at his table, his hands locked behind his head, and his right shoe nudging the white nylon stocking of Carolina Montoya. Her profusion of dark hair flowed as if a fountain from under the broad-brimmed robin's-egg blue Wizard's hat akin to something perhaps worn by the Good Witch Glinda of Oz. Purple and green stars decorated the cone, with curling ribbon streamers hanging down almost to the white brocade-rimmed brim. Rather than his usual attempts to pull her hat down further in the front, Caliban had been contenting himself with the occasional sub-*mesa* leg nudging with his red high-topped Converse All-Stars. He didn't bother to shoot his hand in the air as several others did.

"They both have breasts," Chimayo blurted loudly without being called upon. "but hers are slightly better disguised."

Mr. C was torn when it came to his most vociferous Society member. He loved Caliban's enthusiasm and involvement with almost any subject; yet he rued Señor Chimayo's inability to follow any rules of propriety or courtesy. The soccer player probably had an IQ of over 140, but his social skills consisted of repeated verbal assaults on the senses, whether auditory affronts, or insane interruptions coming at unpredictable moments. Mr. C thought about banning the fifth grader from the Society. But then freedom of speech had to be considered, as did eagerness, spirit, outrageous opinion, and the many other variable characteristics of an untamed participant. When he was in his homeroom class, Caliban was ridden like a buckin' bronco by Ms. Sevilla, and in Library hour Mr. C constantly upbraided his interruptions, disruptions, and unbridled rude behavior. The kid did have spunk and pizzazz, though, and misguided energy often spontaneously infused other interests in knowledge of more valuable nature.

"When I asked for differences between the pair," said Mr. C, walking over to Chimayo and signaling with his finger that the under-the-table nettling was to stop, "I was referring to the painters themselves, rather than any physical attributes or atypical characteristics they might have. And I don't remember you raising any more than a shoe rather than a hand." There was also to be considered the impropriety of a ten-year-old using female anatomy as humorous fodder. But drawing further attention to this off-color remark, Mr. C pondered briefly, would only encourage more of the same.

Caliban shook his head. "Well, then, Rivera puts more collective soul into his work, while Kahlo looked in the mirror too many times."

"Mmh...Mm-huh," disagreed twin Guadalupe De Vargas. She had on yellow patterned socks, one of which was wiggling in a black patent dance slipper at the end of a crossed leg. "Frida wanted to escape a body in pain," she began—"

"Could you speak a little louder?" Mr. C asked the diminutive twin, putting a hand up to cup his ear.

"She wanted to escape a body in pain," she repeated still softly, "and she painted mirror images of herself in hopes of becoming someone other than a victim of physical problems."

"She was a narcissist who studied herself in the mirror more than any other people, creatures, or objects," Chimayo again loudly proclaimed without being called upon.

"Maybe the mirror told her about her creative rather than physically handicapped self," said Antonio Lopez, a year ago one of the many fourth graders in the Society. "I know a couple of narcissists at Coronado who are victims of their own egos. They try to win verbal battles with louder voices and interruptions."

Spontaneous loud applause, whistling, and banging on the tables erupted. No one had missed the drift of Antonio's comment.

The previous week his father had let Antonio know that getting eliminated from the spelling bee was no shame. The hard-working student had placed third, and in future would do better. Slowly, over the last two years of entering the higher three grades of five in school, Lopez's confidence had soared. While most found Caliban's loud, disruptive tactics intimidating, Antonio believed Chimayo to be merely a show-off who lacked social confidence.

"Yah, well I know lots of timid nerds in Coronado who think they're special when they're nothing but mediocre," Caliban tossed out while looking at his hands clasped upon the table.

"Now, now, gentleman," Mr. C cautioned, "what did we say about kindness being the motivation of choice for Wizards? Is either of you being kind, here?"

Caliban crossed his arms, a show of indifference when he knew the Librarian had pinpointed the destructive nature of their skirmish.

"Let's get some more comments about the differences between the married painters," Mr. C intervened to get the group back on track. He scanned those at the front tables. Most of them were gazing at their tabletops, embarrassed for both Caliban and Antonio. Caliban was undeterred, however, wildly waving his hand to comply with being recognized.

"Caliban, you may have the most forceful personality in the group," Mr. C cautioned while looking around at the different faces, "but let's let some other Society members contribute."

Carolina finally looked up from under her good witch's hat, raised her palm sedately to chest height, and was recognized. "The content and size of their works differed a lot," she began. "Because of her lifelong injuries and pain, Kahlo obviously was tormented and self-involved. Yet even though she concentrated on self-portraits, she put animals and plants in many of her paintings. In contrast, Rivera's wall murals made the size of the painting almost as important as the subject matter. It was if he were trying to create maximum viewership."

"Sort of like maximum hair," said Caliban, his arms still folded while he leaned back.

"Now, now, Caliban. I've warned you once. First you need to raise your hand and be recognized. Then you should concentrate on making positive rather than negative contributions. Please apologize to Carolina."

"Sorry," Caliban muttered.

Mr. C knew he didn't mean it. Trying to accommodate the abrasive fifth grader's issues required the Librarian's utmost restraint and patience. And the Wizards Society leader didn't want to point out that the Shakespearean character Caliban was half monster. Highlighting the eponymous character might simply have offered the brash student further excuses for his behavior. Most Teachers refrained from blaming students for any lack of social skills, knowing that home life or lack of same, little guidance and educational encouragement, and often limited care, involvement and love received, drastically affected student motivation, behavior, and well-being. Behind every kid's disruptive nature or lofty learning abilities, were one or more parents, brothers and sisters, aunts and uncles, cousins, grandparents, friends, and myriad other influences. It was a miracle most students from impoverished and incomplete homes could reach moderate levels in the educational system as well as they did.

Guadalupe raised her hand diffidently. "Frida had a lot more pain than Diego," she began. Faces around the tables turned toward the less passive of the twins. Thoughts of Caliban and his outrageous posturing disappeared.

Guadalupe looked down at the green tabletop, hoping to gather courage from some place other than her heart. None was forthcoming. Several times she tried to begin a sentence of explanation. But nothing came out. Her mouth again opened, the others wondering if this time some thought would be revealed. "Um...Sometimes pain is physical and sometimes mental...Frida Kahlo had both." The twin paused, looking at the ceiling, unable to make any sort of eye contact. "Diego Rivera was a big man, big on recognizing the human condition, with big paintings." She put her hands up to rub her eyes. "The subject matter of his murals put him at risk. Certain Americans found his painted political and economic statements too much...Kahlo craved acceptance as a normal person. But when she looked in the mirror, it was apparent she wasn't like everyone else. She couldn't paint herself differently than a surrealistic reality she saw...Rivera couldn't paint the common man as anything but immortal..."

The twin had everyone mesmerized. Not only had she been able to capture some apt differences and similarities between the pair, but she had also been able to express herself aloud. Guadalupe's effusion was so uncharacteristic, other Society members and the Librarian were stunned.

"Well said, Guadalupe," commented Mr. C. The twin deserved far more praise and 'A' for effort, but Mr. C didn't wish to commend any one comment too highly in fear of discouraging others. "I'd like to hear more on the question of differences between the two. But we still have six questions to address. Let's do one more and then have our snack."

The next question asked what each painter's most significant contribution to the world was.

"Finding a mate twice or one-half your size?" threw out Caliban.

Mr. C ignored him and pointed at Matilda. This is going to be good, he thought. Blackstone's quiet demeanor and confidence promised a no-nonsense response. And at that point the Librarian wanted to avoid spending any more negative energy in dealing with the unbridled Chimayo. Forbearance wasn't bliss. But failing to recognize any such outré comments seemed to keep the ship of Wizards on a more positive course.

Matilda Blackstone had a Columbo-esque manner of fiddling with something in her hands, belying that her next remark might be far more insightful and provocative than her nervous habit and soft delivery might indicate. She wore her faded jeans cinched high on her waist, the missing belt appearing to be an oversight. But hiking up those same trousers upon standing up or in strolling through the shelves of books merely became part of her divergent style. Being tall and full-figured contrasted everything about her movements, clothing, and calm demeanor. The other Society members waited, knowing Matilda would steer the commentary back to order.

"All that is necessary to enjoy a Frida Kahlo painting is patience," she began, her hands on the table playing with an elastic hair band. "Her face alone conveys the stoic necessity to endure a life of pain. The eyes have it. And yet the dresses she chooses, and telltale heart painted in 'The Two Fridas,' or the rouge on her cheeks and Rivera's portrait on her forehead in 'Diego and I,' or the complexity and variety of 'The Wounded Table'..." Matilda paused to shake her head, yet still her focus remained on the twiddling hands. "'The Wounded Table,'" she continued, "a skeleton and surgical blood off-set by children and a deer. There is hope and despair in almost all her paintings."

"Chronic complainer," mumbled Caliban, "but she might have been cool as a low rider."

"She left a lifetime of singular paintings," Matilda added, finally looking up and over at Chimayo. "What will you leave behind?"

"No trail of tears, that's for sure," answered Caliban. "She got real in some of her paintings, but she needed to get real with her life."

"Hands raised, please," threw out Mr. C in a cheerful voice.

"She mixed real with surreal," said Antonio after being recognized. "And there was nothing more real than the stories told by Rivera's paintings."

Matilda was nodding. "There may never be anyone who better captures the heart and soul of the Mexican worker. 'The Carnival Life of Mexican Dictatorship' uses a smile to depict the faux concern of a greedy leader. 'The History of Mexico,' as a contrast, captures the hard work, persistence and hopes of all types of peoples in Mexico."

"Yah, but he treated his wife like a crippled peon," blurted Caliban. "He led a selfish life."

"Selfish, yes," said Blackstone, again looking down at her hands, "but the great works he left behind more than compensate for any of his negative behavior."

After this interchange, and while his Wizards enjoyed munching a handful of Oreo cookies, Mr. C had a chance to reflect. *This was the beginning*, he thought. There could be no doubt that Matilda Blackstone was a budding genius; that her single-parent mother had her on track to some sort of intellectually challenging future. Caliban Chimayo was another matter. His inflammatory manner and brusque behavior concealed a germinating curiosity. That inquisitiveness might continue in the childlike negative. Yet there was the chance, Mr. C considered, that the pendulum movement between dedicated accomplishment and accumulated knowledge versus self-pity and self-destruction might be grabbed during the positive zenith of its swing. Then Antonio showed great promise, as well. And if Guadalupe could keep from being distracted by more powerful personalities, she was a potential Wizard in her own right. Carolina also performed amazingly, most probably on the way to a private high school and college.

Each Wizards Society meeting was only one hour twice a month.

Yet with the discovery that any one Librarian could not induce every child to read for pleasure, came a different realization that he or she could infuse a few minds with the magic.

~ THIRTEEN ~

Circumstances can sometimes dictate fate. In the case of Cruzito Diaz, being 17 years of age with no previous record went in his favor. Most of the citizens of his neighborhood were unaware of his farming activities. The ones that did know, for the most part kept their mouths shut. It was a community thing. Some of the residents living in the Village of Agua Fria or in its lower vicinity were involved in activities from which there was no declared income, no federal or State income taxes, and the possibility of confrontations with police or other authorities. Life for arrivals, particularly those speaking Spanish and limited, or no English, was difficult. Jobs paying over the table for those with few skills were hard to get. Under the table payments for day labor jobs or part-time work in construction, etc. were commonplace but at or below minimum wage. The sale of alcohol and drugs augmented incomes for those with part-time, poor paying, or no jobs. Cruzito had that certain look that discouraged supervisors or managers from hiring him. His personality was mostly quite mellow. Yet appearances often prejudiced the ability to consider abilities and experience.

After his house was inspected and the farm products and equipment were confiscated, he was given probation and mandated to see a parole officer, to reenter high school, and to see school Counselors. In a few months he would be 18 and his circumstances would

108

change. But in the interim Cruzito Diaz found himself back in school, and with no income or relatives to pay his rent.

As a contrast, Courtney Ray, with the assistance of his father's lawyer, was able to convince police interviewers that he had merely been visiting and had no part in the growth and sale of the illegal plants. The day after his release, he had gone to school, very few the wiser regarding his arrest.

That afternoon Odysseus learned of the confrontation. Instead of coming down upon his older brother, the fifth grader now idolized Courtney even more. The two were standing in Odysseus' bedroom, their father at work and mother at bridge club.

"So did you freak out when the cops came," asked Odysseus.

Courtney, a gold chain cascading from a belt loop to his back pocket, fell back on the bed with his arms outstretched. "Dude, I was freaked! I mean, here were these two cops looking like they're out of a TV show. Except that it was the real deal, and it looked like there was no way Cruzito was going to keep them from discovering his stash."

"So, like, they searched the house?"

"Yah," answered Courtney crossing his arms. "We were both hoping they somehow would overlook the second bedroom. But no luck. After coming back into the living room and asking him about some prescription pills they found, the guy in sunglasses asks Cruzito what was in the other bedroom that was locked. It was over, man."

"So, they took you to jail down near Cerrillos?"

"You got it, bro. Within an hour dad's lawyer arrived, and he got me out. I think they let Cruz go, too, because he's only 17 and they released him to a neighbor he called who acted like his uncle."

"Do you have a record, now?"

"Not sure, but I got something else for Cruzito to use on whoever blew the whistle." He walked over to his closet and rifled under some T-shirts on a shelf.

"Wow," said an astonished Odysseus. "You're not gonna give Cruzito that hunting knife!"

"I might," he answered. "Right now, I'm not going to do anything. But if I have any future problems with the cops or DEA or the Argenta Principal, I don't know what I might do."

"Dude, just don't do anything crazy. I mean, you have nothing to do with their growing weed and selling it. I'd stay away from Cruzito for a while, you know?"

Suddenly a man with a corduroy jacket and rep tie stood in the bedroom doorway. It was their father.

"Odysseus, I need to talk to your brother alone," said Penn Ray. "Could you give us a few minutes and close the door behind you when you leave?" It was more of a statement than a question, but the next 15 minutes or so, the CMNL physicist realized, could be among the most critical times spent with his son and any discipline issues.

Courtney tried to disguise the horror of knowing what was coming. Usually, his father tried to induce him to play golf, or go for a walk in an arroyo. But this was going to be difficult for Courtney to explain.

"Sit down, son," his dad said, taking a designer chair his mother had chosen, now positioned in the room's corner. He waited until Courtney was sitting on the bed, his hands resting on thin, jeans-clad thighs. "O. K., son, I know it's not easy being the son of a white-bread set of parents when living and going to school in an almost entirely Hispanic area."

Courtney rubbed one thigh, then looked at the fingers of his other hand now as if waiting for a manicure.

"I can't choose your friends, nor do I want to," his father continued. "But I am compelled to give fatherly advice, no matter how difficult it may be." Mr. Ray crossed one leg over the other, glancing at his watch. Courtney had yet to look at his father. "But first I have a question: Who is this Cruzito Diaz? A close friend? A gangbanger?"

The high school sophomore pursed his lips. *This could be the most difficult answer of my life*, he thought to himself. "Um...he's just a kid who used to go to Argenta. He left school because he didn't like it. He was living with his grandmother, but she died—"

"I understand all that. You've told me before. But this police report," he said, shaking a couple of pages in front of him, "says that over 30 cannabis plants were found growing in his bedroom, as well as several baggies with more grass in them below the growing tables. Now, as far as I know, Diaz doesn't have a license to grow or dispense pot for medicinal reasons."

Courtney nodded affirmatively, yet with a sideways jerk of his head, as if admitting tacit agreement brought forth a cornucopia of reasons not stated.

"You're not a member of his gang, are you?"

"No, dad! I just know the guy. I knew he sold pot, but I didn't know he was growing it in his bedroom. I'm not involved, O.K.?"

Penn felt his son was protesting too much, in Shakespearean fashion. Yet the best outcome was some sort of promise that in the future he would avoid contact with his friend. The physicist had been assured by his lawyer that no record of the arrest would remain. But the father was also aware that a second trip to any police station, for any reason, would be next to impossible to erase.

"Courtney, your brother is having his own problems in fifth grade. Now this with you," he said. "I don't know," he added, shaking his head. Penn picked a nit off his coat sleeve. "I know I'm not the greatest father in the world. I'm often gone on trips, about which I can tell you very little. And I enjoy playing golf and your mother plays bridge, both of which you feel to be traditional, predictable middle-class suburban entertainment. But please remember that we are more than twenty years older than both of you. We were kids once. We know how there're always temptations to get into some sort of trouble. We know that. But as a father, I think it's our responsibility to draw the line at our sons being involved with drugs or gang membership. You can't blame us for wanting you to stay out of trouble, and for our wanting the best for both of you."

"Dad, I get it," Courtney replied. "I haven't joined their gang, and most of them don't want any non-Hispanic members, anyway. And I'm not gonna sell drugs, either."

The 16-year-old knew the veracity of most of what he said was in question. Courtney didn't feel he was intentionally lying. There was little chance he would even be offered an opportunity to join the Coldwater Carnívores. And although he had helped a couple of friends get a lid from Cruzito, he didn't want to get involved with selling weed. Yet Courtney Ray was among the many disaffected high school students finding staying in school, the subjects taught, and the discipline involved, boring. He wasn't great at any subject. There was little chance he would end up with a mainstream career and wife like his dad. The idea of ambition escaped him. He didn't want to go to college. Courtney didn't know what he wanted to do. But he did know that following in either of his parents' footsteps was unlikely. And even though Cruzito had little money, his friend had a roof over his head and freedom. Freedom to do what he wanted when he wanted. No parents trying to get him to be the stereotypical chip off the old block.

Across from him in the corner, Penn Ray looked over at his son, and considered that telling any teenager what to do often had the inverse effect. You told them to stay out of trouble; they got into trouble. You tried to set examples of discipline in your pursuits; they went out of their way to avoid any such positive activities. Fortunately, most recalcitrant teenagers simply outgrew their propensity to act badly. If you were lucky, they begrudgingly entered some university hoping to be no more than a party animal, yet somehow rediscovered pleasure reading and a subject or two that engaged them. Penn could only hope his sons made it through their formative and teenage years without injury, expulsion from school, or committing a crime. The master of the household stood up to signal his lecture was through.

"Just remember, Courtney, you and Odysseus have an opportunity to excel both at academics and at life. Your mother and I will do everything possible to enable your success. But keep in mind also, good behavior and kindness are mandatory for peace of mind and success in life."

~ FOURTEEN ~

Since there were 24 Coronado Elementary classes attending one hour specials (Library-P.E.-Music-Art-Computer Lab) within 28 possible class hours in any 4-1/2-day week, each special instructor had several hours of weekly prep time. Mr. C used his 'free' hours to order and log in books, to weed out outdated books, to discover more electronic reading, research, and educational game sites, to shelve books, to design posters and plan book fairs, and myriad other activities. Today he was off at a meeting in the Principal's office to discuss a substantial paperback and hardback fiction books purchase.

Meanwhile, the Librarian's office was a room he seldom entered. The space was used by a wide variety of visiting Counselors because the school's Counselor, whose office adjoined the Library, could not possibly render service to all of those needing help in a school of 550. These Counselors were like doctors on call, and their use of Mr. C's office took priority over other usages scheduled by school Counselor Genoveva Juarez. Inside this office, the shelves spilled over with toys, games, DVDs, and a cornucopia of distractions used initially to relax students during appointments.

That morning Christian De Leon had an appointment with a visiting Counselor originally from Spain. The Special Education student felt relieved that he would be excused from his fifth-grade class for an hour. His classmates were rehearsing for a play they had collaboratively written on one of the Minecraft books, and Christian was glad he hadn't yet been chosen to play a role. He looked forward to talking with his visiting Counselor, Señora Octaviana. She dressed stylishly and exuded a kind exuberance that always put him at ease.

As he turned the corner to enter the Library, these and other thoughts of the impending hour helped him realize that whether he continued to get Tutoring from Señora Octaviana, or not, at least someone in the school treated him with kindness and respect.

Yet when he walked through the Library office open door, the Special Education student momentarily lost his composure. Standing next to the desk in the far corner was Emerald Star, the light through the window glistening off shampooed hair cascading down over a dark green suit. She wasn't wearing the tiara, but the same attentive gaze made him forget all about his potential meeting with Señora Octaviana. The Fairy Princess Tutor seemed to glide into the chair behind the desk, then gestured for him to take the one of two cushioned chairs opposite.

"I hope you don't mind my helping you with your reading this hour," Emerald Star smiled softly, revealing a crescent of brilliant white teeth. "Ms. Octaviana is helping someone else in another office as we speak." Ms. Star opened the book in front of her and turned it 180 degrees, so it was positioned on the desk next to Christian.

He was amazed at how every move she made seemed effortless. In a graceful motion she silently spun round the desk and alit upon the chair next to him, a hint of an exotic perfume enveloping him. He couldn't help but notice her sequined amethyst shoes, white stockings, and the giant cobalt-blue gemstone-edged 'W' centered upon the side of the jacket buttoned over her heart.

"What does the 'W' stand for?" he asked bashfully.

"Wizards," she replied, touching the letter gently with a perfectly polished emerald fingernail. "I'm an honorary member of the 'Wizards Society' at Coronado.

"I thought wizards were mean," Christian said.

"The best ones are kind," she replied. "Their mission is to help people rather than hurt them."

"Like you're doing with me?"

She smiled and nodded in agreement. "And for me to help you, you must believe that together, the two of us will transform you into a reader you thought you could never be, maybe even above and beyond fifth-grade level. Do you believe we can work together to improve your reading?"

Christian exhaled. For six years of elementary school he had discovered that he was falling behind in both his reading and math skills. He tried his best, but somehow words, sentences, and books easily read by others, remained difficult for him to understand. Kids made fun of his mistakes. They laughed when he had trouble answering a question. Sometimes he was tongue-tied, and that just made things worse. Even though she had to deal with the problems of more than 25 kids, Ms. Sevilla tried to help him when she could. She assured him that reading abilities were like walking for a toddler: for some bipedal motion came easily and quickly; others needed to hold onto hands, couches, chairs, and other objects while wobbling forward on two legs. But eventually they walked, and he knew Ms. Sevilla and Emerald Star were right in telling him to be patient and to believe. "Yes," came out of him as if a genie from a bottle. He wanted to add: 'I think I can,' but he wasn't *that* confident yet.

"We're going to read the version by Joe Hayes of *La Llorona* in English three times," she began, turning to the first pages of illustration and text facing one another. "I'm going to read it aloud to you the first time. I will move my finger below the words so you can follow along. The second time we will read the page aloud together, and you will move your finger under the words as we read. And the third time you will do it alone, again using your finger to highlight each word.

"Yet remember, reading is cumulative. The idea is that by the end of a life, a reader, writer, and speaker, makes fewer and fewer pronunciation, grammar, and spelling mistakes. He or she reads, writes, and speaks with more and more confidence. Practice makes perfect. The reader slowly acquires more and more vocabulary to be able to express him or herself. You are that reader."

Her index finger tipped in emerald lightly touched the top of his hand just for an instant, as if magic was conveyed through the tip of this digit. "But we all must be patient. Reading requires a lifetime of practice. Never worry if you don't understand any word or word. On the second time through we will stop when you need to look the word up in this dictionary. For online books, in most cases, merely tapping on or highlighting a word can bring forth a definition. Patience and the ability to learn from your mistakes are your most important helpers."

The effect of Princess Emerald Star's voice upon Christian was nearly overwhelming. No one had spent as much time to reassure him with such ease. His 'Wizard' Tutor exuded caring and consideration. Her aura was more positive than anything he had experienced. The fifth grader had to concentrate to stay focused on what she was saying. He didn't really know what a true miracle felt like. But in their two brief encounters the Special Education student already felt a growing relaxation and confidence. It was as if a past school life of insecurity would slowly lift and be replaced by language skills previously thought impossible.

"Long years ago, in a humble village, there lived a fine-looking girl named Maria," Emerald Star began to read aloud as mellifluously as if singing a ballad. Her long and slender finger glided underneath each word of the story of *La Llorona*. The hue of her skin matched an exotic mocha coffee color of a fine leather belt. There was the fragrance of kindness surrounding them.

Star had practiced storytelling for many years within her Apache father's home, although now living in her mother's Cochiti Pueblo. Children and adults often sat crisscross in front of her on the Earth, listening attentively and being ferried into realms carefully crafted oral or written fiction helped reach. Star loved the myths and legends passed down orally by tribal members. Each story created its own place and time. Each often transported the reader or listener to untold lands of magic and events of wonder. She also loved the challenge of kids like Christian. The barriers he approached and had to overcome, each year becoming more challenging. Yet in her experience at Tutoring, Emerald Star had found attention to detail and delivery of language all-powerful. She had seen those with limited comprehension skills blossom like the rare desert cactus, Queen of the Night, whose trumpet flower blossoms only one summer night a year. Comparable to desert flora simply needing occasional water and nourishment, students like Christian suddenly turned the floral corner of unexpected reading skill.

Within the hour the Tutor and the student desperately wishing to be accepted under any terms had successfully negotiated the story, a tale of a woman whose loss of her husband's affections provoked the drowning of her children. Early on during Mr. C's Library tenure, an observer found his reading aloud of the folk tale inappropriate due to its womanizing, drinking and violence. The observer was unwilling to acknowledge parallels from folk tales like Little Red Riding Hood, many of Grimm's fairy tales, and other scary stories in English kids love. A wolf eating a grandmother or a grandmother cooking a witch in an oven were somehow acceptable, while drowning your children in a river, the story originally in Spanish, somehow was considered inappropriate. Kids speaking both Spanish and English, without prejudice of social correctness, loved the story. And after Christian and Emerald Star read aloud the story three times, it was apparent both the subject matter and Christian's newly acquired skills with letters, words, and sentences sublimated Mr. C's earlier observer's opinion.

"Did you notice that when you read the story the third time that your reading ability and comprehension of the story itself were signs of progress you didn't think possible?" Star asked.

Christian's head was swimming. They had only spent one hour on one story. Yet already he could feel that the formerly impossible was now becoming a growing reality. He nodded. "Yes," he answered, again running his index finger over the last few words of the closing paragraph of La Llorona. "Suddenly, my wish might come true!"

~ FIFTEEN ~

The gods looking down from above knew better. The seemingly innocuous task of making an after-school parking lot run smoothly was a never-ending challenge. Patience and guidance were required. Impatience and disregard for instruction were commonplace. Teacher/monitors daily did their best to get kids on their way home as quickly as possible. Beginning at least twenty minutes before the 2:55 bell, students' relatives began lining up their trucks, SUVs and low-rider sedans along the curb stretching back beyond the small gym and out into Las Vegas Boulevard. Teachers with walkie-talkies asked the occupants of each car which student(s) he or she was picking up. Those same parking lot monitors relayed the information to others near the school's main exit where kids were waiting expectantly. During those 10 to 20 minutes, depending upon car air-conditioners or heaters, how the day had gone for the drivers and other passengers, or lack of movement in the line of vehicles, tempers could flare. Toddlers, little brothers, and sisters could whine. Food and drinks could be dropped on the car floor.

Meanwhile near the school's entrance/exit, students of various grades gamboled round the concrete apron or streaked toward buses even when yelled at to stop. Numbers of kids blithely ignored regulations and sneaked to the forbidden candy truck parked curbside off school property. And as vehicles collected their children and tried to exit parking lanes, other Teachers in SFSD orange vests acted as traffic cops to try and maximize safe vehicle exiting of the premises. 'Organized chaos' might describe the whole scenario.

As fifth-grade Teacher Mr. Penumbra tried verbally to warn a departing parent to wait while a woman in a wheelchair was escorted within the crosswalk, a white car, piloted by an impatient visitor of some sort, refused to wait. The driver floored her vehicle, the passenger door flying open. Another parent in the crosswalk jumped backwards, narrowly avoiding being knocked to the pavement by the door flying out like a metal wing. The irate driver careened through a right turn onto Las Vegas Avenue. Mr. Penumbra wanted to yell, but just shook his head. Most parents and relatives were patient and waited their turn. Yet the whole after-school release was only as safe as its most dangerous or impatient driver. All it took was one parent or relative having a bad day, having had a couple drinks after work, or annoyed with a perceived excessive wait, to cause havoc. Ironically, you rarely saw a kid run out in front of a vehicle. They knew better. It was almost always an impatient, irate, angry, late to an appointment, or omniscient adult who defied instructions from the dedicated monitors in vests.

Honking suddenly erupted from about the sixth car in line to exit lane one. Monitor Katarina Española stood with her arms outstretched to indicate the line should hold fast. She wished she could turn and flip the driver off with her middle finger, but restraint was necessary to avoid pandemonium. Every day those no-win situations: you let one line of vehicles proceed; those in another line felt unfairly restrained in having to wait their turns.

Nearby, Mr. Penumbra considered what the rest of his afternoon might be after crosswalk duties. He would probably need to annotate and file a report on the careening vehicle almost killing a Teacher, person in a wheelchair, and another hapless potential victim. It was one more example of how staff monitors within the white pavement-crossing lines barely could ensure safety. Then at 3:30 Penumbra would have to meet with two parents of a recalcitrant boy who regularly on the slightest whim disrupted the class. There were also the essays to grade on the rights and obligations of U. S. Presidents. Ms. Sevilla had asked the fifth-grade Teachers for a 10-minute meeting sometime before four o'clock. And a decision was required to present to Principal Penelope regarding the purchase of some classroom books and other necessities. His face was already red, but should time permit, he was hoping to acquire a brighter garnet hue while rodeo riding his mountain bike through the nearby arroyo. That enjoyable exercise probably remained iffy.

A Ford flatbed truck with giant fluorescent green monster shocks drew up to the crosswalk, the rumbling of dual exhausts signaling the vehicle waiting its turn.

Mr. Penumbra thoughts came back to reality as he realized the crosswalk was empty of parents and kids. He could now let a stream of vehicles compete with those from parking lane one for the two exit files dodging passing traffic.

"Hey, man," a probable Argenta High student said while leaning out his truck window.

Mr. Penumbra asked another Teacher to shepherd the cross walk while he answered the call of Mr. Monster driver. The young kid had mint green sunglasses to match the shocks and looked down at the fifth-grade Teacher sporting khaki pants and a button-down shirt. "Sir," the young man in the Dallas Cowboys T-shirt said from his high-elevation pilot position. Before using the three-letter entitlement, he had realized Mr. Penumbra's age required some deference. "Waiting at DMV doesn't take as long as this curbside pickup stuff. Can you please let some of the cars through?"

Penumbra knew it was a losing battle. You let one driver impose a request, then others gained momentum by edging out from the line to pass those waiting patiently. Yet to some extent the kid was right. The crosswalk monitor had been daydreaming and lots of drivers in curbside cars with collected occupants were now becoming impatient.

"Pedestrian kids and adults take preference," the gray-haired monitor answered before turning back to put his arms horizontal while Mrs. De Vargas and her two twins crossed over. As soon as that trio reached the parking lot median between lanes, however, Penumbra waved the youthful driver through. Compromise was always a consideration in school life. Spontaneous decisions had to made in unpredictable fashion. Departing kids, adults and vehicles fell into that nebulous realm requiring instant decisions.

"Thanks, dude," the 20-something yelled down at the 50-something Teacher as he passed by.

Penumbra was considered Anglo, though he was primarily of Irish heritage. Yet he felt the Hispanic population by and large treated their senior population with a lot more respect than he got from those with pale skin colors like his own. Most Hispanics, both young and old, tended to the politeness end of the spectrum. Kids often held doors for him. Parents rarely raised their voices even when adamantly concerned about their child. The Teacher smiled as the huge truck tires edged toward one of two lanes leading to freedom.

To the elevated beast's left as it departed stood parking lane one's stream of idling metal-and-glass machines. These eager relatives, students and siblings believed parking in lane one closest to the exit gave them preemptive privileges. The opposite was true. Monitor Española used her hands outstretched like 45-degree wings to keep them from exiting. Vehicles exiting curbside took priority. Sorry, folks. Just another group champing at the bit when 20 to 30 vehicles must funnel into two-car exits.

At that two-car opening in the perimeter fence, three kids having surreptitiously swapped coins for candy at the forbidden curbside truck, darted across. The exit monitor yelled at them, but the slow-est of the three galloping third graders nearly was hit. The driver of an exiting car had been looking left before shooting out between opposing lanes of cars. Just another blip on the daily release-from-school radar screen.

Meanwhile, three of the four giant buses were leaving together like a slow-moving herd of giant yellow-and-black dinosaurs. Their drivers had to be careful: small white buses picking up various after-school club members or special education kids edged in and out of bus lanes.

On the xeriscape gravel below under-watered, stunted trees, one careening Kindergartener fell and hurt his elbow. Nearby two girls were pulling trash items from a standing circular container to hurl at giggling boys. Another girl was sobbing uncontrollably while a Teacher bent over to console her.

"What's wrong, dear?" the monitor asked.

The girl in a navy-blue dress and white blouse stained with chocolate milk, with pink tights underneath for accent, continued to choke into hands held up to her face.

"Don't worry, dear," said the Teacher reassuringly. "We'll go in-side and call your mother to come and get you."

The monitor took the second grader's tiny hand, but the dis-consolate girl looked up at her through oval, black-rimmed glasses. "But my mom's at work. She can't...come and get me now."

The two continued to the front office. "Don't worry," consoled the monitor, "we'll find her. This happens to kids every day. We'll find your mom or someone else to get you."

In the crosswalk, Mr. Penumbra looked at his watch. It was 3:10, just 15 minutes after the bell. Only a few cars remained in line at the curb. Only about seven students still waited for rides. No more relatives were attempting to thread between the white lines to reach parking lot safety. *I wish I could just jump on my mountain bike and shoot off down the arroyo,* he thought to himself. *Dodging Cortez Middle School and then Argenta High School students ambling down the path.* But his many further duties, meetings, gradings, *et al,* called.

Inside the office one secretary, Magdalena, was explaining how a parent's daughter undoubtedly must have taken the bus when she was to be picked up. The other secretary, Blanca, hovered over a phone, attempting to reach the crying student's mother at work.

The entire release process on most days only took 15 to 20 minutes. Yet much like shouting in a stock exchange, or a traffic manager of a news organization, solving the myriad problems arising like carnival shooting targets was complicated. Release could become an ordeal. Or Teachers, and office staff could simply take in stride one problem at a time, prioritizing, answering questions, and directing students as best they could. After-school release was often as complicated as the all-day rendering of knowledge to kids in chairs with boundless desires to move.

~ SIXTEEN ~

At the Principal's conference table sat three women: the Principal, assistant Principal, school Counselor, as well as Rodolfo Mendoziano, one of two popular male physical education Teachers.

In his mid-40s and with experience at several schools, Mendoziano had a propensity for cheerfulness and enthusiasm, yet also a penchant for hugging. The latter was a difficult dilemma in the era of Me2 and other groups and causes now regularly delineating inappropriate behavior by males. For years certain men in Hollywood were known for employing the casting couch. Others in corporations could with impunity chase secretaries round the office. For decades complaints had been lodged, but largely ignored, explained away, or dissipated into the realm of 'he said, she said.'

Yet in the second decade of the third millennium, impunity had flown with the wind for such predators or other males employing inappropriate verbal comments or suggestive touching. Men at large were put on notice that no one, whether at a major television network, in charge of a major film production studio, politician, or film or TV star was exempt from accountability. Males either behaved appropriately or could suffer formerly avoided consequences.

Señor Mendoziano's foibles were proving unique, yet unacceptable. In the gym he would pat nearly fully grown fifth-grade girls on their butts. On parking lot duty, the P.E. instructor tended to hug everyone: Teachers, Kindergartners, young or old, thin or partially developed girls, and anyone with whom he felt familiar.

Principal Guadalajara had used the Library office to warn the affectionate man that he must cease and desist from any such behavior. Over several days a central office observer unknown to him was a witness to many such inappropriate incidents. Several girls had complained to Ms. Juarez, the school Counselor. While some of Mendoziano's gestures might be construed as innocuous, hugging fifth grade girls frontally, patting butts and other inappropriate touching plain and simply were not on.

Now Ms. Guadalajara was placed in an awkward position. Firstly, there was the 'coach's' popularity. Secondly, if Mendoziano chose to dispute the charges, a great deal of time and effort was to be wasted and costs incurred, all because of a male in a position of responsibility's inability to refrain from inappropriate behavior. Hugging a Kindergartener or holding his or her hand occasionally might be acceptable; hugging or patting fifth-grade girls was inappropriate. Ms. Guadalajara had made that more than evident in her first meeting with the physical education instructor.

For those now sitting round the Principal's office table, it was evident each dreaded what was to come. Should Mr. Mendoziano be dismissed, not only would a capable and well-liked instructor lose his job, but he could lose his teaching license and become a pariah in the future. All three women had had to deal with difficult problems in the past. Yet telling a longstanding Teacher he would likely be dismissed would undoubtedly prove more unpleasant than talking to parents, students or Teachers about performance or discipline issues. The coming process was particularly onerous for Principal Guadalajara, who over the years at Coronado had gained a real affection for coach Mendoziano. Assistant Principal Victoria Sandoval sat looking through the case summary, glad she could probably refrain from comment during the tribunal. Counselor Genoveva

Juarez remained stoic. During the session she would be obligated to present numerous unappealing reports detailing Mendoziano's poor judgment, as well as to note subsequent warnings. Principal Guadalajara denoted all parties present and warned them that the recorder she was turning on would record anything presented. There would be no chitchat. The matter had to be on record.

"Mr. Mendoziana," Principal Guadalajara felt forced to begin when she had often used his first name, "this is a difficult meeting for all of us. As you know, from our meeting two months ago in the Library office, you were warned in no uncertain terms that inappropriate hugging or touching of our students had to stop." She pursed her lips and glanced up at him briefly. "Yet numerous complaints from specific students, Teachers, and Counselor Juarez, have been lodged since our initial meeting." Ms. Guadalajara gently put her several-page report down on the table. "Do you have any comments?"

"O. K.," he began nervously, "I know I get a little carried away from time to time. I'm too enthusiastic with hugging. Ask even the Teachers in the school and they will tell you that I hug everyone, and that my hugging is platonic. I mean, I'm sorry if any of the Teachers or girls felt offended—"

"Mr. Mendoziano," the Principal interrupted, "these reports involve far more than just the hugging of fifth-grade female students. And once again, I am forced to remind you of our previous meeting in which past as well as future behavior was discussed. Do you feel you have adhered to the changes in behavior outlined to you from the SFSD code of behavior?"

There were beads of sweat on his forehead as coach Mendoziano looked down at the table. "No." he shook his head sadly.

"You have put the students at risk, as well as jeopardized many of the faculty members' careers if strong action isn't taken. Do you understand that?"

"Well, I still feel my intentions in hugging are harmless and show concern for my students."

Mrs. Juarez picked up her report. "The reports I have detail far more than inappropriate hugging," she began. "The complaints allege 'patting my butt,' 'he said my figure was starting to get curves,' 'held my face in his hands while he talked to me,' 'put his hand on my knee while we sat in the bleachers.' I could go on, but without reading further, I think it clear you have failed to cease and desist from your previous warned-about-as-inappropriate behavior."

"Mr. Mendoziano," said Ms. Guadalajara, gently shaking her head. "Again, your lack of judgment and behavior have put Coronado Elementary, SFSD, and the students and faculty of this school in a difficult position. Our mandate is to protect our students against any such inappropriate behavior. Certainly, you must understand—"

"But...I mean...come *on*, people, this is my career you're talking about, and—"

"I'm sorry, Mr. Mendoziano, not only have you failed to adhere to our earlier warnings, but you now have created a dilemma that most probably will have only one outcome."

"What's that?" the coach asked.

Everyone at the table knew the answer.

"Normally for certain infractions a Teacher in your position and with your history—including inappropriate incidents and warnings at other schools—might be given the option to resign," said the Principal, but in your case those in SFSD central office have admonished both assistant Principal Sandoval and me that a hearing will be convened most likely leading to dismissal."

"Dismissal!" sputtered a red-faced Mendoziano.

"I'm sorry, Mr. Mendoziano," continued Ms. Guadalajara, but your refusal to refrain from inappropriate behavior leaves SFSD and Coronado Elementary school with no other tenable option. A hearing will be held in central office, but we at Coronado Elementary would be remiss if we didn't inform you of probable termination. There are rarely any third chances. Any faculty or staff member of any school with as many complaints lodged against him or her as you have, usually is terminated. I also must warn you that you may also lose your teaching license."

"What!"

"I'm sorry, Mr. Mendoziano, but you will be notified of the hearing. In the meantime, you are to be put on paid leave, and are to gather your things from your office after this meeting and leave the premises."

"But I've got four classes today!"

"A substitute has already arrived and will assume your duties."

~ SEVENTEEN ~

The fourth-grade class taught by Christina Cortez was bilingual. Most of the students spoke Spanish and English, but several knew only basic English words or phrases for communicating in their new country. After all, the State of New Mexico's name more than hinted from where many of its inhabitants were descended. Coronado was one of several south-side schools hosting a preponderance of first-generation emigrant students from Mexico or other Central and South American countries.

At the time Coronado remained part of a system accommodating emigrant arrivals. The school's bilingual plan included two weeks of studies in English alternating with two in Spanish. Many argued either for or against the dual-language approach. Naysayers stressed that every two weeks taught in Spanish put students farther and farther behind in English, the language they would eventually have to master. Those decrying the approach emphasized that the U.S. school system made no accommodations for Chinese, Japanese, African, French, or other emigrants. During English-only classes such students were immersed, without help from their foreign languages.

Those in favor of bilingual programs argued that students fell behind their English-only peers in elementary school, drew even during middle school, and moved ahead during high school. Many

Teachers and observers found those in favor of this approach often failed to present evidence proving its success. Many felt Español should be offered, but only as an elective or perhaps for an hour a day.

The school and its Library took the matter seriously. One entire wall of the Library was devoted to Spanish or Spanish/English dual-language books. Mr. C and others, however, observed that most students, even Kindergarteners tended to gravitate toward the English sections of the Library, even when they could read little of the respective texts. Generally, the younger the child, the more illustrations and fewer words he or she needed. Yet as early-grade students accumulated vocabulary, some gradually moved in the direction of English text-only books. This was partially true because many of the Spanish chapter books centered upon Anglo heroines or heroes and were simply translations of English chapter books rather than written by Hispanic authors. Mr. C believed ardently in getting kids to love reading. To encourage many students, he had slowly acquired more graphic novels, books often combining beautiful illustrations with limited but often challenging texts.

Mrs. Cortez was a quiet but intellectual woman who had repeatedly considered all the above. For her fourth graders, however, she felt her fluency in Spanish, combined with most of her kids speaking Spanish at home, enabled her to conduct class in either language. Most of her kids preferred Spanish. Yet over time, she felt her students able to understand and acquire English better when they could go back and forth. Bilingualism was an advantage. Mrs. Cortez enjoyed the challenge for the most part. Yet every year she inherited a few from third grade seemingly intent upon disrupting her tranquil approach to teaching.

Today she was concerned with getting her kids to understand the basics of the U.S. government. Mrs. Cortez showed some illustrations of the Constitution on the Smart Board, asked specific students what several key rights they enjoyed thanks to the Bill of Rights, and discussed the three sections of federal government, the executive, legislative and judicial. For most of Coronado's elementary students, English language skills and accumulated knowledge were limited, even as students reached third through fifth grades. In Middle School they would spend more time on social studies, history, and other more complex subjects. Learning literacy and math skills remained the focus of elementary school students.

Like most Teachers, Ms. Cortez had to be vigilant. Teaching was somewhat like performing magic tricks or stage acting: you had to control your audience; and you knew when you had them and when you didn't. Signs of inattentiveness were fidgeting, playing with toys and spinners, whispering, throwing paper wads, and a cornucopia of disruptive diversions. Under most circumstances Cortez was adept at enforcing discipline, with only brief interruptions. Yet in most elementary school classes, there always seemed at least one or several disruptive or disinterested sorts who could test any Teacher's patience.

"Luis, I'm trying to conduct a class on U.S. government, while you seem to be trying on non-governmental faces while I do so. Do you think you're making the right decision with your behavior?"

The small boy with the loud voice tapped a short drum roll on his desk. "Mm-huh," he smirked looking over at Francisco and Marcus, each of whom Cortez had placed as far from each other as possible.

"Well, this better be good, for you to be interrupting our class. Most everyone but Francisco, Marcus, and you are paying attention. Do you think Abraham Lincoln would make such faces?"

"With a face and a beard like his, I think he would," he said, looking over at the other two. "Too serious."

"And you think Mr. Lincoln, his actions on slavery, and the subject of government are amusing subjects?"

He nodded, and the other two of his amigos giggled.

"Well, perhaps you and Francisco and Marcus will find some amusement in joining me here for your recess period. Meanwhile I expect the three of you to participate with the rest of the class now in understanding how government is a serious and complex business."

Mrs. Cortez continued by comparing the federal and State houses of Congress. However, she had to fight to regain her composure. She knew that engaging, motivating, and controlling Luis was the key to diffusing many of her classroom discipline issues. He was bright, often defiant, and used a loud voice to compensate for being insecure over his small size. When he felt up to it, Luis could contribute in a positive manner and with relatively good articulation, either in Spanish or English. A combative sister had given him practice at asserting himself. His ability to control a stressful home life and mother suffused him with a unique boldness. All in all, he was a good kid, with huge potential. And Ms. Cortez gave only partial blame to any student's misbehavior. Fueling most negative actions or inactions were behind-the-scenes factors like poverty, lack of employment, lack of housing, insufficient food, one or more missing, abusive, or uncaring relatives, drug issues, and low intelligence quotients. Those and myriad other causes remained factors in poor mental and physical development. Teachers often were expected to provide the inspiration and discipline not coming from homes. A father might be in jail, another deported. Kids might be living with one parent, rarely at home because of working two jobs to make ends meet. Other students might live with an aunt, uncle, or grandparent. Most of these guardian angels did their best with the resources they had. But when 95 percent of Coronado kids were considered from homes below the poverty level, and those same students all received school meals, many reached their classroom desks lacking the same impetus as those fortunate students from affluent surroundings.

"Francisco, what are the three arms of the U.S. government?"

"*Que?*" he answered, having spent the last several minutes folding a paper flower.

"*Tres,*" Ms. Cortez responded walking over to his side of the room. As if she had divined 'let there be light,' the sun came out from behind a cloud, a cascade of light illuminating Francisco's paper flower and hand having dropped it. "Could you enlighten us on the three arms."

"Three arms," Francisco mumbled, nervously looking around to try and summon what had slipped into the ethers while he had been paper folding. "A...three arms like three horns on a rhinoceros?"

Laughter erupted from even the quietest students.

Ms. Cortez shook her head and crossed her arms. She came to a stop on the far side of Francisco's desk. "How many arms do you have?"

"Two," he replied, hoping she was heading in a direction enabling his recovery from attention deficit.

"And how do your arms differ from the number of arms in government?"

"By one."

"Indeed. And what are those arms totaling three?"

"A...infantry, artillery, and armor?"

"Maybe in the primary branches of the military. But we're talking arms of the government, detailed several minutes ago while you were gardening with a paper flower."

More laughter, while someone in the back of the other side of class threw a paperclip hitting Dulce's nose.

"Anyone else?" she asked expectantly, now allowing Francisco respite from his inattentiveness.

After briefly shooting a glare at Luis, who had hurled the missile that hit her proboscis, Dulce raised her hand. The stylish girl's black converse all-star shoe and Wizard of Oz multi-colored sock also were elevating from a crossed leg at the rate of two a second.

Ms. Cortez pointed at her. "Dulce is giving us an example of how a raised hand combined with waving a raised shoe will enable a student to be recognized, using two limbs rather than one."

Marcus convulsed with laughter enough that his chair tipped over backwards. Although his head grazed the linoleum floor, he quickly jumped up and replaced the chair with himself in it.

"And Mr. Marcus has shown us that using two arms to govern breaking his fall is a lesson in classroom management. Dulce?"

"Um, the judicial, executive, and legislative?"

"Correct," responded Ms. Cortez, pointing at a branch-of-government synopsis on the Smart Board. She then walked over to Luis to make sure he was again focused on the matter at hand. "At this breakneck pace, we might all capture the essence of U.S. federal as well as New Mexican State government in less time than it takes Mr. Francisco to divert from his paper flower to a paper trail of government information."

Recently at a staff meeting Principal Guadalajara had talked of classroom management and the need for each Teacher to control his or her own students. Because a disruptive student often required heavy doses of discipline, Teachers and assistants often felt they had gone as far as they could go. This meant sending the student in question to either the Principal's office or the school Counselor. Ms. Guadalajara now stressed that control of one's class meant forgoing kicking such disruptive students out of class or specials to redirect them into more quiet and productive behavior.

Ms. Cortez certainly had her hands full with disciplining unpredictable, unruly cliques of nine-year-old's. Usually, withholding recess, asking them to write a line admitting bad behavior or poor decision making 20-30 times, or for the student in question to miss a field trip, kept even the worst offenders in line. But there was strength in numbers, and when Luis led, and Francisco, Marcus and others followed, normally successful remedies often came up short.

"Why is studying U.S. government important?" asked the Teacher, grasping one wrist with the other behind her back.

Christina Cortez had the kind of placid face, innocently framed by Cleopatra black locks, that could prove enigmatic. Students often were not quite sure what her expression conveyed. Was there an asp in her desk drawer? Was their Teacher on the point of becoming angry? Was she fiddling while Rome or Coronado classrooms burned and four of her male students were up to their tricks? It was a different perspective for nine-year-old's. Some had no problem wearing the harness of educational discipline. Others simply waited for each opportunity when she wasn't looking. A moment when the real issues at hand, the feathers of entertainment and posturing or showing off, could be displayed with impunity. Learning social studies, most felt, was better tolerated by middle school students. Elementary sorts tended to drift if the vocabulary or subject matter became too complex. One large picture of a toothy shark might permit them to absorb a whole paragraph of description. But a page of the Constitution might prove more soporific than birthday cupcakes.

Ms. Cortez and other fourth grade Teachers all were aware of the challenge of holding attention spans while decanting such dry matter. The whole nature of teaching was one of presentation coupled with eye contact, enthusiasm, questions and answers, and the occasional pause to continue the mirage of spontaneity. Teachers, in effect, constantly did a tap dance of educational approach-avoidance: concerted effort mixed with bursts of humor; distillation tempered with elaboration; clear definition contrasted by voluble expansiveness; and classroom wandering versus chair sitting while the *maestra* or *maestro*'s voice incited imaginations rather than wiggling. Every subject required a performance. Some were good at it all the time, some occasionally held sway, and a few bored the pants off any student barely restrained by gravity in a chair.

"Mrs. Cortez," a girl who rarely contributed said while waving a hand in the air.

"Yes, Flor?"

"Luis keeps whispering things to me and pulling my hair."

Mrs. Cortez felt her eyes briefly gaze skyward. "Luis, one might assume you capable of composing the Bill of Rights yourself, since you avail yourself of the right of free speech at almost any inopportune moment."

"Huh?" he said, suddenly feeling his powers evaporating from their usual overwhelming abilities.

"Why would you be talking while I am, and pulling on Flor's well-combed locks?"

His mouth opened but nothing came out. Marcus and Francisco both giggled.

"Do you think President Downton Arby would put up with your nearly constant disruptions?"

"I couldn't reach his comb-over to pull it," replied Luis to the class's amusement.

"The fact that you can reach Flor's hair is a poor choice of focus. I would expect such behavior from a Kindergarten student, yet somehow the lessons imparted to five-year-old's have evaded you. I want you to take your chair and place it in front of the Smart Screen. You will then confine yourself to hanging on every word I deliver on government, or a forgone field trip will be another unpleasant omission detailed in a conduct report. Have I made myself clear?"

~ EIGHTEEN ~

Mr. C could hear them coming down the hall. As new Kindergarteners, and because assistant Elana Tompkins presented an imposing figure, the line of five-year-old's entered the Library with hands clasped behind their backs. They had only been to the cavernous room of paper relics and posters fewer than ten times. They looked right and left, still somewhat overwhelmed by the shelves and standing racks displaying exciting offerings. Ms. Tompkins gazed expectantly at Mr. C.

"They can sit in the corner," he said to her. "Sit crisscross in the corner," he said more loudly while pointing as kids streamed by his desk. The Librarian read aloud to every class, but for Kinder through second grade students he alternated between reading real books in the corner with reading books displayed on the Smart Screen. For the screen, the kids sat at tables in front. His thinking was that particularly younger students needed to familiarize themselves with the real hand-held treasures. Yet as part of their educational world, they, too, needed to see the words, sentences, and phrases on the big screen of modern technology. That way they could match Mr. C's pronunciation with words, and while following along, learn spellings as well as occasional definitions from contextual word juxtapositions.

Mr. C had pre-selected several large easy fiction books, and one small size-appropriate series book on farm animals, to read aloud. Ms. Tompkins was strict, so as they settled in upon the carpet, the 14 kids slowly quit chattering and squirming.

"Now, I wanted to go over a few things before I read a couple books out loud," Mr. C began. "Who can tell me why we are here again?"

"To read," said a young chubby boy, oversized for a Kindergartener. His face was very wide, and upon it his emotions could easily be seen. His hair was clipped as short as a marine's, and his jaws were wider than the top of his head, much like an aircraft carrier's deck stretches wider than its conning tower. A yellow-and-red striped shirt, the front of which had captured much of his school breakfast's flavored yoghurt, covered his barrel-like torso.

"That's right Octavian," the Librarian softly answered the boy looking up at him, "but remember, you have to raise your hand before talking."

Mr. C found Octavian Valdez's enthusiasm endearing. The big Kindergartener often came up and talked to him. The gestures let the Librarian know that Octavian was needy but had a good heart. Yet the stout lad could be quite demanding, and often took what he wanted from other students. His size and loud voice got him his way. The special education student with attention deficit often would appear behind Mr. C's desk, trolling for books, stickers, crayons, and any objects of interest upon the Librarian's desk. Repeatedly Mr. C would encourage him while at the same time redirecting the curious student back to a table.

"Octavian was correct," Mr. C continued on the back carpet. "You are all here to read, or to learn to read. Don't be afraid if you can't read anything at all or can only read a little bit. Slowly, over time, you will learn to read more and more of the books in this Library. But for now, enjoy the pictures and as many words as you know. Also, after I'm done reading aloud, I will pass out the markers. Remember to leave your markers behind when you take a book off a shelf. That way, you will know where to put it back."

Already, Mr. C could see some kids beginning to fidget and whisper. Octavian had lain down upon the carpet to the side. Mr. C shook his head and signaled the boy to sit up.

"Octavian," said Ms. Tompkins from a chair behind the sitting group. "Sit up. Don't make Mr. C interrupt the class to get you to do the right thing."

Mr. C selected a story about kids starting school. He was good at holding up an open picture book facing the kids, while reading it from the side. The book had big yellow school buses, and little Anglo kids painting and coloring in a Kindergarten class. Mr. C wished his Library had more books in English with Hispanic characters. He had a whole wall of Spanish books, few of which had Hispanic characters. Yet most of the publishers of books with Hispanic characters he found offered few English or bilingual books for Kindergarten through second grade. It was easy to read aloud from his upholstered armchair to this English-only class: most were already fluent in speaking and understanding what was spoken.

"On their first day of school the students were excited," Mr. C read to his captive audience looking up at the pictures in the book. The clothing worn by the students in the story was at least a generation old. Yet those kids still wore jeans and colorful shirts, blouses, trousers, and skirts. "Everything was new and fun. Mrs. Judson gave the kids crayons so they could draw animals."

And so it went. As he continued the Librarian could see they were listening. No one was whispering, and several kids leaned one way or the other to see the book better. They liked the story. Still, everything was a trial with Kindergarten classes. Although some classes had an occasional new student, by first grade most of them were familiar with the rigors of schooling. Yet many Kinders had never been away from a parent or relative. They cried easily, sometimes disconsolate over not being able to return to the safety of their known world. They also had short attention spans. Keeping five-year-old's engaged, when most of their bodies wanted playground frolicking or classroom chatter, was challenging. Over his many years in the Library, Mr. C had learned an array of magician's tricks. Yet kids were kids and you had to engage them in short bursts, particularly the likes of Octavian.

"I like coloring," he suddenly said during Mr. C's reading.

The Librarian put down the book in his lap. "That's great, Octavian, but remember to raise your hand if you have something to say. Otherwise, the flow of the story is hard to follow if someone interrupts."

"Yeah, but those kids in the story are coloring," he said. "I want to color."

"Remember," Ms. Tompkins said from her table, "if you want to come to Library, you have to do what the Librarian tells you to do."

"That's right," echoed Mr. C, picking the book up again. "In order to learn in school, sometimes kids need to listen for quite a while. It's not always easy when you want to be coloring or out on the playground. How many kids like the story?"

"Yayyyy," they erupted while waving their hands in the air.

Mr. C looked at Octavian, now spinning his fingers in his lap. "See, Octavian, we are now having what's known as majority rule. Your classmates want to continue the story. Try to pay attention and be kind. In a few minutes you and the other kids will be able to look at books yourselves."

This was one of the trade-offs of 'leave no child behind.' In trying to do so, the thrust of any teaching done could be waylaid by discipline issues with kids like Octavian. Any Teacher had to spend too much time and effort with disruptive children. Yet often as each year progressed, kids outgrew their problem behavior. And if they didn't, they found themselves put in rooms with others unable to remain calm in learning environments. Language learning was abstract, and the study of letters and words proved particularly difficult for those with far greater structural than abstract visualization. Fortunately, stories for Kinders were short, so within several minutes Mr. C was reading from a miniature hardbound book of farm animals.

"Who can tell me what this animal is?" the Librarian said, pointing at a bird pecking at the ground.

"A chicken," answered a little girl with thick, green-rimmed glasses.

"Right," he said, glancing over at straw-scattered ground with a variety of munching animals. "Raise your hand if you can identify some other animals."

"That's a cow," answered a called-upon boy with a bowl haircut.

"There's a horse in that corral," replied another without being recognized.

Mr. C raised his hand while looking at him. Kindergarteners learned by doing as well as saying. Like pre-schoolers, they often were perfect subjects. They had enthusiasm, energy, curiosity, absorption abilities of a sponge, and a desperate need to be accepted by students and adults bigger and older. Yet pictures and information had to be simple, or their attentions wandered. Teachers had to put extra effort into voice modulation and eye contact. Variety in levels and emphasis compared to monotone worked miracles for short bursts. Do any one thing for too long and kids drifted, fidgeted, whispered, kicked, or poked, and generally found themselves overwhelmed by the life force of motion.

Fifteen minutes later the kids were up and gallivanting with their markers round the Library.

"Where do I find princesses?" a little girl in all white asked while pushing glasses up on the bridge of her nose. She barely came up to Mr. C's waist, but he bent over in parallel so he could talk to her better. "Well, come with me," he said, walking over to a wall of white shelves for Kinder through second graders. Each cubbyhole of the shelves contained perhaps 20 tiny books with orange, yellow and light-blue dots to signal reading levels. While some Librarians argued that no dots should be used so that kids could discover the contents of any book on their own. Mr. C disagreed, believing pointing them in the direction of discovering books they could fathom easily made sense. It seemed a waste of good reading time to stand at the shelves or walk to a table, open a book, and then discover the text far too difficult to read. Yet at the same time, adventuresome and early reading sorts intentionally looked at the color chart to find the light green, red, and dark blue that third through fifth graders could read. Certain students who read above level, then could try their luck at harder books simply by selecting a higher-level color code.

This Kindergarten class was the only one of four allowed to check out one book. Each week Ms. Tompkins selected a child to carry a blue plastic tub of books back to the Library. Kinders couldn't take books home: they lost them too easily. Other Kinder Teachers kept a choice of books in the classroom. They didn't want to face Mr. C's periodic overdue list detailing an avalanche of late or lost books.

As Mr. C slid into his high-backed black leather chair, a line of kids faced him. *At least they aren't as pushy as kids growing bigger and more assertive with each year*, he thought.

"What's your name?" he asked a girl barely tall enough to see over the top of his desk.

"Nina," she answered with the innocent smile of those not yet enjoying confidence.

"Well, you've selected a light blue dot book," he said, pointing to the dot. "Can you read second grade level?"

She nodded bashfully.

"Let's see," he said, turning the book 180 degrees so it faced her.

She stood on her tiptoes and pulled the book to the edge of the desk. There was a pause.

Normally, in a wish to mature faster, kids often brought books they couldn't read up to Mr. C's desk. For first through fifth graders, he allowed students to check out one book a parent, brother, sister or relative could help them read or read aloud to them. But one of the two books they check out had to be at a level they could read, so that they could practice their individual reading skills. Kinders were different, however. Most couldn't read anything yet, so their Teacher encouraged them to check out any book of interest, just to inspire the desire to read and the literacy process.

"The mouse looked at his bowl of...oatmeal, and then...picked up a spoon—" the girl began haltingly.

"Very Good," said Mr. C, turning the book back around and closing it for scanning. He glanced down at the class roster, got her five-digit number, and dialed it up on his computer screen. By third grade, kids memorized their student numbers, but some Kinders could not yet remember their last names unless prompted.

The Librarian soon confined himself to caning his way round the Library. "Good job," he said loudly, "I see almost everyone's reading." He knew his comment wasn't completely true. Most couldn't read much if anything, rather contenting themselves with turning pages and taking in the wonderful illustrations and pictures that tell those myriad fabulous stories.

Mr. C then arrived at a window seat with three kids in it. "How many kids in a big window seat?" he asked. "Two," the girls in the corners answered, looking at the middle girl who was last to arrive. Mr. C motioned for the girl to get up and find a seat at a table nearby. "Mr. C, where's zoo animals?" another child with his shoes untied asked. "Follow me," the Librarian answered, his odyssey continuing to the back corner. "Here they are right here, on this middle shelf." The numbers and names of most major Dewey

Decimal System categories were on shelf-edge labels. But he had to remind himself that Kindergarteners could not yet read.

He enjoyed making his rounds. His travels throughout the rolling shelves and Library created a varying diorama of kids discovering a thousand vicarious stories and treasures. Viewing the vivid colors of the covers, the treasure hunt of pulling books out from a line, and the serendipitous discovery of untold two- and three-dimensional collections of exciting new illustrations, pictures, and words were daily unfolding for the adventuresome. Librarians couldn't get all the kids to get it, nor get everyone to love *los libros de la biblioteca*, but collectively they could over time invest thousands of students with an even greater curiosity for vicariously visiting places, characters, people, and the mysterious or unknown.

"Mr. C," I love Library," a little girl said as he passed by her table. She was turning pages, immersed in the excitement of new discoveries.

"Well, good. I'm glad you like it. Every time you come back to the Library, you'll be able to learn and enjoy more and more."

"My mom says if I'm good she's going to let me buy a Sofia book," said a girl sitting nearby.

Mr. C nodded at her approvingly with a smile. *It's like being a doctor on his rounds*, he thought to himself. *While you have to deal with occasional challenging situations, most of your patients are improving and appreciate the efforts you're making.*

~ NINETEEN ~

More than two months had elapsed in the lives of Coronado Elementary school kids growing like cornstalks approaching the fourth of July. Fall with its cool temperatures, light breezes and shortening days, is a favorite season for many. It was the Friday before a Saturday Halloween, and fifth-grade twins Guadalupe and Maria were in their bedrooms putting on their costumes.

"You've only got another fifteen minutes," their mother said as she walked by their room. "Remember you still have to eat breakfast before I take you to school."

Mrs. De Vargas believed strongly in her daughters' education. She herself had been an executive secretary in a bank before a late pregnancy and giving birth to the twins. She was concerned for her daughters. Not because they lacked learning skills, but rather because of their coltish figures. Both were slender, shorter than most 10-year-olds, and had the quiet demeanors undersized children often had. Both loved to read, never failing to have two books checked out from the Coronado Library, others lying round the room they had acquired from the south branch of the city Library, or ones their mother kept buying them. Although identical, Guadalupe was the more dominant personality while Maria was the more artistic. They rarely fought, rather enjoying the camaraderie of spending ten years in proximity. While they often confided in one another, there were few problems to sort out, the pair being well adjusted and liked by their fellow students and friends.

"Mom, why do we have to call Halloween 'Fall Festival?' asked Guadalupe as her mom looked in on the way back down the hall.

"Good question," she answered. "Especially since our family name comes from Don Diego de Vargas, the general who re-conquered the Pueblos. I can understand why they are always arguing whether Fiesta should be held or not. The defeat of the Pueblos by the Spaniards back in 1692 has two perspectives, winners, and losers. The Pueblos have to suffer the indignities of defeat again each year. But a bunch of kids running round in costumes as witches, goblins, ghosts, and other spirits seems innocuous enough to me. I guess it's a religious thing," she said sitting down on the bed. She swept her Anna Wintour hair back from blocking her view and crossed silk-stockinged legs. "Halloween is a contraction of 'Hallowed Eve,' the night before the religious holiday, All Saint's Day, November 1st. Some people in the Christian churches object to evil spirits as any part of a celebration. They think kids dressed up as dark spirits defy God's will. Then there's the whole mixing of religion and State. Holiday comes from Holy Day—never mind," she abruptly added, jumping up. "We don't have time for this discussion now, girls. You need to have your breakfast and get to school."

An hour later it was apparent in Ms. Sevilla's fifth-grade class that many students felt themselves too old for the costumes of Halloween. Most kids were in the mufti of malls, skateboard parks, and cinema lobbies. Still, a Fall Festival parade was to wind its way through the school at 9:00.

The fifth-grade assistant, a college student studying education at the High Desert Community College, had the quiet demeanor and dark complexion of many Native Americans. Yet he was from old New Mexican Hispanic stock tracing back to the Duque of

Alburquerque (sic). Mr. Humberto Salas was a kind young man, attempting to use softly delivered answers and instructions to the 10-year-old's in his charge. The combination of Ms. Sevilla with her years of experience and firm but caring authority, dovetailed nicely with Humberto's gentler approach. The CC student hoped his time spent at Coronado Elementary would be considered both educational and community service time, and that recognizing this work would be the prestigious Harvey College in Las Vegas.

"Mr. Humberto, do we have to march in the Fall Festival parade?" whined Odysseus Ray. To Señor Salas this seemed juvenile coming from someone usually finding outrageously showy behavior *de rigueur*.

"No, you don't," the lanky college student replied. "I will lead the kids in costume in the parade, while the rest of you can stay here and work with Ms. Sevilla."

Odysseus realized his mistake. By forgoing the costume parade, he had unwittingly doomed himself to further classroom work. "Can we march as a fifth-grade student?"

"Officially, yes," replied Mr. Humberto. "However, Ms. Sevilla's rule is that you either have to be in costume or stay in class and work."

In the Kindergarten wing of the school, excitement reigned supreme. Some boys swaggeringly displayed Batman or Superman capes and outfits, and certain girls modeled as dancing fairies or Disney princesses, walking with the agility and attempted sophistication of ballerinas. They were already admiring each other's finery, with most boys and girls enchanted with their own costume selection. Sequined masks, wands, crosiers, and glowing necklaces each generated further excitement. Instead of the traditional 'visions of sugarplums dancing through their heads,' of Christmas time, the miniature ones daydreamed of myriad colorful bits of candy like M&Ms, jellybeans, and chocolate bars. Some five-year-old's were fortunate enough to have had their parents or older brother or sister take them trick or treating before their first school year. Yet new and veteran Kinders looked forward to the thrill of walking door to door during a night with a full moon, chilly air, and untold encountered spirits and costumed kids.

All the Kindergarten classes had watched short Halloween stories on the Smart Board. Their Teachers collectively had decided teaching anything in the hour before the parade to be nearly impossible. As a group they agreed free video stories from internet searches would solve the impatience dilemma. The grand parade was about to begin, and whether they called it Halloween or Fall Festival mattered little to the sprouts in costumes exuding their own magic. In fact, almost all the Kinder through second graders were looking forward to the following evening's Trick or Treating.

At 10 minutes before the hour in her office, Principal Penelope Guadalajara was plowing through the hundred or so e-mails she had received overnight and before school began. There was a notice of a Superintendent's meeting, a future conference of school administrators on security, an explanation of the upcoming testing schedule, and several requests from Teachers for personal days or classroom purchases.

Guadalajara walked with difficulty to a nearby filing cabinet. In her 50s, rheumatoid arthritis had suddenly found its way into her joints. Drug prescriptions had helped considerably, but she contemplated early retirement on the horizon should her condition fail to improve. Like many Teachers and administrators, the pressures of daily existence were enormous. Juggling ten to twenty problems at once was normal. Issues of discipline, parental meetings, staff breakdowns or terminations, and student injuries were just several habitual impromptu duties with which she had to deal. The tricks of her administrative trade included prioritizing in order of importance and time constraints, maintaining equanimity of temperament, being firm when necessary, as well as remaining cheerful and kind for as much of every day as possible.

The whole Halloween and Fiesta dilemmas were well down on her list of ponderables. Fortunately, the Fiesta king, queen, conquistadors, and others had paraded through the small gym without incident and with few kids missing. Culturally most of Santa Fe, including Catholics, Jews, Muslims, and Christians all celebrated Christmas and Halloween as civic and cultural, rather than religious events. There were always certain parents and relatives, however, who objected strenuously to Halloween's nocturnal mix of good and evil spirits. Never mind that kids loved *Little Red Riding Hood, La Llorona* and other scary stories: there were always those who found the whole end-of-October celebration objectionable.

Ms. Guadalajara was able to follow current protocol about the titling of the celebration and parade with costumes. However, she and her school were not about to forgo carved pumpkins, specially designed orange-and-black cookies, and other goodies, dark as well as dazzling costumes, and all the other folderol of Halloween. Kids loved it. Most parents loved it. And as far as she was concerned, during that evening gainsayers could turn off all the lights, draw the shades and curtains, and watch sitcoms on TV with bare minimum light and sound coming from their high-def screens.

~ TWENTY ~

That afternoon Matilda Blackstone was reading one of Louis Sachar's Wayside School books under a standing lamp in her condominium living room. She heard the front door close and wondered why her mother was home early at 4:30.

"Hi," Daniela mumbled as she set down a bag of groceries on the floor.

"Hi, mom," said Matilda, putting down her book. "Aren't you home a little early."

Her mom nodded, plopping down on a floral-print couch. "And I may be home a lot more during the day."

Matilda could feel her mother's comment was said with more than a hint of dejection. She knew her mom both liked her job and was considered competent as a doctor's receptionist. Yet a look of disappointment clouded Daniela's face as she sat with her hands in her lap.

"What's wrong, mom? Did something happen?"

"Yep. Dr. Widdington is moving back to Texas." She shook her head, then paused. "I won't be going with him, so I'm out of a job."

When Matilda looked at her mom more closely, she became aware that their racial difference was not even a consideration. It was their age difference. With a missing father, to 10-year-old

Matilda her plump Anglo mother suddenly looked like a forlorn provider, one who was losing the power of invulnerability.

"Gee, mom, that's a real bummer. What are we going to do?"

Well, there's good news and bad news. My friend Candace who works the drive-through window at McD's says they need a night person. That would be me. The bad news is that I start tomorrow night, Halloween."

On Halloween afternoon the weather appeared threatening. Dark stacks of cumulus clouds were approaching. But the wonder of most Santa Fe storms is that many veer or pass by, leaving zero precipitation. Months could pass in the high desert with little rain or snowfall.

That early evening inside a Silver Arches hamburger chain outlet, situated on a main road not far from Coronado Elementary, Daniela Blackstone was observing a woman operate the computerized system of taking orders. Matilda's mother was told that when things were slow, she might have to both take orders and collect cash and credit card payments. But the Day before All-Saints Day in a Catholic town, especially since it was a Friday, meant a steady stream of customers not wishing to cook when they had to deal with several hours of trick or treaters.

Ms. Blackstone was a rapid learner, having a kind and helpful disposition. Although having lost her medical office job, working as a short-order clerk and cashier in a fast-food haven was all part of doing everything she could to keep a roof over their heads as well as ensure Matilda could come home to a safe environment. Daniela never thought of any job as permanent. If one opportunity evaporated, she made sure another developed. Nor was she judgmental. The fact that most of her fellow employees were young Hispanic women in their 20s and with little more than some high school education made them similar in backgrounds to her own.

She had finished high school yet remained apart from many others not enjoying the privileges of college, by becoming an avid reader. Every night both before and after she adopted her daughter, she would delve into a reading mix of classics and contemporary fiction and non-fiction. Daniela was literate, yet her true educational profile remained relatively hidden to those in her world. While her communication skills were superb, the lack of a formal education had caused the rejection of applications for many higher paying jobs with greater challenge and responsibilities. Yet she never complained, making sure her adopted daughter had every opportunity to remain on the path of advantageous formal education.

At least no rain had fallen, the breezes had quieted, and around 7:00 the girl training Daniela let her begin to take orders electronically on the computer screen and over a loudspeaker ordering process. It was routine stuff, the only big difficulties being either a hesitant customer unfamiliar with the lighted-sign menu or SUVs packed with family members and friends ordering huge numbers of items.

"Two Enormoburgers and a medium fries," came a woman's voice.

"Anything to drink?" answered Daniela.

"Large Diet Coke."

An hour later, probably approaching the end of the Halloween neighborhoods' trick-or-treating gallivanting, fewer cars were coming through. The girl who trained her had warned that it got busy later as more and more people left bars. But she also said that most people would be home tonight handing out candy and goodies, so that traffic most probably would be light.

Two minutes later a man who had simply ordered a large coffee appeared in a low-rider cruiser at her window.

"Give me all your money," he said, pointing a pistol barrel barely above his driver's window.

"Pardon me? Is this a trick or treat?"

He waved the gun up and down. "No, no trick or treat! Give me your money!"

She could now see he had on a Lone Ranger's mask and a stingy brimmed black hat. There was probably a buzzer to push somewhere below her miniature order counter, but the girl hadn't mentioned anything about security. There was nobody nearby to rescue her. She was flustered.

"Aa...sorry, but you pay at the next window. I just take orders. I don't collect any money."

With that his electric window scrolled up, and he accelerated out of line and around the far corner of the building. Daniela tried to get the license plate but the lights illuminating it had been turned off. The mysterious masked man was gone.

~ TWENTY-ONE ~

That day in the cafeteria, manager Magdalena was preparing for the mid-day onslaught. Kinders were to be served in the first half hour from 11:00 to 11:30. They were the most likely to spill food on the floors and their clothing, and were the hardest to keep corralled at their tables. Nearby in anticipation, custodian Ronaldo Estevez and his maintenance crew were chatting behind their waste disposal containers.

Inside the kitchen, food service worker Charity was stirring a large pot of chili meat, soon to be ladled upon sprays of curvy chips on Frito pie day. Somehow years ago, a local five-and-dime store on the plaza began serving the delicacy at its counter, and a following began to develop. Because of an extensive Hispanic regional influence, SFSD introduced several favorites like quesadillas, burritos, enchiladas, and Frito pie to their menus. With shredded cheese on top, pinto beans on the side, and lettuce salad available to create fiber to help the meal move through growing digestive tracts, the meal was relatively nutritious. Certainly, the Frito chips might not be all that healthful. But then it could be argued many of the meat, canned veg and fruit meals derived from mainstream America wouldn't pass Weight-Watchers either.

The first Kindergarten class of fifteen hungry critters entered the large gym, converted to a cafeteria for the noon meal, at a walk with hands behind their backs. Soon, however, the fragrance of Frito pie and empty assigned tables at which certain seats were more desirable than others, the five-year-old's spread out and broke into runs. "Walk, walk!" yelled their assistant instructor as they darted for favorite seats along their assigned table's benches. As this melee was happening, another and then another of the four classes entered with much the same enthusiasm.

Minutes later, Charity stood at the cash register as another tray of lettuce was placed in a glass-covered serving area. Food service workers began to accommodate both lines of kids with trays including the Frito pie main course and pinto beans; the kids then used tongs or ladles to serve themselves lettuce and either canned pineapple or half bananas. There was often a certain amount of crowding, pushing, and shoving. Kinders could barely reach the bars on which their trays slid, however, so actually were better behaved than their schoolmates a couple of years older.

The whole lunchtime experience was a balancing act. Food service workers had to get up to 150 students served in 30-minute increments, with the least amount of spillage possible. The kids had to go through the serving lines like streams of ants, before downing these delectables inside of 10 to 15 minutes. The process was a recipe for spills and thrills, especially for the youngest ones. Milk and chocolate milk were the most likely to find unpredictable homes upon jeans, blouses, and jackets. Yet eating Frito pie required the dexterity of seamstresses, with lumps of meat, corn chips, cheese and lettuce all needing to be carefully conveyed upon a fork from tray to open mouths. The fronts of clothing, floor, and tabletops enabled the gym to transform into a war zone. Most kids, however, simply went about the business of filling bellies for a busy day of caloric expenditure.

"Sit down, please, Octavian," Teacher's assistant Margarita Sandoval warned the careening Kinder.

But it was too late. The barrel-chested boy smashed into class-mate Gwendolyne's tray, some of it tumbling down her dress, and the rest crashing noisily onto the floor.

"Ewww!" a couple of kids groaned, having witnessed this mid-day entertainment.

Gwendolyne just stood in place, tears rolling down her cheeks. Ms. Sandoval was quickly at the scene, as was custodian Ronaldo rolling a mop in a yellow bucket toward one of many daily dilemmas.

"Don't worry, Gwendolyne, it wasn't your fault," Margarita consoled the small girl. "We'll get you cleaned up, sponged off, and get you a new tray."

The crying Kinder seemed more concerned about her clothing being ruined than eating.

Nearby a boy wearing an *Aeropostale* hoodie hurled a Frito chip that hit Javier on the side of his head below a bowl haircut.

"Ernesto, don't throw food, or you can join Octavian sitting in the bleachers," said Victoria while handholding Gwendolyne back to her seat.

Teachers' assistants found their daily lunch duty pushed them to their limits. Infractions such as running, food throwing, or fighting could happen elsewhere, as well. Yet growing kids needed three meals a day, providing them lunch with a tray of objects and additional hurling devices such as spoons and forks creating a whole new host of potential disasters. The assistants wanted to sit kids apart from others when the incidents occurred, but then every student needed his or her calories with dispatch. Lunch time became a conundrum every day.

"Alright," this table line up," said Ms. Sandoval, pointing toward the end of the gym with the exits, "and I do mean walking not running." In class she might have chosen kids being quiet one by one. But time constraints with the next crowd coming at 11:30 meant accelerating any process. "Steven, do not grab Alfredo's arm while you're sitting in line. Thank you, Daphne for sitting quietly...thank you Edwin for sitting quietly..."

That was another conundrum. Schools were fastidious about wiping down tabletops and chairs with clean sponges and damp rags, yet often allowed kids to sit on carpets and floors with untold deposits and smears upon them. It then takes little imagination that the backs of those pants, skirts and dresses then sit upon chairs with nearly infinite transference possibilities. Then those possibilities don't even address what kids pick up during falls on the playground when frolicking, running, tackling and ball throwing. Mixed messages on hygiene were constantly being sent. It was important to bathe, wear clean clothes, and to clean the tables and chairs. But it was also O.K. to hit the playground dirt and wood chips and merely dust oneself off or apply disinfectant to scrapes and cuts. And it was permitted to sit on dirty floors and carpets upon which hundreds of contaminated shoes have walked.

The noise levels, both at the tables and in the sitting lines they formed near the doors, continuously peaked with a cacophony of chatter. Up to 150 kids all talking, eating, and spilling simultaneously could reach the decibel level of a cheering football stadium. Teachers' assistants as well as maintenance and kitchen staff all got used to it, just as refuse pickup workers get used to crashing cans and bottles, banging plastic recycling and refuse containers, and the thunderous noise of the trucks lifting loads heavenward for disposal.

Outside was a warm early November day, the normal blue skies ever so slightly occluded by smoke from one of the last dry-year fires annually reducing to ashes forested pockets of the Southwest. No cloud cover was to be seen, and serial groups of Kindergarteners arrived excited to a smaller contained playground near their classrooms. Beyond the fence, scrub piñons and the many varieties of green and gray flora that can survive with little precipitation stubbornly hung on to their arid patches of high desert soil. Only a few five-year-old's had the same tenacity. These were difficult circumstances, for clothing, skin, and for sensitive minds and bodies spending their first time away from mom or other relatives. Recess periods required the patience and restraint only those mandated to educate kids have experienced serially in all types of weather and circumstances.

~ TWENTY-TWO ~

The end of the hour and the school day was rapidly approaching. Mr. C gazed at his watch and realized he had survived another ten hours of coffee, news, e-mails, robo-call announcements, showering, driving with his favorite jazz station soothing his journey on the 599 high-desert highway, turning on all the cavernous Library lights, eating a breakfast tamale cooked in a nearby microwave, putting books away and discovering those thrown helter-skelter, hidden, or put upside down or backwards almost anywhere, tens of discipline issues, hundreds of questions, readings aloud to each class with enthusiasm, lunchroom and office trips, parents paying fines, assigning computers, logging in new books, and the several hundred scannings helping young people lead vicarious lives through those magic pages. It all worked, but Librarians needed the patience of sidewalk homeless in the sun to get through a day among the paper relics.

In the back of the Library, three tall fifth-grade girls were chatting while pretending to be looking for books. At a rectangular table near the map room, Ms. Sevilla was attempting to do some planning at her computer while answering the questions of two hovering students. The school's most-revered Teacher used most of her 'essentials' hours, when kids went to Library, art, music, P. E., and computer lab, to prep. Yet because Mr. C was a paraprofessional rather than licensed Librarian, union and district regulations required a licensed Teacher to be present. Ms. Sevilla took this addi-tional obligation in stride, using the time for the most part as prep time like that accomplished while cloistered in her empty class-room. But there were interruptions and disruptions with 28 kids spread out in the brightly illuminated catacombs of knowledge.

Behind Mr. C's crescent-moon desk two of six students surrep-titiously were playing game sites on the Library computers, hoping that the Librarian was too busy to notice they were avoiding his mandated e-reading sites. Their real-life game was more creative than the electronic games. Clever kids not particularly adept at reading went to the computers when they heard their names called, not to further literacy skills, but to mindlessly watch colored objects make their ways through mazes, or superheroes shoot their way out of lethal circumstances.

"Mr. C, can I go to the bathroom," asked a student whose glasses nearly overwhelmed his head.

Deceptive, quickly deduced the Librarian. It's 2:50 and the kids lined up at 2:52, making it easy for the requesting student simply to escape through a side door to a car with a relative waiting outside, without ever returning to the Library.

"No, you'll have to go on the way out of school," Mr. C answered as if routine, knowing the student would not stop at a bathroom during his aborted early but late exit.

That was another trick to learning the Librarian ropes. Mr. C and others had quickly to decipher what requests were legitimate and what ones had more devious outcomes in mind. For instance, one girl would ask to go to the bathroom. The girl having been ostensibly reading at the opposite end of the wide window seat would wait several minutes and then, while the Librarian was busy with at least three or four students in front of his desk, ask to go to the bathroom, as well. The Librarian then had to remember there was already another girl in the lavatory and that indeed her window seat partner was now conniving to join her.

The eight rolling shelves containing fiction and easy fiction were aligned for viewing, like spokes of a wheel, with the main desk as the hub. This ensured that while kids could hide between the ends of shelves or sit on footstools hidden from view in the back corner, there were few spots in the Library the Librarian couldn't see while craning his neck or rolling his desk chair slightly. Of course, it was another real-life Library game certain kids thrived upon. Mr. C often was busy checking in and out books at his desk while answering questions from as many as four and five students at a time; these interludes provided opportunities for inventive students to slide down behind the backs of shelves, or chat while pretending to look for non-fiction books along the back wall. If Mr. C caught them after being previously warned, they might have to sit in the 'time out' chair in front of his desk, or they might lose computer privileges. But many kids considered the risk more than worth it. Punishments were sometimes simply badges of courage to resist the known and explore the unknown.

"O.K. It's time to line up. Put your books away, push in your chairs, and walk to the front of the Library."

This announcement was little different, at the end of the day, to the starting gun of the Kentucky Derby. In minutes kids would reach the sunlit real world outside. The world of trucks, SUVs, big yellow buses, and afternoon freedom. Some pitched their books on top of the nearest row of books, or put them back anywhere nearby, leaving their colorful plastic markers in place. They wove between tables at full tilt. More strict Teachers might have refused to let them line up and demanded they return to tables. But it was the last class of the day, and Mr. C was too tired to slow down the exit process. A few admonitions of 'Walk! Walk!" was all he could manage. Instead of a finish line in Kentucky they reached a jumble of backpacks in

Santa Fe. The sounds of opening zippers and increasing volume of chatter further infused the excitement of day's end.

Meanwhile, Coronado lost a lot of books to theft, graduation, and family relocations. Mr. C could tell which books were most popular simply by matching the number of copies his computer said should be in the Library, with the actual number on the shelves. At one point he was supposed to have 31 copies of *Diary of a Wimpy Kid*. He could only find 17 on the shelves. The theft of the four books of the *Minecraft* series, *Essential Handbook, Construction, Combat*, and *Redstone* was so prevalent, Mr. C kept them on a shelf behind his desk. Microsoft had apparently paid $2.5 billion for the electronic game and four books, an idea of where contemporary vicarious pleasures were heading.

"Can I just look at a *Minecraft*?" a kid with two overdue books outstanding would ask.

"Nope," the Librarian would answer. "You can only check them out and then return them at the end of the hour. In your case, you can't check out anything until you return your books or pay for them."

Somehow, Mr. C decided that today, close inspection of departures was necessary. The Librarian stood up and walked with his cane over to the motley assemblage of scrambling and chattering kids. Normally he'd attempt to straighten the line and quiet them down, but with the barn gate ready to open, he became more tolerant.

His last-period students were required to leave their backpacks near the front door in hopes of eliminating these decorative containers for schoolbooks, lunches, water bottles, candy, and furtive Library treasures filched when opportunities presented themselves. Most kids didn't steal. But the ones that did often made up for each ten to thirty kids who didn't.

His roving eye, vigilant because of recently losing a key expensive book on minerals, and in the last few days finding several book covers empty of their stolen treasures, suddenly spotted what inevitably and clandestinely occurs. It required an eagle eye, but he saw it.

Odysseus shoved two *Dork Diaries* in his bag.

Not more than twenty minutes earlier Mr. C had declined checking out two other books for the defiant fifth grader because he had two books totaling $20 outstanding. So, the Librarian knew what was being shoved into the Superheroes backpack was contraband.

"Aa...excuse me, Odysseus," Mr. C said as if some sort of simple change of location, "could you bring your backpack over here."

Odysseus had a look of hesitation upon his face, but he quickly realized that refusal would merely implicate him further. He walked over behind the Smart Board and dropped the bag on the mint green-colored linoleum floor. Behind him most kids were still stuffing books into or tugging jackets out of their backpacks, all while jockeying for positions closer to the door and oblivious of the nearby contretemps.

"Open the zipper," said the Librarian.

"Why?" Odysseus asked, suddenly aware of what was coming.

"Because I *told you to*," said Mr. C with his arms crossed.

By now kids in line were beginning to get the drift and one by one were quieting. They shifted from one foot to the other, sensing Odysseus was in some sort of serious trouble.

"Why?" whined the petulant fifth grader. "It's just my books and some personal stuff."

Don't argue, Odysseus," said the Librarian more forcefully. "Students don't debate what I tell them to do. Just do what I say! Open the bag."

Odysseus shook his head from side to side, refusing to bend over toward the bag. By now the entire line of kids were staring at the pair. The defiant fifth grader hoped the bell would rescue him.

"Alright," said Mr. C nonchalantly. "Then we will wait for Ms. Sevilla."

The bell rang, as if some sort of redemptive diversion.

No one moved. All the fifth graders realized an explosive delay was only just beginning.

Ms. Sevilla walked up alongside the line of kids.

"Did you hear what Mr. C said, Odysseus?" the Teacher said with the authority every student in the school knew meant business. "Do what he tells you! Open the bag."

The tension at the front of the Library was palpable.

"Why! There's nothing in there but the books I checked out and some other stuff!"

"I'm going to count to five, Mr. Ray. If the bag isn't open and its contents dumped on the floor, you, your father, and I will meet in Principal Guadalajara's office tomorrow.

No one in line was breathing. Every student now sensed the outcome of this whole exit-delaying episode.

There was a pause while Odysseus considered the comparison of possible outcomes being bad versus disastrous.

Suddenly, however, he reached down, shaking his head as he did so. The whole process, had it been viewed carefully, was simply an exercise as if to say 'there's nothing unusual in my bag. You're both just acting unreasonable.'

Then out plopped the two *Dork Diaries*, a miniature skateboard and keys on a chain, and an empty candy wrapper. Most of the kids felt their classmate had won, revealing nothing of consequence.

"What about the *Dork Diaries*?" Mr. C said, his arms still crossed and Ms. Sevilla surveying the items on the floor with look of disdain.

"I checked them out!" Ray shouted, glancing at the kids behind him in the hopes someone would confirm his actions.

"No, you didn't," said Mr. C, with gravity.

"Yes, I did!"

"If Mr. C says you didn't, then you didn't," said Ms. Sevilla, moving closer to the recalcitrant student.

"I did, I did!" he shouted, grabbing the sides of his head with both hands in futility, yet internally realizing weaseling out of this would almost be impossible.

"No, you didn't, Odysseus," the Librarian said more softly. "You have two books, totaling $20 outstanding, and no fewer than 15 minutes ago I told you there would be no more checkouts until you returned the books or paid for them. So, Mr. Ray, you are caught in the process of stealing two Library books."

"But I checked them! I checked them!" he shouted, beginning to sob.

"And even worse," added Ms. Sevilla, "you are lying. You stole two books and then are lying about checking them out."

Many of the kids in line were looking down at the carpet. It was apparent their arrogant classmate was toast, even though a well-deserved toast.

"I for one, have had enough of your antics," said Ms. Sevilla, who in her more than 20 years of teaching was used to one or more such devious sorts each year. "Mr. C, I would suggest you not only report this to Principal Guadalajara, but also that a report be made to the Santa Fe police. It's the end of the school day, so perhaps a police officer could join the three of us in Ms. Guadalajara's office at 3:30." She motioned for the class to begin filing out. "Come with me," she said to Odysseus.

Mr. C phoned the police, who said officer Nestor Ortiz would be sent to the school. Although from experience both Mr. C and Ms. Sevilla were aware that in New Mexico, larceny of under $250 was a misdemeanor petty theft vs. misdemeanor theft, and felony theft if over $500, on rare occasions they wished a police officer to come to the school to add gravitas to a student's conception of his or her offense.

Odysseus Ray fell into just such a category. Bullying, disruptive classroom or Library behavior, inattentiveness, poor efforts at almost any field of study, tardiness and absences had all pushed Ms. Sevilla to her limits. First, she called his home number, but a message indicated his mother was playing in a championship bridge tournament that afternoon. An alternate number enabled her to reach Ray's father, Penn, at CMNL. Fortunately, he was just finishing a meeting with federal energy department officials in Santa Fe and said he could be at school by about 4:00 to join the meeting in progress regarding his son. He was not pleased.

"So, Odysseus, Mr. C and Ms. Sevilla have informed me you tried to steal two books from the Library," Principal Guadalajara stated at 3:45. She had left the student at a time-out desk in the outer office to contemplate his fate and to give his father and the police officer more time to arrive. Privately she felt assured that officer Nestor Ortiz, now sitting beside her and opposite Odysseus Ray, was familiar with the accused student because of his brother's earlier near drug bust. The officer knew the right things to say to a 10-year-old to infuse the appropriate fear of reprisal and avoid any future similar infraction.

"I didn't! I didn't!" he pleaded, more for effect to temper the accusations before his father arrived.

"Let's get something straight," Ms. Sevilla said. "Everyone in this room is familiar with your *modus operandi* of lying to escape consequences for your behavior. Let's have no more lying, Odysseus. Face up to the fact that you were caught stealing two books from the Library."

The whole ordeal was a sad example of what can derive from unfortunate social and often financial circumstances. Kids were always greatly affected by their environments. Parents, relatives, friends, and enemies all contributed to their behavior. Teachers knew that misbehavior derived more from poor parental or relative supervision, lack of home monitoring, as well as lack of inspiration and motivation, than most other factors. A 10-year-old child is not an adult. Yet students had to be taught accountability. Consequences existed throughout all of life. Students had to be taught respect and proper behavior somehow, and that sometimes meant painful consequences to all concerned, even Teachers and administrators.

Penn Ray arrived, briefly put his hand on his son's shoulder and then took the remaining seat at the table. He shifted several times in his three-piece midnight-blue pinstriped suit, obviously stressed out further by this confrontation.

"Mr. Ray, as you were earlier informed over the telephone, within the last hour your son Odysseus was caught trying to steal two books from the Library," said Principal Guadalajara. "We appreciate your taking time off during a busy day to be here.

"Officer Ortiz, you've had some experience in the consequences of such matters," continued the Principal. "Do you have some comments?"

He nodded, gently shaking his head from side to side. "Odysseus, because of his age and circumstances, your brother was given the benefit of the doubt in a drug bust at a local home of his high school friend. I've talked extensively with your father, and it is apparent to me your parents are doing everything they can to both encourage your education, and to build respect and tolerance for others. At the same time, your Teachers at Coronado and your parents have tried to instill a sense of ethics and values during your time spent at Coronado Elementary School. And now this." Ortiz pursed his lips and looked further at the young student, whose eyes were downcast. "Stealing of any sort, no matter what the age of the thief, is the beginning of a trip down the wrong path. You may be thinking, 'So what, it's only a couple of books.' But it's not just two books, it's an indication of a lack of respect for doing the right thing."

"Odysseus, if this were high school or even middle school, suspension might be an appropriate consequence," Ms. Guadalajara added. "However, my colleagues and I feel suspension often simply leads to more problems. Supervision at home is often a challenge with parents who work. And then the students in question simply miss more classroom education and activities, as well. Accordingly, the consequences you face, especially because of the seriousness of this offense, will be a month of two days a week of detention after school, and several sessions with our school Counselor, Ms. Juarez."

Tears were rolling down the fifth grader's cheeks as he gazed downward.

"Think of this as an opportunity," officer Ortiz said with his hands interlaced. "You have two choices here, Odysseus. You can either choose to feel this session and these consequences are too harsh and to remain sad and angry. Or you can choose to see this point in time and all our concerns round this table as an opportunity to create positive change. I'm sure your parents are now disappointed. But any negativity that has evolved from your past behavior in school can change. It's up to you."

~ TWENTY-THREE ~

Weather in the high desert is usually predictable. Most days are very bright on the Kelvin scale, the high elevation sunlight heating up even mid-winter days into the 40s and 50s Fahrenheit. Most of the soil, even though imported deciduous trees often survive successfully, lacks much in the way of nutrients. Rainfall generally is sparse. Yet in July and August what are called Monsoon thunderstorms arrive late afternoons or evenings. Late in September first the world's largest single living organisms, aspen stands, begin to turn from green to yellow, and by October other fall colors mean winter's cold nights are about to arrive like uninvited guests.

It wasn't yet time for a future thousand-year rainfall with massive flooding. However, oddly, in early November, when snow or rain may occasionally occur, it was strangely warm on a Friday. Many kids forgot to wear their jackets home when released at 12:35. And during that night it rained perhaps two inches, a veritable deluge for the dry mountainous terrain.

On that Saturday, Coronado fifth grader Antonio Lopez rode his bike to the new, big Walmart at the south end of town. He enjoyed riding his mountain bike part of the distance on the dirt arroyo trail continuing from the concrete bike path to Las Vegas Road. The nine-year-old wanted to buy a couple spare skateboard wheels and lubricant so that he and his friends could try some frontside and backside pop shuv-its and other stunts.

After locking his bike outside the garden center, Antonio walked back through household cleaning, paint, and automotive sections to the sports department. He was imagining an afternoon of boarding with some Coronado friends. Unexpectedly, however, he came to an abrupt halt to avoid a woman using a cobalt blue wheelchair/ walker. He recognized the woman in her 70s as a volunteer for third graders at his school.

"Oh, hi, *Abuela*," he said, not knowing if he should call her 'grandma' instead.

After they exchanged brief pleasantries he continued his mission, dodging lots of loaded shopping carts as if in a video game. The store didn't have the exact wheels he wanted but within five minutes he had both new wheels and the lubricant.

While weaving his way through house wares and furniture, Antonio suddenly spotted grandma trying to reach a towel on a top shelf. Her arthritis prevented her from standing up completely straight, and she was using a long set of grip tongs to grasp the towel.

"Here, let me help, you, *Abuela*," Antonio said, reaching up and pulling a floral towel from atop a pile. "Do you want one or two?"

"One will do, thank you," she replied, sticking the towel into a compartment under the walker seat.

Antonio knew she didn't remember his name but didn't reintroduce himself to avoid embarrassing her over having forgotten.

"I have a mop at home, but I have trouble using it. There's lots of water in my sunroom from last night, you know."

"You mean from the rain?"

She nodded. "Mm. I thought maybe a big towel might be easier to soak some of it up and then wring it out."

"Maybe I could come over and help mop it up," Antonio said with a smile.

Grandma could walk yet displayed the side-to-side wobble those with a weaker leg cannot avoid. Like many women in her seventh or eighth decade, she dyed her hair. Unfortunately, while brown shoe polish coloring gave its recipient a slightly more youthful appearance, the change was offset by wrinkled and sagging skin more closely revealing one's age. None of this mattered to Grandma. Her husband had passed away from a stroke several years earlier, and she only saw her daughters occasionally when they drove up from Albuquerque. But she often went to lunch at a senior center, volunteered at Coronado, and enjoyed watching soap operas and sports on her aging TV. She was bilingual, speaking mainly in Spanish because of less proficiency in English. She used both languages in speaking to a variety of mainly female friends. They often went to the cinema, also enjoying chatting at length on the happiness their lives had brought them.

"Oh, I couldn't ask you to come over to my house. It's way out of your way."

"No, I know where it is," he answered, his metal supermarket basket paralleling hers. "I'm on my bike and I could zip over and help you get it cleaned up."

"Are you sure? You've probably got better things to do on a Saturday."

"See you there," he said, pushing his cart off toward checkout.

Twenty minutes later Grandma unlocked the battered door of an old adobe casita in the traditional Agua Fria village part of Santa Fe. The home's walls were cracked, a slightly bent chain link fence surrounding a rectangular dirt yard with some scattered ceramic flowerpots devoid of plants. Antonio leaned his mountain bike against a front wall under a portico with peeling white paint.

The interior of the house was tidy but forlorn. It was obvious the retired woman lived alone, her two daughters grown up and living in the Duke City. A three-dimensional cross with a crucified Jesus upon it gave one wall a mournful appearance, while a rocking chair with a faded serape draped upon its seat and arms looked well used. An older box TV sat on a battered wood table nearby.

Most of the water on the floor of the back sunroom had filtered out into a small back dirt yard featuring a flagstone walk to a corner garden with some sagging Russian sage. Antonio spotted Grandma's walker sitting in the kitchen on the way to the sunroom. He asked if he could grab the mop and pail from a kitchen closet so he wouldn't have to use her new towel. Minutes later he had the remaining water in the pail. The cycling ten-year-old would be a little late for his skateboarding, but he had always been friendly with *Abuela* and was glad he could help her out. Ms. Sevilla stressed the importance of community service. Antonio wasn't sure if cleaning up an elderly woman's floor was helping the community at large; he simply had the ability to think of others rather than just himself.

"That should do it," he said cheerfully, returning from dumping out the water into the back garden. He put the pail and mop back into the closet, along the way noticing Grandma remained standing while he was there. It was evident to him that many people of her age wished to remain a part of daily life. They didn't want to be marginalized to a life of watching television and pre-packaged meals. Pride of participation was important, particularly to those having lost some of their mobility, memory, loved ones, or the energy of youth and middle age.

"Thank you so much, young man," she smiled at him.

"You're very welcome. It only took a few minutes," he said, realizing she wouldn't feel comfortable sitting until he left. "And besides, you'll need plenty of energy for helping out third grade this week at Coronado."

~ TWENTY-FOUR ~

One of the benefits of being a Title 1 school was the installation of state-of-the-art computers. The SFSD had a school board that did what it could to rectify inequities in schools servicing less affluent neighborhoods. Coronado's computer labs were equipped with large flat-screen Apple computers. The Library had nine more, six of which could be used by the students. Another 90 Chrome pads were provided from rolling carts, not only enabling electronic testing, but also student reading of books on free or subscribed electronic sites.

On a Monday Mr. C inadvertently walked into the Library's adjacent office. Although a plethora of dinosaur VHS tapes were stored there, he rarely used the room. The Librarian needed to be out at his circulation desk, dealing with student requests and check ins and outs, or logging in new books. Supplementing the school Counselor's heavy workload of cases, visiting Counselors often gained the quiet space they needed for talking with distraught students. Toys and games brightened up some of the shelves. Particularly younger students rarely had the ability to begin talking about home problems with a stranger. Playing with games and toys acted as diversions to put them at ease before such important matters were discussed.

Mr. C was looking for a three-ring punch. He knew it was in

the faux-wood desk somewhere. Yet as he pulled a drawer open, he noticed something was missing. Then he saw it. Blue and white cables coming out of a desktop port were connected to nothing. The Apple computer was missing. His first thought was that it had been borrowed for some purpose. Perhaps the Principal had needed it. Then he had another thought. There was no metal security cable alongside the power and system cables. He realized all the other computers were locked down with those cables to prevent theft. The missing Apple hadn't been locked.

Later during a free hour, he knocked on the Principal's door. He could see she was reading e-mails on her computer, and she waved him in.

"Did you borrow the computer from the Library office desk?" he asked.

"No, I didn't," she said, looking away from her screen for a moment. "Why?"

"Well, it's missing. I hope somebody didn't steal it."

"When did you notice it was missing?"

"I'm sure it was there last Friday. Maybe somebody took it over the weekend."

"Well, there's a security camera on the wall of the Library and another one outside the front doors. Let's have a look at the recordings."

Minutes later, she had turned her monitor so that Mr. C could see it and was high speeding through the weekend's recording from the wall of the Library. Nothing. Yet someone with a security key could have exited the Library through the adjacent Counselor's office out of line of sight from the wall camera.

"That's funny," the Principal said as she looked at her screen. There is no recording from the camera over the front doors." She made a quick call to the cell phone of the head of security, and he joined them in minutes.

"That's strange," the security man said, unable to provide an explanation why the camera over the front doors hadn't provided a recording. "Let's go down and take a look at the camera."

Soon he was up on a ladder outside the doors of the Library and the Counselor's office. After removing one of the sound baffling panels, he fiddled with the camera up above.

"It doesn't seem to be working. Let me go in our control room. It's just down the hall.

Mr. C went back in the Library and checked some e-mails. Minutes later the security man returned.

"Well, I've got some unexpected news. Of all the cameras in the building it is the only one unplugged."

Both the security man and Mr. C. knew what this meant. The theft was an inside job. Over the past six months numerous security and construction workers had key access to all areas, at all different hours of the day. It occurred to Mr. C that someone with access must have pulled the plug, knowing that he or she could then carry a large flat-screened desk computer out the front door of the Library. The removal almost inevitably must have occurred during the weekend and during darkness so the wall camera on the outside of the building could not detect the theft.

Did someone need drug money, or a several-thousand-dollar computer to sell on the black market for cash? As far as Mr. C and Principal Guadalajara discovered, determining a culprit with so many outside workers with key access was going to be a near impossibility. Neither could the local police spend much time on the theft, with much larger problems needing investigative talents.

Mr. C also considered the fact that undoubtedly he was under suspicion. A Librarian with pay of $15,000 per year has a computer disappear from his office. Any investigator would look closely at him, probably assuming he needed money and not knowing he had begun collecting social security payments augmenting poor pay. Yet he had worked as the Coronado Librarian three years without anything other than books having gone missing. That would stand in his favor. He drove an old Subaru, so that would help to diffuse thoughts of someone stealing significant items to support a lifestyle. He didn't do drugs and rarely, except for surgical recovery, had been absent from his job. Mr. C was an active mountain biker on an old beater bike. If he had had a $4,000 newer high-tech bike, people might have asked how he could afford it. No, Mr. C felt assured, given his lifestyle and lack of possessions, few would consider him absconding with a computer. Besides, there was the unplugged camera, a major clue of how anyone with access, excluding the Librarian, could leave the building carrying a flat screen and base more than 24 inches wide. The computer was replaced, but someone had gotten away with felony larceny.

~ TWENTY-FIVE ~

Counselor Genoveva Juarez's small room beside the computer area of the Library contained a round table and chairs, her cluttered desk, and shelves full of colorful games, puzzles, books, document boxes, and some wall posters, all intended to provide a warm environment for listening to students recount those subliminal or obvious factors that contribute to mental or physical problems. In that room, Ms. Juarez had heard tales that made her internally cringe while at the same time act with calm and concern. Most of the students knew the convivial yet stern woman. She was known for a no-nonsense approach to almost anything. Yet her listening skills had been honed by years of research, formal education, and thousands of interviews with students, parents, and other relatives or guardians. Teaching as well as counseling could not be learned overnight or solely in a school. Each year brought more experience in the human condition, myriad tricks of the trade developed through endless trial and error, an ability sometimes to right wrongs, to alter a child's destiny, and the reassuring process that some kids could be rescued from seemingly impossible dire straits.

Today's slate of appointments made Ms. Juarez more than uncomfortable. The lowlight of her day would be a meeting with Odysseus Ray and his mother, Ashleigh. The mother was one of the most pretentious Anglo women the Counselor had ever met. She had a condescending manner to anyone with the slightest color in her or his skin. Mrs. Ray was pretty in a sylphlike way, her clothes and shopping always purchased during excursions to the east coast. Yet her arrogance, based upon an honors degree in art history from Lake Forest College and several bouts of travel to Europe and a semester in Paris, remained intentional and overbearing. She didn't share her husband's need to immerse their sons in a less affluent area of Santa Fe. Ashleigh Ray much preferred hobnobbing with birds of a feather found at society fundraisers and gallery openings. She was tall with perfectly coiffed and sprayed hair, and always artificially employed an unassuming friendliness and boundless joy to initiate any conversation, even among those lacking her respect.

As a contrast, Mrs. Juarez had her doctorate in Social Welfare from Northern New Mexico State University, and the third-generation New Mexican had spent 25 years listening to and observing elementary students. She had two grown daughters and an insatiably curious grandson, so plenty of first-hand experience had also increased her abilities to help mentally, physically, and emotionally challenged children. Women of means and private formal education, such as Ashleigh Ray, remained judgmental. They could not understand the celebratory culture of those with severely limited financial resources for travel, lavish housing, and the accouterments of the rich.

Yet it was Odysseus that Ms. Juarez had scheduled first, in order that as much information as possible might be gleaned without the overshadowing presence of his mother. Children, as well as many adults, were far less revealing when dominant familiar figures inhibited difficult social opportunities for them. Ms. Juarez was intrigued at why, given the family's resources, Odysseus felt compelled to steal. Undoubtedly the older brother was a substantial influence. Yet when he arrived, the younger son and fifth grader was nervous, obviously aware that Mrs. Juarez's report to the Principal, to become a permanent part of his record, would affect his future in ways he couldn't begin to fathom. The Counselor could see the student was apprehensive, his blond forelocks hanging indiscriminately as a partial mask to obscure his expressions.

"Thanks for coming in," Mrs. Juarez said to reduce the initial tension as she slid into a chair at a round conference table nearby her desk. Odysseus was too old for icebreaking games. The Counselor still wished to put him at ease, or perhaps put him under less stress, again, to facilitate obtaining as much information as possible before the imposing lead figure of the family appeared. "I'm sure all of us make mistakes we later regret. I'm guessing you might periodically have reconsidered your poor decision to take two books from the Library." Her intent was to provoke some sort or revelatory response while at the same time sympathizing with the student over his foolish action.

"Yah, I was pretty mad at the Librarian for refusing to let me check out two books, even if I did have a couple of books outstanding."

"Why, Odysseus? Should Mr. C ignore the rules of overdue or lost books preventing further checkouts?"

"Well, I'm not saying he should ignore the rules. But he could have made an exception. I mean he didn't ask me why the books are missing."

Mrs. Juarez looked up from her interlaced fingers on the green tabletop to meet the glare of a young boy attempting to persuade her of an exception being made. "Whose fault do you believe the missing books are?"

"Mine. But what neither Mr. C or you know is that my older brother's girlfriend is a nerd, and she took the books to read and doesn't know where she put them."

"Yes, but does that exempt you from the responsibility or returning the books or paying for them?"

He reluctantly acknowledged her point by forgoing an answer.

"And if you had it to do over again, what might have been a better decision than stealing two books?"

"Stealing four. No, just kidding. Look, I know the rules, and I know all the arguments against stealing books from a Library, the main reasons being cost of replacement and the fact that no other students can read books if you keep them. But my brother takes stuff all the time from his school and from shops and stores. He's cool and he doesn't get caught."

"What if he does?"

"What if he does?"

"Right."

Then he's grounded for a month, and he'll probably go to jail or to a different school because of the grow house warning. But I would have brought the *Dork Diaries* back. I mean, it was more like I was borrowing them."

Counselor Juarez knew this was a bogus attempt at legitimizing taking something from the Library with no accountability. Odysseus Ray had no intention of returning the two books. The theft most probably centered upon a rite of passage to prove to Courtney that he had the *cojones* to do so. But that wasn't the sort of admission she wished to try to get him to make. "What about your father. He must be disappointed."

He shrugged indifferently. "Sure, he's disappointed. Disappointed that neither Courtney nor me is a chip off the old block. We don't play golf. We don't want to learn to play golf. We don't spend all our spare time reading books on U.S. history and politics. I don't want to wear pinstriped suits or work in buildings with other nerds and boring dudes who talk about nuclear potential and atoms and mathematical equations all day." Odysseus ran open hands up and down his pants legs below the table. "My dad thinks his engineering job at CMNL makes him cool. But I wouldn't want his life of meetings, golf, boozy luncheons and reading endless newspapers. Besides, he doesn't really care."

"Why do you say that?"

Odysseus shrugged.

"What kind of life would you like to create for yourself."

"I don't know. But I know it would mean not going to school. School is boring and you have to study all kinds of useless stuff."

"What about your mother?"

"What about her?"

"She will be here soon. How do you feel about her?"

"I don't know how she got through college. She's a ditz who likes shopping, playing bridge with a bunch of posers, and reading *New York Times* best-selling books she doesn't understand."

"So, you don't care for her."

"How can I care for someone who spends her life playing cards?"

"She cares enough about you to come and talk with me."

"She thinks I'm worthless and my life is a waste of time."

"What is your life?"

Odysseus swept his forelock onto the top of his head, but it slowly slid down in front of his face. "Well, this is all a part of it I don't like. Reading, mathematics, paying attention to stuff that is boring. I mean, what's the point?"

"Would you rather be skateboarding or hanging out at the mall, or..."

"I'd like to be playing Minecraft."

"Yes, but if you keep playing Minecraft enough, eventually you may wish to do something more meaningful in your life."

"You mean like working."

"Absolutely," said Mrs. Juarez, pausing a moment to allow contemplation. "Is there something constructive outside of school you might like?"

"Mm, maybe overhauling engines."

And with that his mother knocked on the glass panel in the door and swept in. She had on a midnight-black suit with a skirt that displayed thin ivory thighs. Her lavender Jimmy Choo's matched her broad-brimmed sunhat. She removed her sunglasses and put them in her purse. "May I sit down?" she asked the Counselor, who gestured her to join them at the table.

"This whole business could be resolved far more easily without my coming in," she said, peering intently at Mrs. Juarez. "I mean, Odysseus assures me he only took the books because of being denied checking them out. We would have paid for the books."

Mrs. Juarez pursed her cheeks. With most of the children's mothers or fathers she saw she was able to reach a certain rapport. But with Mrs. Ray, her immediate impression was that not only was the woman annoyed with having to come in regarding her son, but that it was one step up from a distasteful trip to the third world.

"I'm sorry that Ms. Sevilla couldn't attend this meeting, but the school appreciates your effort in taking the time to meet with us," said Mrs. Juarez, slightly lifting some pages in front of her to add some gravitas. "I know it's difficult for everyone concerned, including Principal Guadalajara and the police, to become involved with any sort of stolen items, petty theft, or larceny. Yet you did take the books from the Library without checking them out, didn't you, Odysseus?"

He nodded, obviously wishing to react as little as possible in front of his mother.

"Yes, but as I've already alluded..." his mother attempted to assert.

"Mrs. Ray, it seems to me we have an opportunity here to point a student, your son, in a more opportune direction in terms of his remaining in this school," Mrs. Juarez said, meeting Mrs. Ray's gaze. The intent was to convey the gravity of the situation and Mrs. Ray got it. "The police were called for a reason, and as you are aware, this isn't the first behavioral incident regarding your son."

"Yes, but—"

"Mrs. Ray, do you wish Odysseus to continue his education at Coronado Elementary School?"

"Well, I'm not sure," she said, stalling for time as she contemplated how to trump this woman already having made several points quite different than during a bridge game. "Odysseus, do you wish to stay in school here?"

He shrugged, unsure how to react. If he said he wanted to go to another school, going there could be worse; if he said he didn't want to go to school, his dad would flip out.

"Counselor," Ashleigh Ray responded further, not having taken the trouble to remember with whom her appointment was, "my husband has made several substantial donations to this school. I understand Odysseus has made an error in judgment, as well. But I would hope we could all move beyond this childish mistake, with the assumption that it won't happen again."

"But that's just the point, Mrs. Ray," said Mrs. Juarez. "Ms. Sevilla, Principal Guadalajara, and others have all made that assumption several times regarding your son. His judgment apparently hasn't altered in the positive way we had hoped. Consequences, of course, are realized from either positive or negative behavior. Odysseus, in this matter, once again has merely shown himself unable to improve either his judgment or behavior. Still, Ms. Sevilla, Principal Guadalajara, and I all thought asking you to come in and join your son in a discussion might help to create a more positive future direction for him."

"See, Odysseus, this is what happens when children are given too much," Mrs. Ray erupted, crossing her legs to the side of the table and leaning forward. "This is the kind of thanks your father and I get. I'm in the middle of a challenging tournament that gives me a chance to do something you and your brother might admire, and it is simply scoffed at. I'm looked at as nothing more than a consummate shopper. But apparently you have gone one step too far." She looked up at the ceiling.

"Odysseus," Mrs. Juarez said as if it were time to get to the heart of the matter, "as I said earlier, behavior creates consequences. It seems to Principal Guadalajara, Ms. Sevilla, and me, even though consequences are required, that there are several possibilities and/or opportunities. Firstly, and most advantageous, would be changing your ways. Your Teacher, your classmates, specials Teachers and others in the school might see a transformation sometimes seen in children having several times gone down the wrong path. But that of course would be up to you. Secondly, you could be suspended. However, suspending any student generally puts them further behind other students, and gives them free reign outside of school to get into further trouble. Thirdly, and I think appropriately, you should pay for the lost books and will attend detention classes after school, twice a week for a month."

Mrs. Ray shook her head in disgust.

"This is a difficult situation for you," Mrs. Juarez said to the fifth grader. "However, it isn't the end of the world. You have made a mistake and there are consequences. Yet the future still holds unlimited opportunity for you, Odysseus, should you make a conscious decision to change your ways. Not everyone likes school. But it is required for all young people, and it works best when each student assumes an attitude of doing the best he or she can. Think of this point in time as one at which you are going to turn a corner into a land of opportunity, rather than one of disappointment and frustration. Your future is important to your family as well as to all of us here at Coronado. Only you have the power to change your current course to a positive one." She paused to clasp her hands, and then concentrated upon the beleaguered student in front of her. "Do you feel you can change your attitude toward progressing in a positive way?"

Odysseus nodded as if a deposed nobleman facing the guillotine. It was apparent to the two adults that taking the path that is best often remains difficult. Anger, feelings of futility and hopelessness can get in the way. Assuming responsibility for one's destiny, especially for a child, is a precarious business.

"Odysseus, you had better do what the Counselor says," Mrs. Ray spoke with an edge to her voice. "Your father and I will expect nothing less. You will be grounded on weekends and lose your allowance for a month, but should there be any more trouble, your father and I will have to think about a different school, maybe even in a different State."

~ TWENTY-SIX ~

The Coronado Elementary budget meeting for the next school year was held in the office conference room. The meeting was open to any staff member wishing to participate, creating numerous opportunities to be heard for those needing supplemental materials or any other financial consideration. The budget's major expense encompassed Teacher salaries, but there were perhaps a hundred other considerations like maintenance, cafeteria food and operations, field trips, bussing and transportation, computers, Chrome purchases, security, *et al.*

That day's meeting would involve both explaining all the major categories' allotments, as well as trying to accommodate requests made for additional funding. Those attending arrived with the usual convivial repartee, yet most were aware that a major announcement was in the offing.

"Just to get started," Ms. Guadalajara said, standing behind her chair at the end of table, I want to go through each of the components of what makes Coronado financially able to do what it does."

The opening descriptions of costs normally could be wound up in about twenty minutes. Mrs. Guadalajara had done this sort of exposition for years, and at another school long before she assumed her Principality at Coronado. During her presentation, most of the

Teachers and several assistants in a group of about thirteen listened with reasonable concentration. Most of them restrained from interrupting with a raised hand, knowing that later opportunities to express themselves would be more advantageous. All such meetings were political in the sense that decisions had to be made and could only be altered with enough comments from those wishing those changes. With half of the meeting completed, Ms. Guadalajara had agreed to take several requests into consideration. Finally, there was a pause in the flow of requests, discussions, and subject matters that all needed to be heard.

"I know there have been many rumors regarding this year's budget, even though technically it is already in place," began Principal Guadalajara. "Most of you are aware that the current federal administration's approach to reducing environmental restrictions to accommodate more oil and gas drilling is in full swing. While it is not difficult to predict that the environment will once again deteriorate over time, predictions also indicate the State Land Endowment Fund will increase substantially due to oil and gas drilling licensing. Still, New Mexico repeatedly vies with Mississippi for the poorest per capita income, and there are many squeaky wheels calling for additional funding. Unfortunately, Santa Fe School District has indicated that Coronado's further enrollment drop this year, due for the most part to two new schools having been built in our area, means we may have to lose one Teacher." She raised her eyebrows, giving everyone at the table a chance to digest this speculative information. "This reduction in staff isn't a given but is still likely. Meanwhile, I'm doing everything in my power to avoid having to let a staff member go. One option is that we need an interventionist. Hopefully, if a Teacher must be lost, that individual could become the interventionist."

There was more, but not much. Speculation would be rampant, yet Ms. Guadalajara was aware her staff needed to be apprised of a future probability. The blow had to be softened by advance notice. Then there were several possibilities, most of them not good. Last in, first out might be an option. Yet the latest four Teachers added were bilingual, while others speaking English only had more seniority. Given the SFSD's current approach to bilingualism, it was difficult to say what arguments local union officials and SFSD administrators might pose regarding any decision. Mrs. Guadalajara and her Coronado staff had to hope that last-minute funding diversion from the Land Grant Fund might avoid any such reduction. But that might depend upon State legislators in January agreeing to draw either more money from the fund, or to take a larger percentage of the budget for education. Other districts in the State would be facing reductions, as well, and then SFSD's poor test scores could well influence legislators in a negative way.

It was all very complicated, confusing, as well as the part of her job Mrs. Guadalajara liked least. Every summer, staff members elected to retire, move to another school, or to quit teaching to pursue less stressful and more lucrative occupations. Certain others were not asked back due to insufficient competence. In her experience few Teachers were lazy, but some were just plain unable to teach up to certain standards. This meant endless interviews, hirings, firings, and diplomacy all Principals, Superintendents and other administrators had to conduct and develop. It was a challenge as difficult in scope as Eisenhower's decision of when to cross the English Channel. Mrs. Guadalajara was among the best, yet still dreaded having to let an occasional Teacher go; to hire one person over another when both were capable and enthusiastic; and to deliver the sorts of bad news associated with adequately staffing her own little domain. Yet the staff was now aware, and she could go home and have a glass of wine with her husband before spending a restless night of further contemplation. A Teacher's or administrator's life is tough, but if you were capable, durable, kind, caring, decisive, considerate, disciplined, and persistent, you eventually retired, leaving the *Sturm und Drang* of the struggle to impart knowledge behind before the great silence that must eventually come.

~ TWENTY-SEVEN ~

Citizens habitually tend to complain that public schools are underfunded, and Teachers underappreciated. It would seem in even remote areas of the country public school budgets could be more substantial. Yet surprisingly, in the second decade of the new millennium, generosity harbored in many invisible non-profit institutions was waiting to be awarded. Money for schools was out there, and not just for private schools or schools for the wealthy. Not only did most State legislatures do their best to provide funding opportunities for many creative projects, but they also were forced to spend the largest percentage of their annually contrived budget for education. Enticing good Teachers to come to an underpopulated, undereducated, and underfunded State was always a challenge. One chip-making company even brought its own Teachers to Albuquerque.

Citizens and legislators alike often asked, 'what are we getting for this huge expense?' And when school test scores were among the worst in the nation, it was then misguided to hold tight reins on annual education budgets. The State's destiny was certainly an apparent conundrum or Catch-22: without good schools, industry and commerce were hard to solicit; without more commerce and industry taxes paid, better education was hard to fund. Corporations of note, notwithstanding mining and farming, wanted good

192 - P. J. CHRISTMAN

transportation, excellent schools, highly trained work pools, plenty of water, moderate weather, and numerous other amenities to locate headquarters or major hubs to any State. An agricultural State that was fifth largest in landmass, with a population of only a little more than two million, faced several dilemmas, none of which was easy to solve without boatloads of money. School enigmas were no different.

Yet relatively hidden from many who could avail themselves of their services were myriad philanthropic institutions with money just waiting to be dispensed. Mr. C was one employee that had churned the internet and perused newspapers and periodicals to learn of several benefactors that might provide his Library funds. In his several years at Coronado, he had invited a Hispanic female filmmaker from Las Vegas, New Mexico, to the Literacy Committee's Literacy Night. Thanks to 'Funding 2 Schools' Coronado had been able to pay her per diem, hotel, travel allowance and a small honorarium for showing part of her film and providing an inspirational talk. The same organization had funded two sets of Library shelves. Yet now he had landed an impressive gift from 'Givers Choice,' an extremely generous funding source where online donors could elect either to be revealed or to remain anonymous. This special benefactor funded most requests of up to $1,000 and some for more.

At some mysterious point in time Coronado's Library line budget had disappeared like occasional dust storms on interstate highways. Now you see it; now you don't. While the State's biannual Book Bond bequests provided Coronado several thousand dollars to buy books in alternate years, the Library sorely needed several thousand books for its offerings to be brought up to date. Those who originally set up the school provided a cornucopia of attractive hardbound books. Unfortunately, many of them disclosed middle school reading levels rather than K-5. Then almost all the fiction and non-fiction information and stories were peopled with Anglo characters. With Coronado being 95 percent Hispanic, it was then difficult to identify with the *Hardy Boys* and *Nancy Drew* series more appropriate for middle or high school readers in the East and Midwest. Most of the stories were written or illustrated in styles reminiscent of 50s, 60s and 70s America, when anyone with color in his or her skin rarely could be discovered as leading characters in mainstreams books and films.

One day during the previous school year fourth-grade Teacher Cristina Cortez mentioned to Mr. C that his students felt there were very few Spanish chapter books, or stories in which characters faced different challenges in serial episodes, to read in the Coronado Library. Several translations of English chapter books were available, but again, they centered upon life in the twentieth century when these students had yet to be born. By e-mail Mr. C had been informed that a Teacher was receiving materials through a grant from Givers Choice. It occurred to him that he should explore their website. In doing so he learned that those grant requests of under $1,000 had a more-than-seventy-percent chance of success. He chose Spanish titles *Diario de Nikki*, *Diario de Greg*, and *Casa de Arboles*, all of which were translations of English chapter book favorites. Mr. C also requested two Spanish fiction packages for fourth and fifth graders. By the start of the current school year the Librarian had received almost all the perhaps 70 books requested and had logged them into the district's book tracking system.

The skies were overcast during a November day when Ms. Cortez's fourth–grade class appeared in the Library during the final hour.

"Mrs. Cortez told me recently that many of you felt there weren't enough Spanish chapter books to read in our Library," Mr. C began while standing in front of the Smart Board. "In response to her comment, Coronado Library applied for and has been approved for a grant providing almost $1,000 worth of Spanish chapter books and other fiction. You can find most of these new titles at the bottom of our *Libros de capitulos* shelves over here," Mr. C said, gesturing to a column of shelves in the Spanish wall of books. "Some are third, most are fourth, and others are at fifth-grade reading levels. Since you are a bilingual class, most of you hopefully will be able to find a book or two you want to read. We have translations of *Diary of a Wimpy Kid, Dork Diaries, Magic Tree House, Judy Moody*, and many other fiction selections."

Shortly after he read out loud the English version of *El Cucuy* by Joe Hayes to the class, Mr. C noticed a scrum of students on the floor below the Spanish chapter books. One by one they were discovering titles that were familiar from having earlier read the English versions. As always, Mr. C was pleased to see any student reading any book in his Library, no matter how far behind or ahead of the reading-level curve that student might be. From vacuum tubes, came transistors, came circuit boards. From all-illustration books came heavily illustrated gems, occasionally illustrated works, and then the truly magic realm of the imagination, text-only stories. The Librarian felt that while the level any child was reading remained important in educational terms, it was more important that they were improving that level, with the eventual possibility of finding the world of abstract language as fascinating as that of the world of picture books. Some fourth graders were reading at a second- or third-grade level, perhaps at the level of heavily illustrated Berenstain Bears books; a few could read Harry Potter or Matilda with far more challenging texts.

Several minutes elapsed while kids pointed out books to each other as well as assumed the window seats and remote tables first, always opportunities to chat while reading. The shelves arranged in spokes enabled Mr. C to check out books, answer questions, and survey the vast expanse for those accomplishing more whispering than reading. He had the option of strolling through the Library to put away books and have a few words with those ignoring the no-talking rule. But then he was away from his desk and as kids began to queue up to check out books they began chattering. The more students convened in any one area, the greater chance arose that little reading would be done and a lot of standing around or vocal diversions take place. Mr. C felt you had to mix it up. A few firm commands from his desk often worked. If he had forgotten a name, he could quickly scan the class roster to refresh his memory. Calling a child by name let the student know he or she couldn't misbehave anonymously.

"Luis, do not use your marker to hit the overhead posters," he said to a boy jetting across the back of the Library. "Esmeralda, no talking to Carmela."

"O. K., chicos," Mrs. Cortez said as Mr. C resumed his seat behind the desk to check out books, "you've got five minutes to check out books, because we've got to go American Dance Academy introduction for a half hour." ADA was a nationally funded group that used dance and movement to instill teamwork and confidence in elementary school children. Soon Cortez's fourth-grade class had each checked out their books and then lined up at the front doors for departure.

Meanwhile for the second half hour the Librarian had scheduled a first-grade class having missed their usual specials hour due to a field trip. Carolina Contreras' first graders arrived quietly, their hands behind their backs. Mrs. Contreras looked at Mr. C expectantly, wondering if the kids should sit at the tables in front of the Smart Board. Since he generally alternated between reading stories from the electronic board and from paper books, he had K-2 students sit on the back carpet in the reading area. There they could hear stories up close and personal as he sat in his rocker.

"They can sit crisscross in the back corner," said Mr. C while he checked in books from a line of miniature students diffidently waiting in front of his desk.

Mr. C looked forward to reading aloud in the back corner. It always seemed more intimate with kids looking up at either the pages of the book he held facing them or making eye contact. He could read the book from the side as it was held up in front of the kids, or while turning it right to left in front of any array of third through fifth graders sitting at tables in the front of the room. When the older students were spread out, however, the reading-aloud process lost a little bit, primarily due to the distance from certain students to the book and its illustrations.

The Librarian carried his perforated glazed silver can of markers and four books to the back corner. He settled into his cushioned chair and blew his PEACE harmonica to signal kids should raise two fingers in compliance of quieting down.

"Very good, students," he said, "I liked the way you came in quietly." He held up a plastic marker. "Don't forget to use your marker when looking for books later. Which reminds me, I will continue to put out new books each week. We have lots of them. Don't forget to check for new books each week on this stand here, that stand over there, and the stands on top of the K-2 green, white, and tan shelves," he continued, gesturing as each location he mentioned, "as well as the stands on top of the Easy Fiction shelves." He then put the marker he had been using as a pointer back in the can and pulled up a book nestled beside the chair arm below. "The first story I'm going to read—"

"Attention," suddenly came the intercom and Ms. Guadalajara's voice. "This is a shelter in place."

"Alright, students," said Mr. C, "we just go on doing what we're doing, but do so quietly. Hopefully, I can read aloud a story or two and then you can find one of our new books and settle down to some silent reading. Remember to use your markers, and no talking."

The Librarian had a weird feeling about this shelter in place. It was almost inevitably a drill, but the school had just had a shelter in place rather than a fire drill several weeks earlier. They were mandated to have so many drills a semester, but Mrs. Guadalajara's voice hadn't repeated that it was a shelter in place.

"Who can tell me what lightning is?" Mr. C asked them as he held up a tiny series book with lightning bolts and dark skies on the glossy cover. As usual, hands flew up before his kids even knew what the question was.

"Um...um...it's a light that comes with a storm."

Mr. C pointed at another raised hand.

"It comes from clouds and rain."

"Well, all of you are right. It's actually electricity, but it does come from clouds and during storms."

It wasn't precisely the Socratic method, but to hold kids' attentions Teachers had to get them to participate as well as to listen and watch. Slowly in the next few minutes, the Librarian mixed reading aloud with questions about the causes of lightning and thunder. He held up a small hole he made with thumb and first finger to demonstrate the typical one-inch lightning bolt's diameter contrasting its 6- to 10-mile length. Show-and-tells from the book elicited 'wows' from the kids.

Several minutes later he was reading aloud Five Little Monkeys Reading in Bed and had the kids in stitches over the monkey's shenanigans while defying mama and reading after being told to turn out the lights. The Librarian liked starting younger students with a non-fiction book when their attention spans were still fresh and then reading aloud something wacky, scary, or amusing when they were starting to fidget more and more. Holding their attentions for twenty minutes was his general goal before releasing them into their own world of the vicarious.

"This is now a lock down," the Principal's voice suddenly came calmly but firmly over the intercom. "I repeat, this is a lock down."

~ TWENTY-EIGHT ~

"O.K. kids," said Mr. C as he arose from his desk, "I want everyone sitting quietly in the back corner under the wall of non-fiction books. I think most of you have done this at least once, so you know how we all have to be really quiet now."

Ms. Contreras, in her first year of teaching after completing her degree and credentialing, silently directed her kids to the opposite book-lined back corner as Mr. C found some pre-cut black paper to cover the front and back door windowpanes. "Eduardo, can you get all the lights."

As the student scurried to flip all the light switches, Mr. C began covering the back exit single door glass pane with black paper secured with book tape. Fortunately, the venetian blinds surrounding the reading corner carpeting and window blinds were all drawn. Mr. C quickly moved back up to his desk to grab the rest of the black paper to cover the panes in the front doors. While doing so he reached outside the door to lock the entrance. Two minutes later he walked back into the dimly lit room to check on the students. Several were whispering and giggling.

"O.K. people," he whispered softly, "it doesn't matter if this is a drill or a real occurrence: you need to remain quiet. That means complete silence and holding still." Ms. Contreras warned all of them in Spanish, as well.

They sat that way for twenty minutes and nothing happened.

Usually, they end the drill by this point, thought Mr. C. *Then again, maybe Ms. Guadalajara and Sandoval are walking around the entire school to check on things.*

More silence.

Slowly as time elapsed whispering began to reoccur. While Mr. C began moving among the kids with his cane, suddenly they all heard someone wiggling the metal door handle of the back emergency door.

The first graders quieted down in similar fashion to when Kindergarteners put their heads down on desks. Mr. C knew that during the many drills he had participated in over the years, no school drill conductor had ever tried to enter through an exit door or window.

More handle wiggling.

Mr. C used his outstretched arm to signal further silence and stillness.

Abruptly thundered a loud crash, as someone outside the door smashed through the windowpane. *This is it,* thought Mr. C. *No drill. A real intruder.*

A hand reached through the broken pane and tore away the black paper. A small stream of light came through the tear in the paper as a hand turned the handle to open the door.

In stumbled a man who looked as if his dirty khaki pants were a size to big. His blue chambray shirt was stained with oil, and as he slammed the door behind him, the man wobbled from side to side as if off balance. In one hand he loosely held a switchblade.

"Where's Nina?" he mumbled, looking around as if his head was attached to a rusty neck. "Where's Nina?'

"She's not here," Mr. C answered, not completely sure the person in question wasn't. "Is she a student?" he asked, walking over to stand to shield the children. The Librarian furtively glanced over at them. All were sitting with their heads down behind him along the wall of books. There was just enough light coming through the hole in the black paper to partially illuminate the back reading corner. The man continued to wobble from one foot to the other.

"Of course she is," the intruder replied, trying to lean to one side to look behind the Librarian. "She's a first grader here and she told me...I think she said...she told me she always went to some...special class or something...before lunch and recess." He burped, as if he had been drinking beer.

I think he's drunk, Mr. C thought. *What's the best approach to dealing with someone like this?* He tried to remember what the police presentation to the Coronado faculty had been. Forty or so employees were told 'go, throw...' He couldn't remember the third bit. But it didn't matter. The man had a knife and there was no way he could safely get more than twenty kids out through any of the front or back doors. Meanwhile throwing a book at the man would be a waste of time: hitting the knife out of his hand was a real long shot.

Behind Mr. C, Ms. Contreras was hugging a sobbing girl grasping her suit skirt. "Nina's not in this class," the Teacher said. "I think her class is in the computer lab right now."

"Move over and *shtand* aside," the man slurred, gesturing for the Librarian to get out of his way so he could see who was behind along the wall.

Mr. C complied, all the while considering that he should be doing something to deter this man. *He's at least close to drunk, and all I have to do is catch him off guard*, thought Mr. C.

But the man pointed the knife at him while wobbling by and began looking at each face in the line. With the pauses a blind man might make he slowly surveyed all the kids and shook his head. "O. K.," he said, holding the knife up in the air and twisting it for all to see. "We need to get her here...*now*."

"*Niños!*" the man said, holding his forefinger up in front of his lips as he swayed back and forth. He then began to follow the Librarian to the front desk.

Mr. C nipped behind it, all the while wondering if he should make a grab for the knife. He still wasn't sure just how intoxicated the man was. Nina's father or relative had waved the knife enough that a mistake in trying to disarm him might get someone cut or killed. *Maybe I can do it now, while he's away from the kids.* But several times when he had tried to get closer to the man, the intruder had kept away just far enough to maintain distance and control. *At least he can't kill too many if he becomes enraged*, the Librarian thought. The man was watching him carefully from the corner of the desk. The Librarian had a cell phone in his pocket but didn't want to reveal it. There might be a way he could use it when the drunken man became distracted. Mr. C picked up the desk phone and dialed the front office.

"Carmelita, it's Mr. C in the Library. Do you know where first grader Nina Villanueva is? Mrs. Contreras thinks she might be in computer lab." The Librarian glanced over at the man with the knife. There was no way he could even whisper something about the actual situation into the phone.

"Let me check my rosters for first grade," the secretary answered.

Mr. C put his hand over the phone. "She's checking where she is," he said to the anxious man, now wavering back and forth from one foot to the other. The Librarian took his hand away from the phone. "Could you please send her to the Library when you find her."

He didn't wait for a response. He hung up the phone, now knowing there was little time to avoid any impending disaster. If Nina was found and directed to the Library the man might take her as a hostage, or even kill his own daughter, depending upon how angry he was with his wife, his child, the school, her Teacher, or any number of unknown factors. He then remembered what he thought the police had said to do if you can't go or throw: *fight*. He had to try something soon. With the intruder and his knife behind him, they walked back to the terrified kids sitting in the back. Ms. Contreras was sitting between two six-year-old girls, trying to console them. "It will be alright," she said, not hearing the approach of Mr. C and what might well be Mr. Villanueva, Nina's dangerous father.

"I need the bathroom," one slender girl whimpered from the corner. She was undersized as a six-year-old. Her knees protruding from a navy-blue jumper were shivering, even with slender arms grasping them tightly.

O.K, this is it! Mr. C knew. *I can take her to the emergency potty and nip into the office to make a call on my cell phone.* It was a long way to the makeshift five-gallon paint-can toilet with a plastic liner and absorptive sand in the bottom.

"I need to show her where the emergency toilet can is," Mr. C said. "It's in the locked storeroom by the computers."

"O.K., but don't try...anything funny," the man said. "Remember, I've got the kids and...their Teacher," he said, again waving his knife to emphasize his point.

Mr. C grabbed the little girl's hand and quickly jerked her to her feet to escort her back to the front of the Library. *The man knows I won't leave the Library and the six-year-old students behind. But what if he comes up to check on me. Doubtful. Most men don't want to have to deal with a child's potty use.*

Quickly he grabbed the makeshift plastic toilet under the sink near the desk and unlocked the storage room door. "Go in and use the toilet in here," he said, putting the container down just inside the door. There's sand and toilet paper in the bottom of the plastic liner."

He then moved to the adjacent office, unlocked the door, went in, and silently closed the door behind him. He flipped open his clamshell phone and fortunately it lit up. He dialed 911.

"Santa Fe Police Department. What is your emergency?"

"We have an intruder with a knife in the Coronado Elementary Library at Las Vegas and Airport Roads," Mr. C whispered into his phone. "He broke in through the back exit door—"

"Could you speak more loudly, please."

"Can't," he still whispered into the black device. "Send armed men. But use the back door. If they use the front, he might injure or kill some children. Please get here quickly. Intruder's been drinking."

"Is the door open now?"

"Closed. But they can reach through broken glass and turn handle." Mr. C could now see the first-grade girl standing outside of his office door's glass pane.

"I can't talk. Got to go."

He opened the office door, grabbed the girl's hand, and quickly made his way back to the group huddled in the back corner. When the man saw them, he appeared satisfied he still had control.

"Mr. C are you there?" Carmelita's voice came over the intercom from the office.

"Yes," Mr. C answered loudly, as the speaker and microphone were at the other end of the room.

"Nina will arrive at the Library shortly. She's finishing a test in the next five minutes in the computer lab and then she will come down."

The Librarian now was hopeful. *A first grader normally wouldn't walk alone all the way from the other side of the school alone. She would be escorted by another student.* Carmelita hadn't mentioned 'she will be brought down.' Maybe the police had called the Coronado office and alerted them. *And maybe they're now checking the camera on the wall high up on the Library wall opposite my desk.* If they did, in the dim light they couldn't see much behind all the shelves in the back corner. But they could keep an eye on things and report back to the police periodically or keep an open line.

"She'll be here soon," Mr. C tried to reassure the man. "It won't be long."

"It better not," he muttered, separating a couple of venetian blinds against the far wall, then briefly peering out. He was obviously looking for anyone outside. Fortunately, he hadn't seen any police. "Got to get her...out of here."

Soon Mr. C's personal calm was beginning to evaporate. What if the police couldn't get to the Library in time, and the man became enraged when his daughter didn't arrive? Surely the office by now knew the scenario and wasn't going to send her down to possible captivity or harm. The man seemed to be losing patience. The Librarian wanted to try to find out more. Yet the man was at least partially inebriated. Being interrogated in any way might simply enrage him into violence. Mr. C knew he might have to try to disarm Nina's relative, even if the man stabbed him and then possibly many others.

Before the man could react, a hand silently reached through the door, turned the handle and three policemen dressed in all black, helmets, and flak jackets burst in.

The intruder tried to escape to the front doors, but soon was tackled and subdued by the trio of armed rescuers.

"Let me go," he yelled, "or I'll kill you. Got to get my daughter out—"

Scuffling sounds and it was obvious the four were struggling.

"Ow! You're hurting me!"

Fortunately, the armored men were highly trained and not about to lose the battle with one drunken man with a knife. Quickly they had the man handcuffed on the floor.

"You can make this easy, or hard," everyone heard one officer tell the man. "Do not say anything further unless requested to do so, as you may further scare the children."

"I don't care! I want my daughter!"

"Sorry, sir, but you won't be seeing your daughter just now," another voice calmly informed him.

Mr. C peered over the shelves and watched as two of the three escorted the handcuffed man dragging his heels out the front doors of the Library. Nearly invisible in his black flak jacket, the third officer walked back to the petrified children, Librarian, and Mrs. Cortez.

"It's all over people. You're safe. I'm sorry this had to happen, kids. But if we wait five minutes, your Teacher can take you safely back to your classroom."

The officer took a large walkie-talkie off his belt. "Zozobra Seven and Central HQ, we have the Coronado Library secured. No injuries. The suspect is in custody and two officers are escorting him to the parking lot. Have several patrol cars and an ambulance waiting. And please inform the Coronado Elementary School front office."

The man couldn't see the front parking lot, but it looked like a war zone. Five squad cars and an armored personnel carrier surrounded the area of the gym adjoining the Library. Although sirens had been turned off during the final approach to school, lights were now flashing. The man was quickly placed in the back seat of a squad car. This time disaster had been avoided.

~ TWENTY-NINE ~

Students were sent home that day, and school resumed the
following day. Within the next several weeks there were security
improvements, e-mails on security, staff meetings on security, and
classroom admonitions regarding security. School shootings had
become commonplace in the third millennium. Death or injuries
had been avoided this time, but within 24 hours a potentially violent incident had shaken the community. Although the students at
Coronado Elementary had avoided the deaths, injuries, or mayhem
associated with gunfire, students and faculty alike found themselves
increasingly preoccupied by thoughts of future unpredictable possibilities. The argument against automatic weapons was easy, but with
millions of shotguns, rifles, and pistols already in existence and easy
to buy on the internet or in sporting goods stores, how were things
to change? Faculty members spent many long nights contemplating
how lucky they were the rhetorical chamber had been empty in
a game of Russian roulette. Who knew when and where the next
distraught child or adult would take it upon himself to go on a
rampage?

The actions having been taken at Coronado were dramatic but
concluded with limited violence. There was no need to further
frighten the students. While each class was addressed, administrators
and Teachers were careful to downplay the recent event. Additional

door–to-floor locks were installed, security card scanning devices put into the front office, and students of all grades drilled on what to do should another such situation occur. Even arming Teachers became a consideration. Yet every adult knew that an enraged intruder, even with minimal knowledge of school building layout and security, could manage to get in. Breaking windows, concealing weapons in backpacks, devising explosives detailed on the internet, were just several possibilities that could create potential tragedies difficult to prevent.

As a contrast, Christian De Leon began to have an excellent day in Ms. Sevilla's fifth-grade class. His Teacher had a wonderful malleable ability to motivate and entertain, while quickly transforming to enforce strict discipline when necessary. For a big woman her posture was just one favorable gradation below military bearing, yet she remained relaxed and confident except in rare instances. Ms. Sevilla recognized a distinctive change in her special education student. His diffidence was still there, but the terror of his fellow classmates and talking in front of them was slowly subsiding. Ms. Sevilla had only met De Leon's Tutor in mufti, so thought of her as an informed, well-educated Native American Pueblo of Cochiti extraction. The fifth-grade Teacher was unaware of the Counselor/Tutor's Apache father. Ms. Sevilla began to see increasing evidence of her work but hadn't seen Emerald Star in her female Wizard-like regalia.

Star had somewhat modified the dual-capacity Clark Kent/Superman approach. Rather than ducking in a closet to change into her more ethereal garb, she used the faculty bathroom just down from the Library. Few others had seen her in her fairy-like attire, most public appearances as a mythic character avoided by making appointments with children and having them come to a Library office engagement rather than picking them up at their classrooms.

While still in class Christian De Leon had surprisingly, yet with typical restraint, answered a question on which planets were gaseous as opposed to solid. When called upon he initially hesitated, but suddenly a vision of Emerald Star reassuring him appeared mentally. "Jupiter, Saturn, Uranus and Neptune," he then found himself responding in an uncharacteristic voice everyone in the room could hear. The class burst out in applause and internally Christian was jubilant. He now knew his two hours a week of intensive Tutoring was already paying dividends.

A few minutes later he made the short walk to the Library office. Inside Emerald Star stood up to greet him with a handshake. She could see by the way he had entered there was a change in his usual apprehensiveness. She tapped him lightly on both shoulders with her wand tipped by the three-dimensional sparkling emerald-green star conveying magic through its touch. The Fairy Queen was wearing the matching emerald tiara in her hair, while cascading below, its long wavy jet black captured De Leon's attention. Recently applied green lipstick and nails completed the image of an energy source capable of transforming even the most difficult subject.

"How has your day been going?" she asked, gesturing for her subject to take a seat on the other side of the desk.

"Good," he answered in a singsong manner. Sincerity without inhibition had yet to pervade his delicate soul. Immediately upon answering, however, the fifth grader recollected his improvement to responding in class. "Well...I answered a question in class..."

"And how did that go?"

He hesitated. But hearkening back to his response and the applause gave him strength. "I did it...in a loud voice."

"Tremendous!" she enthused.

"Yah, I think the reading you're helping me with really is giving me confidence."

Emerald Star was amazed. It was one of the longest sentences her subject had been able to enunciate in an audible range. His unexpected enthusiasm gave her hope.

"Everything at home O.K.?"

"Not really," he answered, visibly slumping in his chair. "My dad came home for an hour."

"And what happened?" Star could tell Christian really didn't want to talk about it, but that doing so would help him get beyond any difficult encounter.

"Mm, the usual telling me what to do and how my going to school was a waste of time."

"Nothing physical, though."

"No—well he did slap me up on the back of my head. But I think my dad thinks it's necessary for me to learn discipline."

His father had probably been drinking, Emerald Star considered. Hopefully soon he would head south to El Paso, find employment there, and seldom return. She knew Mrs. Juarez, the school Counselor, was going to visit Christian's grandmother soon. Many of Coronado's students had challenging home lives that occasionally changed for the better. Maybe Christian's luck would turn, away from school as well. Ms. Star had also chosen not to broach the subject of the recent incident in the Library.

"Anyway, Christian, since your father will occasionally appear in your life by necessity and will probably have to be endured, at least for the immediate future, let's turn to a more productive topic. How's your reading going?"

"Good," he responded, but with a little more emphasis. "I read the first few chapters of *Matilda*," he continued with more enthusiasm, "and I could read everything by myself and understand it."

"Brilliant! And it would seem your newly improved reading skills are helping you become more active in the classroom."

"I want to try *Sideways School* after I finish *Matilda*," he said, scanning the books Star and other Counselors had nestled on one of the shelves without toys behind her, "and maybe even *Harry Potter and the Sorcerer's Stone.*"

~ THIRTY ~

Permanently attired in golf or T-shirts and Bermuda shorts, Coach Baca was a hardy middle-aged fellow who carried some extra pounds around the waist but moved with the alacrity of a post-man in a hurry. His rubicund face made his look Irish, yet he had a long Spanish family history and could speak both English and Spanish fluently. He was generally a jovial sort, but spoke with most people only briefly, always on a mission to create his next method of getting kids to use some of the energy they desperately needed to expend. Classroom learning always took precedence, but reading, physical education, art, music, sports, band, choir, dance, and many other activities in school helped students become informed and well rounded. Coach Baca liked being one of those contributors. He had a solid 25 years in within SFSD schools, liked helping kids, and his son would soon be entering college on a basketball scholarship.

That P. E. day was going to include volleyball in the small gym. Nets, stands, and various paraphernalia had to be set up. Often the Coach would solicit help, usually from fifth graders, and on that day, he zipped into Ms. Sevilla's fifth classroom as her kids were just settling in for the start of their day. Coach Baca's first hour was free, so he had a little leeway in setting up everything.

"Sure, we can get a few in our class to help you out," Ms. Sevilla replied while scanning a last e-mail on her computer. She then stood up in front of her chattering classroom before calling them to attention with her harmonica. With the first harmonic chord, they slowly quieted down and stood in place or slid into chairs.

"Coach Baca needs some help in the gym. Who wants to help?"

Most hands shot into the air. Not only did kids enjoy helping Coach Baca because of his enthusiastic nature, but also because helping any Teacher served as an excellent diversion for getting them out of class.

Ms. Sevilla began pointing over the heads of the kids' waving hands and arms madly. "O. K., Manuel, Christian, and...Odysseus."

The fifth-grade Teacher usually avoided choosing Odysseus because of his periodic but recurrent infractions. Yet he had been rather quiet lately, and she had heard from Mrs. Juarez of the difficulty he was experiencing in dealing with his socialite mother. His self-worth had plummeted after the incident with the books and the Library, as well. Ms. Sevilla felt it was time to give him an option of showing another side of his character. Baca had had his own issues with Odysseus Ray, but easily had concealed his surprise when Ms. Sevilla had chosen the student with a troubled existence. The Coach was aware of the stolen book's episode, but he, too, believed in giving young students second and third or even endless chances. With a wave of Coach Baca's arm signaling them to follow, the four departed.

In the gym the three lads hopped to it, knowing there was no hanging about with Coach Baca. Heavy metal stands were rolled out from storage, nets were unraveled and strung up, balls retrieved from storage boxes, and tape applied to the floor to create outlined courts.

All the while Coach Baca gave periodic orders, many of them from a distance requiring a loud voice. The four were about 20 minutes into setting up, when Christian tripped over one of the stands and came down with a loud thud onto the parquetry court.

"*Uh-oh, here we go*," thought Coach Baca. In his many years of managing kids often running at full tilt he had seen just about every kind of injury. Chipped teeth, scrapes, cuts, bruises and even a broken arm were all part of the risk of strenuous activity. Yet preventing kids from injuries was like driving cars without the occasional occurrence of fender benders and more serious accidents. The Coach began walking quickly toward Christian, the reticent fifth grader now rubbing his arm and trying to use his other arm to get to his feet.

"Here, let me help you," a voice said calmly while taking De Leon's hand and helping him get up. As they approached, Coach Baca and Manuel were both surprised to see the normally defiant Odysseus assisting Christian. "Are you O.K.?" Odysseus asked as if he were a guardian angel.

"Here, let me see your arm," Coach Baca said, gently manipulating the point the injured fifth grader had been rubbing. "It's just bruised. You'll be O.K.," he said reassuringly. "When you go back to class, stop off at the nurse's office to get some ice to put on it."

Coach Baca wasn't a doctor. Yet over the years he had acquired many of the analytical skills of those in the medical profession. If you wanted to keep kids moving, you had to deal with injury occurrences quickly, yet with the confident ability to diagnose and differentiate minor scrapes, cuts, and bruises from more serious mishaps.

The physical education instructor noticed a subtle change in his latest injured student. Christian De Leon was one of the more hesitant boys he encountered each week. Fifth-grade girls often gained far more height than boys during their last year at Coronado. Yet partially due to developing testosterone rather than estrogen, boys often proved to be more aggressive than their generally taller female classmates. Christian was an exception. Usually, the reticent boy stayed in the back of any group, rarely volunteered for any physical game or endeavor, and for the most part tried to remain invisible among his peers. Recently, however, the student with a verbally abusive father had begun participating at a more active level. Most of the physical diffidence was still there, but Baca could see incremental improvements that could sometimes signal a life in transition. The Tutoring he knew De Leon was getting must be helping him gradually to leave reticence behind.

Odysseus was another surprise. Seeing him doing anything that didn't involve self-absorption was miraculous. Coach Baca was aware of the influence his older brother, and former Coronado student, had upon him, as well as how his father with the best intentions was unable to bond with his youngest son. Baca hadn't met the mother, but the word was she was an arrogant socialite with little concern for her children. Still, the Coach felt what Odysseus really needed was a good boot in the butt. No one in a school was allowed to physically discipline anyone, and Baca took care never to lay a non-affectionate hand on a student. Yet if there was ever someone upon whom verbal instructions and advice had little positive effect, it was Odysseus Ray. The kid from the affluent home had already spent too many years of elementary school screwing around rather than applying himself to developing tools he would need in middle and high school, not to mention life itself. To counteract that omission, he acted out, treating others with the lack of respect he felt for himself.

Still, the three fifth-grade boys proved indispensable. The collective energy of ten-year-old's got the whole volleyball set up accomplished in thirty minutes. Had they not assisted, Coach Baca might have overextended himself and probably would have had more than his usual two Gila Monster beers while watching Thursday night

NFL. Over the years his back was becoming more and more dicey. Aggravating it while lifting too much or too often was occurring with regularity. Baca wondered just how long he could stay as active as he needed to be as a physical education instructor. He had only just turned 50, but his back periodically made him feel 70.

When the trio returned to Ms. Sevilla's classroom the day continued to progress without significant incident. With just a half-day on Friday to follow, her students generally were far more congenial knowing the weekend was coming. She gave them extra recess for good behavior, knowing that any expenditure of pent-up energy rather than disruption of the classroom was good. Kids needed to move. or their energy often erupted in negative ways when they were forced to remain calm and focused on the classroom subjects at hand.

"Ms. Sevilla, Iván hit Odysseus in the back with a textbook," said Carlos.

The fifth-grade Teacher had been looking at a lesson plan on her computer screen while the students were supposed to be doing some silent reading. She was aware of revenge sometimes being a motivation. Carlos wasn't allowed to be a part of a small coterie of boys including Odysseus, Caliban and Iván, and was jealous. The previous day Iván had tattled on Carlos for an innocuous infraction. Ms. Sevilla had told him to spend more time on his work than tattling on his peers. Now the shoe was on the other foot, and it was just such seemingly minor discipline issues that brought to bear the necessity for fairness and quickly devised consequences.

"Gentlemen," began their Teacher, "do you think you are wisely using your time? Or squandering it by being mean to one another and wasting my time as well as disrupting the other students reading quietly. Iván, I could ask you why you hit Odysseus in the head, but I would ask you instead if doing so was a wise decision?"

He shook his head from side to side. "No," he muttered.

"Odysseus stole his book while Iván was trying to read it," a soft voice came from nearby.

Ms. Sevilla was stunned. Not only had the voice come from her most diffident student, Christian, but he had done so without his usual fear and apprehension. The entire class stopped what they were doing and stared at the special education student.

"Did you see him do it?" she asked. Ms. Sevilla wanted the whole matter to disappear like a fire drill ending, but she was so surprised by Christian's contribution that she wished to encourage him further.

"He wouldn't have done it, except for Odysseus taking his book first," Christian said, looking over at her.

"No way!" answered Odysseus in a loud voice while staring at Christian with his usual angry and dismissive attitude. The former's usual *modus operandi* was to increase volume for effect. It worked for some of the kids, but it didn't work on the seasoned Sevilla.

"Alright, Odysseus, we've discussed telling the truth when these confrontations occur."

"It is the truth! I was just looking at his book!"

Their instructor could see the anger upon Odysseus' face. Iván said nothing, as much like Christian, he said little to anyone and often acted as Odysseus' silent sidekick. Ms. Sevilla knew Christian might well face consequences from her most defiant student on the playground.

"Alright, we've already wasted too much time on this repetitive aggravation stuff in class. Let's see if everyone can be more kind to one another rather than spiteful." She walked over to Iván and Odysseus. "I want each of you to apologize to the other, *right now*."

"Sorry," said Iván.

"Odysseus, say it like you mean it."

"Sorry, Iván," he said with emphasis conveying the opposite.

"The two of you will spend your recess with me in the classroom," she summarily announced with conviction.

The incident was just one of several each hour most Teachers had to face. The overall effect was to drain the energy from even the most intrepid instructors, as well as from the students, many of which had no actual part in the confrontations and were trying to stay focused. Mrs. Sevilla did her best, when she had the time, to take recalcitrant kids just outside the classroom door so the other students would have the disruption remain minimal. Yet she felt most classroom behavioral issues could be avoided simply by reducing class sizes to fifteen. Twenty-five to thirty students meant spending a geometric increase of time on discipline issues. The State legislature was always complaining of insufficient funds, when oil and gas-leasing revenues, particularly from the southeastern part of the State's Permean Basin, had built the Land Endowment fund to over 18 billion dollars. *Oh well,* she thought, *other citizens of the country simply looked at New Mexico as an impoverished agricultural and under-populated State with among the worst schools.* She knew money didn't solve everything, but fewer students per classroom and higher pay to attract better Teachers could be beacons in a hurricane.

That evening when Odysseus arrived home from hanging out with his friends and their mountain bikes in the arroyo, his father was home early. The fifth grader's mother was off at a women's club meeting of some sort, so the two of them were home alone.

"I got a call from your mother that she had received an e-mail from Ms. Sevilla."

Odysseus made no comment, glancing at an ornate clock standing against the wall in Mr. Ray's antique-filled office. The son knew what was coming from the father: one of the usual talks on discipline, applying oneself, etc., etc.

"It would seem there was another incident in class today," Penn

Ray said, pausing to look up his son playing with a Lego man from his pocket. "What happened?"

Odysseus merely continued fiddling with the Lego man.

"Do you want to tell me about it?"

"No," came the sullen answer.

"Son, your mother and I have tried to understand what goes on in your head. You and your brother both have high IQs and apparently the capacity for good scholarship. Yet there was the pot incident with Courtney, the book stealing matter in the Library, and I could go on..."

Still nothing from Odysseus.

"If you won't tell us what the problem is, it's difficult to help you with it," Mr. Ray said, picking up a paperweight and putting it down again. "Now I came home early today to try and spend some time with you, and yet as always, it is difficult to get you to reveal what's going on in your head."

A tear began rolling down Odysseus' cheek.

"What's wrong, Odysseus? Tell me."

"Everything," his youngest son suddenly blurted, furtively dashing away the tear. "I hate school, I don't want the life you and mom have, you think Courtney and I are losers, and I'll never measure up to what you want me to be no matter what."

"Son, your mother and I want the best for you and your brother, no matter what that may be. We both know you don't want our life of country clubs, charity fundraisers, art openings, the Metropolitan Opera live from New York at the Lensic, and playing bridge. But unless you find something to motivate you other than spending your time being disruptive and negative, neither your mother and I, nor you, can help alleviate the problem."

"But I don't know what I want to do! I just know what I don't want to do!"

"O. K., I phrased the matter incorrectly. Certainly, a ten-year-old rarely knows a course of direction to want to point toward for the future. That's why there is school. It's a place where, by studying different subjects, interest in one or several eventually comes. You have to give it time—"

"You and mom always have the answers," he moaned, "but I find studying, reading, and writing boring, boring, boring! I'm forced to learn millions of things about Anglo men and their accomplishments. What about Latin men and women and their accomplishments? What about all the scandals in Federal and State government? We live this privileged life while most of the kids in my school are lucky to get a free breakfast and lunch."

"Well, our privileged life, as you call it, is better than poverty, is it not?"

"That's not the point," his youngest son snarled. "Your lives are so yesterday." He shook his head from side to side. "I mean, you're still spending your days tinkering with atomic energy and bombs that are more destructive than anything misbehavior in school might cause. Yah, you make a lot of money. We have a big house, two suburban vehicles, and enough money to go to Geronimo if we want to rather than Chili's for dinner. But are you and mom happy? Do you fit in to this south side community?"

"I think your mother and I have our moments that only come from years of sharing. She's not perfect and I'm not perfect, but I think we both make contributions to the community and our fellow man. We don't have all the answers, but as you'll hopefully find out some day in this troubled world, each of us does what he or she can to make life better for ourselves and for others. And then Santa Fe's the great melting pot. Sure Hispanics, Anglos and Native Americans are still in the infancy stages in terms of social interaction. But it's better than it was in the twentieth century. It's better than—"

"Sounds like something our politicians say every day. The State's so poor everyone's got his or her hand in the till. They are all doing more for themselves than for all the poor in this State. It's a big bag of crap. But anyway, why would any of us want to grow up and be a part of the whole downer cesspool of greed and corruption? I mean, build a wall to keep out more than half of my school? Are they building a wall between Canada and the U.S., or do we only need a wall to keep out people of color?"

"You know I'm not in favor of any wall," answered Penn Ray. "All I can say is that for every corrupt politician you read about, there are nine doing the best job they know how, just like at Cottonwood Mesa. Sure, physicists sometimes take long lunches and drink too many cocktails. But who is going to provide the safeguards the country and its schools need without technological development? Somebody's got to make decisions, and sometimes they're wrong or they go in the wrong direction. But trying's the thing, son. Trying's the thing."

"Yah, well I've tried the school thing for six years now and my attitude still hasn't changed. I mean, at least the Library has some newer graphic novels with characters I can identify with. Like, most of the fiction is about Anglo kids in the South or Northeast who are, like, so yesterday. I mean, why would I want to sit and read a book with text only when I can play Minecraft or Fortnite or watch superhero movies on an iPad, or watch the Cowboys annihilate the Broncos?"

"Lots of kids don't like school, Odysseus. I didn't particularly like it. But I stuck with it. Eventually you absorb more and more vocabulary and you become aware of the great complexities of making communities or societies work. Again, Santa Fe's not perfect, but if you think things are imperfect here for people of color, try almost any area of the world you can think of, and education is the problem. Those with the best educations get the best jobs and make the most money. But I understand where you're coming from, son. Right now, making money may be the farthest thing from your mind. You say, 'why do I need reading and books, when visual activities are so much more exciting?' I hear you. But no matter what you do, playing sports, digging ditches, learning Minecraft, or trying to make yourself understood by adults like me, you need language. And to learn language you need words whose meanings are learned through reading. It doesn't matter what. Just reading everything and learning all the communications skills you can, through books, magazines, online articles, newspapers, and signs, or listening to others speak. Why do you think you have all those colored dots on books in your Library? To convey that learning and reading are gradual processes, not overnight sensations. I know you think the whole school regimen is futile, but stick with it, Odysseus, stick with it. Sticking with learning anything and everything you can, including Minecraft. Doing so will help develop passions, and you and your brother need passion in your lives. Remember, knowledge is power."

Mr. Ray didn't want to mention how he agreed with the exclusions of people of color. Sure, moving through the education process helped them get better jobs and to be a part of the American Dream. But racial barriers and preferences still remained strong. Cottonwood Mesa physicists and engineers in positions of power were mainly all Anglo and male. Clubs tended to remain racially divided, or gender specific. But while he had been to many parties, events, and bars where the ethnic mix remained primarily white, people of color descended from Africa, Mexico, China, Diné, and a potpourri of places all continued to increase the evolutionary social changes that were inevitable. Yet deep down almost everyone preferred his or her own kind, whether it be racial, religious, educational, work- or gender-related. Social harmony was as slow to develop as changing the North Star through the precession of the Earth's axis taking 25,770 years.

Although determined to be different from his parents, Odysseus Ray surprisingly could read well. He read instructional material for games such as Minecraft, articles on local corruption in the *Reporter*, and enough to get minimal grades and test scores in Coronado Elementary School. He tested quite well in math, and with only a minimal amount of additional effort, could be reading at sixth- or seventh-grade level. To the fifth grader, however, reading and school learning merely forced upon him the probability of following in his father's footsteps, a path as appealing to him as his mother's bridge friends. He swept his intentionally unkempt locks back over the top of his head.

"Dad, just give it up. I can't speak for Courtney, but I don't think either of us is every going to get into Harvard or Princeton. Not that we want to. I only want to go to school until I don't have to, and then..."

Then's the problem, son. Then will come, and without a good formal education right on through college, you will be lucky to find a job as a tradesman who can't afford to buy a home."

"Then is now, and now is then. I don't like the life of a student."

His dad shook his head. "Your mother and I have been talking, Odysseus. Maybe High Desert Academy or an Eastern prep school might suit you better."

~ THIRTY-ONE ~

Somehow the New Mexican legislature perennially seemed to tighten rather than loosen the State school system budget. Maybe it was because schools required over fifty percent of the annual total. Maybe it was schools with perennial low ratings preventing New Mexico from growing like Arizona or a sunflower in September. The legislation of change was inevitable, but an impoverished agricultural State with hundreds of years of Native American and Spanish colonial tradition often moved with the speed of a sloth going to sleep after eating. Occasionally something new on the horizon such as Rail Runner from Santa Fe to Belen, arose as an innovative project to offset the status quo. But far more quickly came the comments that it lost money, that it was too slow, and that we should scrap the project. Seemingly no one had a vision of how to make the train break even. Suggestions of train times extending further into the evening, commuter routes skipping some stops to match automobile travel times, or hotel/restaurant/dramatic play packages in both directions between the capital and largest city fell on deaf ears. Change was an interesting concept, but too much too soon, brought an alteration in the possession of power, and for many, this was a poison pill to swallow.

Inasmuch as the Coronado Elementary annual line budget for the Library had disappeared, and Book Bond grants only occurred every two years, money from somewhere was needed to purchase books. Grant solicitations, even though limited, could prove generous and helpful. But having 6,000 to 8,000 books, of which eighty percent or more were out-of-date, had unimaginative plain covers or covers with high school students from the 1940s, covers, jackets, and pages ripped, book taped so many times you could hardly read the spines, and non-fiction books with antiquated information, all spelled less and less book reading by every elementary school student unable to identify with the Anglo leading characters and second millennium presentations. Granted the school was blessed with Chrome pads for reading electronically. Yet over time, Mr. C had found most of his students returned to the real thing: books with current covers and illustrations like Raina Telgemeier had imagined with *Smile*, *Sisters*, *Drama*, and *Ghosts*. Transforming a Library took both time and money. And one Librarian, and one non-budget made that transformation challenging.

Initially Mr. C held one for-profit Academic Book Fair a year before Christmas, and one buy-one-get-one-free ABF in the spring. The idea seemed to create a win-win situation. Kids buy books, and if your school's sales are $2,500 or more, about half of the total was credited to that school. The ABF dollars earned could then be used to purchase books from the ABF catalog. Associated problems, however, were several. The second ABF might have worked, if kids bought books. Yet more often, given a limited currency from home of $5-10, they bought magic pens for $3.00, UV pens writing invisibly until the purchaser shone black light from the pen upon the writing. One year Mr. C sold 300 at one ABF. Other purchases included currency erasers, sharpeners, pens, note pads, and other novelties costing between 50 cents and $2.00. With only several dollars from home, few kids bought actual books costing between $5-10 or more. Accordingly, the buy-one-get-one-free was limited in scope and put few 'free' extra books into the hands of kids. Quickly by changing the giveaway ABF to for-profit, the school then made from its two ABFs between $3,000 and $4,000 a year with which to buy books. The second problem arose when Academic's catalog had a far more limited selection of books than the bigger sellers of books like Mackin or Follett. Still, Mr. C put his whole soul into providing a visually exciting fair during which the kids could come to and surround themselves with a delightfully vicarious world.

Yet particularly for the December fair, during which garlands of multi-colored bulbs crisscrossed below the fluorescent lights, purchasing holiday gifts for others played a big part. By holding a school Art Walk and one to two Winter Music Concerts during ABF week, parents strolled down to the Library afterwards in a festive mood.

There were always stalwart kids who loved helping. Mr. C enlisted five or six students from Mrs. Cortez's fourth grade to assist with the Friday setup during the final class two hours one week from winter break. There is no substitute for the energy of elementary school dervishes whirling around to unload books from boxes, opening the rolling shelves that line two walls, and the madcap decorating that always included an ABF theme. This one was Fairyland in the Snow, and lots of standup cardboard figures were placed strategically throughout the Library to further heighten the feeling of the holidays.

To Mr. C it was somewhat like directing the invasion of Normandy. Just where everything was placed was crucial. The tables were covered with green and red or other theme cloths, empty book boxes wrapped in colorful paper to provide a central book stand for each table, while using only two-thirds of the Library made the room feel crowded with potential gifts.

Security was always an issue. The cash register was placed on a table by the door, and students had to show receipts when leaving with purchases. On that table were packed all the books and boxes with desirable toys inside. Those items could only be examined at that table, unless purchased, as taking boxes and books with novelties in them to a circle of chairs ringing a Christmas tree merely tempted kids who couldn't afford them, as well as some of those who could, to pocket them. Pilferage was expected, however, and ABF and Librarians planned accordingly. There were plenty of small inexpensive items for planned removal without paying. It was a form of social welfare, ensuring that even the most destitute children managed to take something away from the Book Fair. These planned disappearances remained unspoken, of course. Backpacks and jackets had to be left outside on carts to ensure taking items without paying became more difficult. Book Fair monitors, with badges hanging round their necks surveyed the room constantly, particularly the novelty item table nearby the cash register. Those items were not supposed to travel to other parts of the room, either, to help avoid theft.

Meanwhile on the Friday before BF week the fourth-grade volunteers were placing and wrapping and decorating with esprit. The tree had gold and red metal garlands and strands of candle-flame bulbs. A star on top punctuated the thought of Christmas. For after all, even though church and State were mandated not to mix, in an area where 95 percent of the population was Catholic, Hanukkah and other religious festivities remained limited in school-wide celebratory activities.

"Mr. C, where do these books go?" asked Dulce, holding a large box of books with a label 'Cookbooks' on the end.

"Put those in that window seat over there."

Cookbooks, as well as a few coffee table biographies more for young adults than elementary students, were put at one of the tables far from the cashier's table. There was little chance of anyone taking them. They were large, expensive, and cumbersome, and Mr. C almost felt it would be a miracle if any of them sold. Books over

$20 were like precious gems at Tiffany's to students with few if any expensive books in their homes.

"O. K., Luis," the Librarian eventually said while placing books strategically overlapping one another on a red cloth covered table, "let's concentrate more on putting books out than standing there reading them."

Elementary school students had short attention spans. Teachers didn't want to discourage curiosity, but another part of the job was keeping students focused on the work at hand. Setting up a book fair after most kids went home at 12:35 on a Friday took constant attention and direction, or his volunteers tended to drift. Throwing paper at one another, reading books taken from boxes, spending too much time putting up a decoration or wrapping a box, all were slowdowns for the train of completion. Yet the kids worked like miniature adults, paid bonuses for piecework. They fought to obtain the set-up volunteer jobs, knowing that a magic pen or part of the cost of a book they couldn't really afford was a reward at hand.

It was early on Wednesday afternoon during BF week, when Mr. C gave one of his Academic Book Fair introductory talks to a fifth-grade class.

"O.K., welcome back to the Book Fair," he said, making eye contact with an array of his students, now sitting on oak chairs in an oval around the Christmas tree. Fake wrapped presents nestled below the tree; festive displays designed to spur holiday sales. "Most of you have been to many of these, but we've got a few changes." He turned and gestured toward the cashier's and novelty tables. "Items on the cashier's and the small item tables may be examined at those tables or purchased. However," he paused for effect, "they can't be taken to the rest of the room. All the rest of the books in the room," he said, pointing at the rolling shelves and tables through-out the room, "may be taken to chairs, examined, and then put back or purchased." Mr. C then addressed where book prices could be found, inexpensive, yellow-tagged sale books and where to find them, maintaining quiet while shopping, and saving their receipts to show as they left the Library. "Oh, and please don't steal. When you steal, you are stealing from yourselves, because one of every two dollars the Book Fair takes in comes back to us in the form of Academic Dollars, which we then can use to buy books for the Library. So please do not take anything you haven't paid for."

Twenty minutes later the noise levels had risen to that of tailgate parties at the opera. Several times Mr. C asked kids to quiet down, but he knew their enthusiasm, while sometimes misguided, spirited them to buy unpredictable choices of attractive books, erasers, pens, and other objects that effectively made a child's day. Getting kids to obey all the rules, especially those destined to complete their Coronado journeys within six months, was a novel idea, but often unenforceable. The very name 'Fair' connoted excitement and displays of unique items in brightly colored surroundings. Remaining calm, even for ten-year-old's, was not on the agenda.

Sales of the smaller items, even bolstered by reordering, were generally brisk, many of them having been scooped up during the first three days of the ABF. Gummy bear erasers for $0.99 were the most popular, and those purchasing anything for $1.99 or less resembled lines of impatient souls waiting for food handouts after a hurricane.

Nearby the cash register, one of the monitors at the door stopped a fifth grader at the door.

"I saw her put these bookmarks in her pocket," monitor Carolina Montoya told the Librarian finishing up a sale. A fifth grader looked down at the floor as Carolina held out an array of 3D bookmarks depicting a white unicorn. Many of the bookmarks were $0.50 or $1.00, but the 3D ones were $3.95 each.

"O. K. Evelyn," Mr. C said, recognizing a quiet girl from her sixth year at Coronado, "stealing is a serious offense that I just talked about earlier."

In reality, stealing was a multi-faceted diamond in the rough. The items taken told him which items were the most popular. Motivations were simple. Many kids stole things because they wanted them and couldn't afford them. Certain boys took things to show off to friends that they could get away with doing so. A third motivation conveyed the desperation of those wishing to participate in the American Dream of owning beautiful things. Another projected the right of passage of young boys accepting risk to prove bravery and an adventuresome spirit. Mr. C knew he'd have to bestow appropriate consequences and her Teacher assign related punishment. He could ban her from the Book Fair. He could make her sit shamefully by herself in a chair near the off-limits computers. Yet somehow the plight of the underdog always arose from challenging circumstances.

The ABF kept open after school and right up to the 5:30 to 6:30 evening concerts. A homebound flyer sent two weeks earlier requested parents and relatives to stop by the Fair either before or after the concerts. Doing so presented an ideal opportunity for those relatives to show their children they believed in education. Many bought one or several books for their daughters or sons, as well as several of the smaller items providing so much pleasure. Both evenings probably brought in an extra $1,000 total, lifting the 4-1/4-day ABF's total sales to just over $4,000, slightly more than half of which could be used to buy books for the Library.

The same helpful fourth graders helped with breaking down the Fair when the Fair closed at 10:00 a.m. sharp on Friday. Found at large in the back of the room were brand new books hidden under shelves or lodged among existing Library books kids planned on retrieving later. The popularity of certain books created unfortunate disappearing destinies.

Through the glass panels of the Fair-ending locked front doors could always be seen occasional students knocking, those who failed to listen to the many announcements that the Fair would be open from 7:00 a.m. each day, but that the whole idyll would disappear like a mirage on Friday promptly at 10:00 a.m. Some delight is always predicated upon brevity. By noon all the Library's rolling shelves, tables and chairs had been put back into place. It was as if the Academic Book Fair had been a fictional episode from one of the Library's stories.

~ THIRTY-TWO ~

Periodically throughout the school year field trips were planned, and students gained a partial day's adventure into exotic realms yet to be explored. The most exciting destinations proved to music or dance performances at the Lensic, a renovated theater providing the community with a cornucopia of everything from Lannan-sponsored interviews of famous authors to music derived from throughout the world. Meow Wolf was a newly created possible destination molded from the transformation of an extinct bowling alley. The impetus had come from George R. R. Martin, a popular philanthropic resident known for his Game of Thrones books and related television series. Through artistic visions, Meow Wolf morphed into an imaginative set of dimly illuminated Alice-in-Wonderland or Adams Family rooms filled with black-lit dinosaur bones or fluorescent trees, refrigerator, oven, or closet doors, leading to thrilling unknown spaces, and a wondrous array of captivating worlds of visual entertainment.

The South Side Library was less an exotic destination in an even more vicarious sense, yet it was the fervent hope of Teachers and the Librarian alike that students would continue reading and discover new worlds throughout the summer or during holidays. Public libraries provided particularly young students with opportunities not only to fill the void when their school libraries were closed, but also a whole new world of books they hadn't yet been able to explore. Some spent half days in summer school, but there were always certain days and weeks when the availability of other sources for reading materials proved bountiful.

Second grade remained an important journey during which most kids learned to read. If, by the end of that year, they couldn't read and write sufficiently in English or Spanish, there remained the unpleasant likelihood that they would never be able to enjoy the magic realms reached by those who used a 26-letter alphabet to take them there. New Mexico's legislators were aware of this discrepancy disgracing their State. It was a stunning land of out-of-doors opportunity with distressingly limited mental opportunity for those of limited financial resources. Yet the various possible solutions to this dilemma were allowed to remain nebulous rather than attainable. No one would admit the travesty of limiting a whole class of people's education. The belief was somehow allowed to stand that the State Land Endowment Fund of more than $18 billion was insufficient to accomplish the changes necessary to create life-long opportunities for small children.

Still, Teachers throughout the State carried on, as if the miracle of great education was still within reach. With nervous anticipation Ms. Angela Montaña's first graders entered the South Side Library with hands behind their backs and eyes scanning twenty-first century walls and rooms full of paper dinosaurs. They still felt the optimism of Kindergarteners because few of them had experienced any worlds beyond nearby neighborhoods. The six-year-old's quietly filed into a room on which they were asked to sit on a carpet-covered elevated platform to receive their introductions. One of the female Librarians, appropriately peering out from behind red plastic reading glasses, brightly began to describe their adventuresome surroundings.

"Many of you have never been here before," she began, aware that most of her charges might not take in all her English explanation. Total immersion was necessary, she felt, more quickly to imbue any child with a new language. Bilingualism certainly had its place throughout much of the world, including New Mexico. Yet this volunteer, retired from an affluent life of housewifery, believed the ability to feel at home in any environment was predicated upon being able to chat with anyone as if you had known them since time immemorial. Librarian Mary Davis was convinced that she would carry on with almost any group as if they understood this necessity. "It's a wonderful place, loaded with books that can take you to the world of your imagination."

After five minutes during which most of the first graders understood occasional drifts of what they were being told, the excited kids were allowed to begin their labyrinthine excursions. Miniature students in jeans, hooded sweatshirts, and some wearing shoes with soles illuminated by movement, reached up and withdrew books from shelves. Energetically they began to bound between them, disappearing from those examining books in the next aisle, and from the real world outside. Mammals, reptiles, dinosaurs, and princesses were among their favorites. Quickly the first graders were permitted to take books to colorful cubby seat areas in which to feel the isolation and immersion of their own imaginations. For most of them, pictures still enveloped their minds, yet some could read just enough to take in words sprinkled like fairy dust among the visual delights.

Later a female Librarian sat them down in another room for several stories of adventure and pleasant outcomes, including animals with the admirable traits of Peter Rabbit and Franklin the turtle. Then one by one Mrs. Montaña distributed Library cards she had been given for each student, the equivalent to first graders or young adults getting their initial passports. The tiny students were also shown the stacks of books in another huge room, in order that they would further learn reading was an ongoing lifelong process of exploration. They were not taken into the small decorative room filled with donated or outdated treasures selling for 50 cents or $1.00. Six-year-olds rarely had any money at all, the equivalent of viewing the shop probably being akin to sitting in the Violet Crown movie theater lobby without the funds to see a Disney film.

Their two-hour sojourn ended with an uplifting talk. A seasoned Librarian told them of all they could experience within the confines of a giant treasure chest, packed with stories to be read and untold destinations to be vicariously explored.

~ THIRTY-THREE ~

The SFSD Fitness 5K Run/Walk was an attempt by the current Superintendent to stress the importance of exercise for everyone. Families with limited incomes often found food as one of their few enjoyable entertainments. Rather than meals out in the more expensive downtown restaurants, many of the residents of the south side spent Sunday afternoons at backyard barbecues or at local favorites and chain restaurants. Over time this meant carrying some additional weight, the price paid for focusing more on fast foods and large soda drinks, rather than salads or protein and vegetable meals. For this reason, the Superintendent herself discussed with others in the SFSD hierarchy what could be done to reverse this unhealthful trend. School meals had for the most part dropped desserts and cookies while stressing protein, salads, fruit, and vegetables. To counteract any indulgent third-millennium behavior, talks were given on fitness and hygiene during physical education classes and at special assemblies. Elementary students also were given more recess time. Yet eating shared meals, snacks, treats, and other tasty delights remained paramount in many lives of poverty and stressful existence, as valuable as the pursuit of expensive travel and restaurants enjoyed by the affluent.

The Superintendent was among those wishing to shed a few pounds, concluding that a series of district-wide fitness runs might be just the signal that movement and physical fitness should be viewed as important as mental development in everyone's future. She wouldn't be able to run the SFSD Elementary Fitness 5K through the streets and fields near Argenta High School, but she could certainly walk the course. The Run/Walk was scheduled early on a late March morning when only a few wildflowers would be blossoming along the course. Ribbons and T-shirts were to be awarded for completion, and giveaways would tentatively hold people for awards at the event after completion.

Antonio Lopez awoke that morning with excitement. He and his father Juan had been jogging in the arroyos late afternoons, and they both looked forward to finishing the 3.1 miles well ahead of most of Coronado's other participating students, staff, parents, and relatives.

The pair got to the Argenta football field quite early when there was still a high-elevation bite in the air. In the distance the Sangre de Cristo snow-capped range hovered as a backdrop better glimpsed once the fitness dervishes got out onto the dirt and scrub-tree flat desert terrain during the middle of the race.

"Yo, Odysseus," Antonio said hesitantly, not knowing how to react to the volatile classmate he was surprised to see. Antonio had seen Odysseus excel in certain P. E. class events yet was unaware his classmate was a runner. Then again, most kids who were active could somehow get through several miles. Antonio felt assured he could beat whatever effort his sometime antagonist could make. But that's why clocks were used. You never knew just who might come up with an unexpected performance.

Odysseus Ray nodded, unwilling to extend himself in a greeting. Juan Lopez had gone back to the car to leave his warm-up jacket and pants, so Antonio watched as Odysseus largely ignored him and strutted over to some fifth-grade girls. *This might be the day I show the hotshot how hard work pays off*, Antonio thought. Yet he was unsure.

An ankle sprain he had gotten while stepping on a rock hidden by a chamiso plant shadow might act up. He had figure-eight wound an elastic bandage around the ankle, but running on irregular surfaces could bring unexpected encounters, especially when you were running harder than normal. The 5K wasn't being billed as a race, but there were those participating feeling compelled to avoid being beaten by others considered to be less fit.

It was very easy to go out too hard in a distance race. While at sea level a runner could go into oxygen debt by starting too fast, that harrier could also recover quickly in the oxygen-rich air. At altitude, however, there was less margin for error: burn too much energy or expend too much lung capacity at any stage of the race and it often became impossible to recover. Antonio and his father settled back into the sixth row at the start. They could see Odysseus in the front row, shifting nervously from one foot to the other.

Over the slight hill round the front of Argenta HS, Odysseus only had one or two middle or high school boys in front of him. With less than a half mile of the race having unfolded he felt good. Entering the dirt path traversing high desert open space, he kept his leg turnover high. *This is easy*, he told himself. *Piece of cake.*

Unknown to him, however, fifth grader Carolina Montoya was running much like a Kenyan. In fact, she was wearing a T-shirt with a 'KENYA BELIEVE IT!' logo. Distance running came natural to her, and she couldn't wait to get to middle school where she could participate on a cross-country team. Early in the race she had left her taller and heavier friend, Matilda Blackstone, behind. Carolina could run longer and faster than most of the smaller boys her age, and in this 5K she found herself among some older males and grown men under rapidly warming spring blue skies.

Antonio's father had fallen behind early. The fifth grader gradually began to move up among those starting to slow approaching the completion of the first mile. Patience was the key. Knowing your own pace and abilities, then parceling out your energy incrementally to enable reverse splitting over the second flat half of the course. His ankle was sore, but it was holding up O.K. He could see Odysseus a good hundred yards ahead of him, unsure whether bravado or fitness was carrying his brash classmate much faster than Antonio believed possible.

Ten males and perhaps one tall female runner remained ahead of him as Antonio passed the one-mile sign. He wasn't sure who the female was, but he thought it might his classmate Carolina. *There's still 2.1 miles to go*, he told himself. *Take it easy. Run your own race.*

The course was basically a large desert field loop extending out from the Argenta buildings and football field, with the last 300 yards to be run on the stadium track. By the 2M mark Antonio could see the school and mountains behind it in the distance. He was running under control and had now closed the gap from Odysseus down to about 20 meters. At one point his adversary glanced over his shoulder and saw him, then picked up his pace, unwilling to have anyone he knew threatening to overtake him.

Earlier Odysseus had been startled when Carolina Montoya drew up alongside. He struggled to match her stride for stride, realizing his lack of training meant he would be unable to keep up. Neither said hello to the other, each wishing to stick with his or her uninterrupted plan. It was evident to the boy, however, that his taller female counterpart had expended energy more evenly, as gradually she began to draw away. He was disappointed to be unable to stay with her, yet at the same time knew she was properly trained, and he wasn't. Besides, she was a girl.

On the return the dirt trail had a slight ascent to it, and most of the runners were sweating more heavily as the cold morning gradually warmed from the intense rays of the sun, the effect more powerful with perhaps thirty percent of the atmosphere missing at nearly 7,000 feet of elevation.

That Lopez dude is not going to catch me, Odysseus thought. *There's only about a half mile to go, and I'm still gonna kick his ass.* Yet Ray was beginning to slow, and he knew it. With just general fitness carrying him, 3.1 miles was a long way to run. *Don't worry. He can't catch you. He's as tired as you are.*

But seeing Odysseus begin to slow ever so slightly gave his harder working classmate renewed impetus. Even though his ankle was beginning to tighten Antonio shook it out a couple of times with that foot in the air, and it seemed to loosen. *There he is,* he thought, seeing Odysseus just a few strides ahead of him. *I wonder if I should try to power by him fast or draw even and make it look like I have very little left in the tank.* He chose the latter, and the shock upon his rival's face when Antonio silently arrived alongside gave a brief adrenalin surge to the mild-mannered lad having chosen to wear Steve Prefontaine's favorite color: purple singlet and shorts. Antonio could see Odysseus immediately get angry. The tiring kid's elbow flew out as if they were in a finishing chute with room for only one runner. Lopez felt a sting in his arm, but pain only fueled him to ramp things up and pull away. Odysseus again hit him in the back in one futile release of fury, knowing he could do nothing to stop his better-trained classmate.

Antonio slapped palms with the Superintendent—having walked the course before the race—when he finished eighth in just over 20 minutes. A good 20 seconds and several places later Odysseus stumbled while reaching the finish-line tent. He refused to slap palms with the Superintendent, pretending he wasn't aware who she was.

Antonio stood off in the distance sipping a bottled water, knowing shaking hands with the kid he had beaten would be refused. He did bump palms with Carolina, who not only had finished first female, but also fifth overall. Mr. C, who used to be a decent runner, but no longer could either run or walk without a cane, congratulated him enthusiastically. Then his dad, who had finished in about

26 minutes, and Antonio slapped palms and bumped chests as if NFL players.

Almost everyone on the football field was in good spirits. The day was illuminating like only rarified air at altitude can, with a brightness high on the Kelvin scale and virtually no smog or haze.

Odysseus Ray, however, kept his distance from anyone he saw possibly moving in his direction. He was humiliated, but the humiliation manifested itself as anger. *I'll get revenge on Lopez no matter what. Just wait.*

~ THIRTY-FOUR ~

A week later in early April during which it had again snowed lightly with no accumulation, Mr. C was weeding outdated books from the Library. It was a job he enjoyed, because in looking at the publication date of each book he silently relived its fading grandeur. He realized how even many great authors' works began to lose relevance over time. Few elementary school kids today were aware of who Edgar Allen Poe or Tom Sawyer and Mark Twain were. Cannery Row by Steinbeck and Twenty Thousand Leagues Under the Sea by Jules Verne hovered, dust covered, untouched on shelves. Mr. C did his best to keep Alice in Wonderland by Lewis Carroll or other classics in place. Yet almost every cover more than thirty years old had wistful young Anglo women or men. The pages were so yellowed and old they had almost turned to parchment in the dry air, with Library cards in folders glued in the back upon which the Librarian once wrote the names and dates of those checking out these relics. Well into the millennium's second decade, most hadn't been checked out since the twentieth century.

As Mr. C snapped another hardback book shut and placed it on his rolling red Library cart, he thought of the great tragedy of these vestiges of the past. They were no longer relevant. Covers and modern stories with lots of bizarre illustrations of lanky, daffy girls and nerdy boys, were now the thing, those or fully illustrated comics now known as graphic novels. Books of 200 or 300 pages of abstract language were virtually as extinct as brontosauruses. And while these bygone artifacts took up a whole room, the virtual reality of the internet and e-books could be contained in an electronic harbor no larger than a small box of jewelry. In current times, taking up shelf space was passé.

Pleasantly surprising, however, was that particularly some of the fifth-grade girls still made the effort to read and enjoy the wordier tomes. There was a certain status to checking out a larger book with a dark green sixth-grade dot on it, even if a student couldn't really get through all of it. Over time J. K. Rowling, Roald Dahl and Jerry Spinelli's books still got a lot of play, particularly after Mr. C would read a couple of chapters aloud to fifth graders. There were just enough readers of abstract language left that the Librarian found respite when he replaced those books on the fiction shelves, knowing some of their readers still had vivid imaginations.

His philosophy, again, was to get kids reading and enjoying books, no matter what the content, difficulty, or lack of same. If it meant ten-year-old's still reading at seven-year-old levels, so be it. The Raina Telgemeier phenomenon gave him hope that such small steps could lead to larger ones. *Smile, Sisters, Drama, Ghosts,* and the *Baby-Sitters Club* books were in constant circulation, and or stolen. His students, however, checked out few of the twentieth-century fictional work more than thirty years old. And it was his job to purge these relics. While he was still extracting such outmoded examples from the shelves, the school's computer program installer arrived to help him with a program.

After joining her at the front desk, the pair sat at his computer and while she solved his dilemma Mr. C began to tell her of his reading philosophy for the Library.

"I agree with you," she said. "My two teenage boys started with graphic novels. They love them. But now they're reading text-only classics. It took a while, but kids do change their tastes over time."

After assisting him in solving his program issue and further discussions of reading for elementary school kids today, she was on her way. Mr. C felt reassured that her sons had indeed begun more challenging reading odysseys with the easier, highly illustrated graphic novels.

Before he had time to leave his desk and return to weeding, however, a couple of fifth-grade girls arrived to return books. The two were Matilda Blackstone and Carolina Montoya, and they were both wearing their *Superintendent's Fitness Run/Walk 5K Finisher* T-shirts. The Librarian scanned their returned books, *Harry Potter and The Goblet of Fire*, and a *Sonia Sotomayor* biography.

"Ladies, I'm going to return to my weeding of books in the back. When you're ready to check out new books, let me know."

Minutes later Mr. C was sitting on a chair in front of the PIN through SEA fiction section of books, again pulling them one at a time for examination. Nearby Matilda and Carolina whispered from time to time as they surveyed the shelves for new reads. They had already checked out contents of the two tall black metal revolving stands in the front. There, the Librarian constantly put new books for third through fifth graders, many of them highly illustrated.

Blackstone and Montoya, however, prided themselves on the more difficult text-only works found on shelves like discovered gold flakes while panning. And like most textual readers, they would open books and read various parts to see if the complexity, difficulty, and subject matter resonated. Stories of certain natures were desirable, but students had to be able to read them.

The Librarian was back in his reveries as he examined one of a series of thick rural-life tomes from the 70s he had decided were too outdated for his students. He heard loud whispering from the girls before Matilda walked over to him.

"This is weird, Mr. C," the tall girl quietly said, handing him a folded note. "I found this hanging out of one of the superhero books in graphic novels."

The Librarian unfolded the note and began to read.

"I'm Going To Kill Them All!" it said in bold letters scratched with a pointed black marker.

Mr. C shook his head. He didn't want to alarm the girls, so he said: 'Probably some crackpot third grader. But I'll turn it into the Principal's office."

He refolded the note and put it in his shirt pocket. Mr. C wished to treat the note as if nothing more than a piece of trash found on the floor to be tossed in the wastebasket at the front later.

As he opened another book for scrutiny, however, and as the girls resumed their search, his mind began to consider the potential seriousness of the note. The Librarian often found notes and drawings, many of them of a violent nature: hangmen, stick men jumping off walls, messages about how so and so was a jerk, the occasional profanity, and faces with tongues stuck out. Most of them were harmless, yet this six-word message in bold had a threatening resonance to it. The letters weren't cut and pasted from different sources. The words still offered the threat of evil. He also knew the girls would tell their friends about the scrawled message. Most of them would write off the note as a harmless attempt by a young boy to impress his friends. But none of his kids needed even any hint of additional stress in their lives, particularly given the recent incident with the drunken parent. Considering the many incidents of violence in schools throughout the country, and schools constantly drilling for such eventualities, he would report it.

The following morning, he had a free hour and used the opportunity to go up to the Principal's office. As he looked through the door, he could see Ms. Guadalajara sitting at her computer, most probably going over e-mails. She looked up, saw him, and waved him in.

He took a seat in a chair right in front of her.

"What's up?" she asked, signaling she had time to listen to him, but not a lot.

He pulled the note from his shirt pocket, unfolded it, and handed it to her.

She quickly read it, took off her light-blue framed reading glasses and lay them on her desk. She shook her head slightly from side to side.

"If this were ten years ago, I would have chuckled at the simplicity of this sort of nonsense, pitched it in the trash, and thought nothing more of it. But now, particularly after the drunken parent incident..."

Mr. C had crossed his arms, not knowing what to say, given the tragic scope of the recent history of school violence.

"Of course, I take it seriously. But where can we go from here? If we start questioning kids as to who wrote it, we start scaring them. Yet if we don't and something happens, the public will say we should have investigated. I mean, these are five- to ten-year-old students." She pursed her lips in consternation. "If I told you the number of these sorts of notes I have seen or had turned in to me over the years," she added, again shaking her head, "I would need a citrus fruit box to contain them." She looked up at the Librarian while still holding the note. "Any idea who wrote it?"

They both knew the answer. There were easily 10-20 boys, and possibly even several girls, in third through fifth grades capable of scrawling the note. And it wasn't always the meanest, loudest, or aggressive kids, either. Sometimes one of the quietest boys made his misguided attempt to impress other boys he'd like to call friends. A boy angry at his mother or grandmother, tired of being bullied, or one invisible on most days to others bigger, smarter, faster, taller boys, or a cipher to those having the confidence to speak easily in front of others like he lacked.

Mr. C shook his head. "I could probably name ten it might be. Then again, it could be the boy you least suspect. The note could be harmless and an attempt to impress friends. Or it could be the effort of a frustrated student nearing desperation. I wouldn't even want to guess, though from the spelling and words, it's most probably a third-through-fifth grader. It looks like whoever wrote it didn't use his usual printing—like it has a sort of fake slant and varied styles among the letters."

"All right," she said, signaling with a glance at her computer that her usual surfeit of obligations needed attention, "just go about your normal routine in the Library. Keep your eyes and ears open. Watch anyone sullen or behaving badly or oddly, carefully. Meanwhile, Ms. Sandoval and I will individually put out the word for vigilance to the third through fifth Teachers and to Counselor Genoveva. For now, however, we'll just pay more attention. I'll tell all the Teachers to look for anyone writing notes, acting badly, or seeming to withdraw from others." She tapped her pencil on her mouse pad. "I wonder if Odysseus wrote it," she said, looking at her computer screen.

"Nah," they both shook their heads before Mr. C departed. The kid with attitude was too obvious.

~ THIRTY-FIVE ~

The nine-month school year had only four more weeks. The weather was warming, every day it was getting lighter earlier and later, and the horses, so to speak, could see it was a great day for movement. Several Kindergarteners had made Mr. C's day by telling him how much they loved the Library and reading. The miniature people darted among the shelves dwarfing them, asking him expectant questions while gazing up at this enormous adult towering over them. Their fresh and optimistic exuberance always made his day. It was a Thursday, the week was almost over, the year concluding, and his sore back and limp seemed to be improving with each beaming five-year-old he encountered.

As he briefly returned to his desk from an odyssey of questions, smiling comments, and disciplinary warnings to those running, talking too loudly, or putting books on top rather than using their markers, Mr. C felt quite good. There had been no more notes or strange behavioral issues that week, no contretemps to fulminate over late night in bed, no major disruptions to his Smart Screen readings aloud from Arbordale, Mackin Via, Oxford Owl and Epic. This week he had Kinder through second graders sitting in the corner, and his readings and visual displays of books on *Lightning* and another on *Chickens to the Rescue* had gotten him 'oohs,' 'ahhs,' toppling-over giggles, and even two rounds of applause.

Literacy test scores, collected from the upper three grades, had improved 50 percent, albeit from a 10- to 15-percent rate of those reaching national standards. The school was not even close to any kind of zenith just yet, but it was improving modestly. Based upon student test performances, Teacher evaluations, but also upon numerous factors like parent participation, extracurricular activities, nutritional changes in student meals, and other improvements, the school had moved from a C to a B. Renewed optimism seemed to be the buzz in the Teacher's lounge, as fifth-grade instructors of Hispanic, Anglo and Spanish descent hovered over plastic containers of bland concoctions saving them the expense of cafeteria food they often looked upon with envy. There was something to be said for Frito pie versus a homemade container of day-old rice, dried chicken shreds and soggy vegetables.

Kids on the playground shot baskets, chased each other to temporary exhaustion, swung to the heavens trying to defy gravity, and endured cuts and bruises for the thrill of catching others on their daily exuberant gallops. Ronaldo Estevez was emptying his cart bag of trash outside at the recycle and trash bins and thinking how his maintenance job had enabled him to buy the Ford truck he had always wanted. Christina Cortez was reading aloud from a biography of Supreme Court Justice Sonia Sotomayor to her fourth graders actually paying attention. Secretary Maria Vargas was helping a parent sign in to deliver a lunch and backpack forgotten by her young son. The front office was relatively quiet for a Thursday, few kids were out with flu or allergies, and the nurse's office pallets were empty of the usual repeaters wishing to avoid classes they couldn't comprehend. A new enthusiastic music instructor and the veteran art Teacher were outside in the hall collaborating between classes over their imaginative and colorful bulletin boards. Mrs. Guadalajara had spun through her e-mails, prioritizing as she went, in a quick twenty minutes. The exhilaration of spring was in the air for students and faculty alike.

Internally, however, many kids still led lives of suppressed wistfulness. They wanted to be smarter, quicker, faster, and always desirable for playground games and lunch table seats. Some of their parents were unemployed, others on drugs or alcohol, several were fighting deportation problems, and many hoped for the miracle of an unexpected windfall. Money was almost inevitably in short supply. Hope of improving almost any family's financial picture, job, purchases, was always lingering. Each day, few of the faces waiting outside on the front apron of the school and in cars and trucks showed the same smiling effervescence of the residents of say, Boulder, Colorado. Still, the sun was high in the sky most days, and many took solace in their children and their hopes for their offspring's education and futures.

Odysseus Ray, however, even with all the advantages of educated parents and affluent surroundings, was hitting a nadir. Losing the race to Antonio was just one more perceived failure to be someone special. In class that day he further realized his interest in school was non-existent. He knew he was relatively quick and bright. Yet his lack of application had set him back far enough, his test scores might even merit retention in fifth grade. Moving on to Cortez Middle School held no interest; he had few friends; his parents understood very little about him; and his older brother was doing not much better in Argenta High.

Every day he awoke exhausted, and on that Thursday, Odysseus went home to find his brother Courtney alone in his room. He saw his older brother quickly stick something into an athletic bag usually containing a variety of sports equipment. Courtney slowly dropped a copy of the *New Mexican Times* on his bed.

"Did you see the paper today?" Courtney asked, his wiry body slumping down upon the bed's black comforter.

"Nope," Odysseus replied. He rarely looked at the paper, although he did sometimes read news stories online.

"A 64-year-old Anglo guy was shot within a hundred yards of Coronado."

"What?"

"Yah," he answered, shaking his head, and looking downward. "I know because I was there."

The younger brother dropped his backpack on the floor and squinched up his eyes. "What are you talking about?"

Courtney shook his head. "I was with Cruzito, another dude and two girls, and we were walking up that lane behind your school to Airport Road from hanging out in the arroyo. This dude was walking his dog toward us, but we didn't move over, and he kept coming with his big dog on a leash stretched out and blocking our way. Cruzito wasn't going to move, and the old dude wasn't going to move. The guy let his dog's leash get tangled around us.

"'You might have moved over instead of walking five abreast,'" the man said.

"'You might have moved that mutt over to the side, *gringo*,'" Cruzito muttered. I could tell from his voice he wasn't going to back down from the old man. After Cruzito got untangled from the leash, he tried to kick the dog. I mean, it was a quiet, big dog. It wasn't barking and it didn't try to bite anyone."

"'Listen, *punk*,'" the man said, as he pulled his dog in on its leash. But the five of us were already walking past the old McDonald's that's now closed.

"'Hey, I'm talking to you!'" the old dude yelled after us.

"The next thing I know, Cruzito pulled out a pistol and shot him. The guy was yelling about being shot in the leg, but we just kept going. Cruzito told us on the other side of Airport Road that he was trying to shoot the dog. He didn't mean to shoot the guy."

"So, what happened to the guy?"

"That's what makes it worse," Courtney said, still slumped on the bed. "The paper says he bled to death. Some people came out of a church to try and help him. They used cloths to try and stop the bleeding. Apparently, the police came soon and an ambulance, but he died in the hospital."

Odysseus slumped into a chair and neither said anything.

"Dude, what are you going to do?"

Courtney shook his head. "Everyone promised they'd tell no one about it. But what if someone talks? And that's not the worst of it. Cruzito gave me an automatic pistol. He wants me to shoot some dude that gave a member of the *Agua Fria Carnívoros* problems."

"You're not going to do it, are you?"

"Are you kidding me! I don't have the *cojones*. I'm out! This whole thing has scared me so much, I'm telling Cruzito I'm out. No AFC membership for me!"

Oddly enough, the first thoughts into Odysseus' mind were about getting that pistol and shooting Antonio and some of the other kids he couldn't stand. Just as quickly he tried to sublimate those negative thoughts. Like his brother, he knew he lacked the courage of the gang members on the south side of Santa Fe. Some didn't care if they lived or died. Then he realized he didn't care either. His life was meaningless. He hated school and living with his parents. He also knew that for his brother and Cruzito there was no going back. Courtney hadn't done the shooting, but he was there. Now he had to hope no one told. And he had to live with knowing that a dude from outside the 'hood was shot by a Hispanic kid. Who wasn't alone.

~ THIRTY-SIX ~

When Antonio Lopez awoke, he felt surprisingly energetic. His daily runs were going well, his fifth-grade work in Ms. Sevilla's class was sailing smoother than expected, and it was a Friday. That meant a half-day and getting out at 12:35. Soon it would be summer, and he would help his dad paint the house. He felt fortunate to have a father who really cared about him. Others he knew were not so fortunate. Some parents were even in jail, or dead.

Antonio tried to avoid thinking negatively, however, and usually he was successful. The previous evening, he had found two Library books he thought he had lost. They had been behind the front couch. One was *Minecraft Redstone*, and the other a biography of *Diego Rivera*. Antonio had no discernible talent in art class, yet he loved Rivera's murals combining peasants with conquistadors and Aztecs, Detroit industrial workers with massive automotive production, and even those of Emiliano Zapata. He had considered telling Mr. C that the biography was lost and paying for it. But it would take him a long time to save up the $20, and besides, Mr. C always stressed that keeping books beyond when they were due or stealing them deprived other kids from reading them. The Librarian and school budget, as well, couldn't afford to replace all the missing books.

That day Antonio Lopez was riding his *Specialized* mountain bike to school. It was only around 50 degrees Fahrenheit when he set off, but it was a short ride, and in the afternoon, it would be in the 60s or even 70. Getting to Coronado he took a combination of back streets and an arroyo bike path. Although there was a bike lane down Airport Road, using the busy thoroughfare made riders or joggers take risks, even with bright clothing or flashing head- and taillights. Most rode bikes on the sidewalks to avoid vehicles seemingly always desperate to compete for speed or arrival times. It was quicker for Antonio to ride to the school from his home west of the South Side Library.

On his way he passed a woman parked on the side of the road with a gasoline can in her hands She had beautiful long black braids offsetting a deeply tanned face.

"Out of gas?" he asked, stopping his bike just behind her car.

She nodded. "Yes," she smiled, "and it looks like I'm going to be late for school."

"Are you a Tutor at Coronado?" he asked, thinking he recognized her from seeing her come out of the Library office with kids during Library hour.

She nodded again politely. "And I have no idea where the nearest gas station is."

"I'll get you some," he said, extending his hand. "There's a station just a few blocks away at Airport and Las Vegas Roads. My name's Antonio Lopez, by the way."

With the can in his hand, he mounted his bike to begin pedaling.

"I'm Emerald Star." She leaned against her car, quite sure Antonio was a fifth grader along with Christian, a boy she often tutored.

It only took Antonio fifteen minutes to return with a gallon of gasoline. Ms. Star thanked him profusely before they both agreed upon the need for speed.

An hour later Ms. Star found herself wearing her normal school attire rather than the magic costume she used with Christian and one or two others. There was the possibility that SFSD would object, should they learn of her select unusual appearance, yet she relied upon walking in the hallways in clothing they would consider more appropriate.

This morning she had picked up and had brought to the Library office a second grader who had a speech impediment in the form of a periodic stutter. Emerald Star felt that Mariana Solis' stutter was almost entirely prompted by feelings of inadequacy. Her father had left when she was very young, while her mother drank beer excessively and lived on welfare. Star had talked with the mother several times, and upon each encounter Mrs. Solis had beer on her breath. Ironically, she believed in her daughter's education, but the mother's volatility interfered with Mariana's development of confidence, general learning, and social skills.

Today Mariana and the Tutor/Counselor were building a tower of blocks on the Library office desk. A block at a time was removed, the purpose being to distract the second grader from a feeling that she needed to talk about herself. It was a game, but a necessary one of many designed to get to the bottom of a child's true feelings.

Today the woman with a Mescalero Apache father, yet currently living with her Pueblo mother in Cochiti, looked much younger than her 31 years. Her faded jeans were tight and cinched with a turquoise-and-silver belt. The Counselor's hands and slender fingers always drew attention away from her upper torso, even as from out of glistening cobalt blue sleeves magnetic digits grasped the arms of the chair. Emerald Star's entire demeanor always conveyed care and kindness, there never being any sense of annoyance, impatience, or indifference. Particularly young students were disarmed by her reassuring voice. Star leaned back in her chair, creating some distance between the two.

"Don't worry if you pull a block out and the tower collapses," Star told Mariana. "Building the tower is much like school. When a student's confidence disappears, he or she, or each of us in life outside of school, simply begins to build it again."

Mariana carefully leaned right and left to determine her best course of action for her next removal.

"That's not wh-wh-what my mom would say."

"What would she say?"

The second grade withdrew another block, the tower maintaining its stability. "Sh-sh-she would say I'm doing it all wrong. She would s-s-say I always am doing things wrong."

"You know that's not true. You're doing much better in school this semester," said Star, hesitating before withdrawing another block. "Besides, your mother is under a lot of stress financially. You've told me she drinks too much. Do you think she really means what she says about you? Or do you think she rather is being critical of you because of being unhappy with herself?"

It was a rhetorical question, but the Counselor felt confident that Mariana needed to be led out of the abyss of her home life to at least a temporarily safe environment. Various county social services organizations were not able to remove her from an incapable mother, but Mrs. Solis had agreed to begin to receive treatment regarding her drinking.

"How do you feel you're doing with your reading?"

The Counselor realized she had pressed one of the stress-release buttons that only spontaneity occasionally brings about. The nervousness evident in the second grader's facial expressions and uncomfortable movements suddenly relaxed.

"I was able to read a whole paragraph in class without stuttering," she beamed. "We have this really nice substitute and she said I read it perfectly." What she didn't realize was that her sentence of explanation had gone perfectly, as well.

Ms. Star smiled her usual radiant beam transmitting kindness and affirmation. "That's a really big improvement for you, Mariana."

The Counselor deliberately didn't mention that the girl's stutter had evaporated temporarily. There was no need. Doing so might bring the stutter back. Extending any time frame of confidence was the most important focus. Emerald Star could only hope that in the final month of school Mariana would find herself stuttering less and less. The Counselor felt assured that if they could get the mother off alcohol, far more dramatic improvements were in Mariana's near future. Yet home lives were tricky. Just when you had a child believing in his or her own progress, incidents outside of the carefully constructed parameters of school appeared like dragons with fire shooting out of their mouths.

~ THIRTY-SEVEN ~

Things were going almost too smoothly, thought Principal Penelope Guadalajara on that Thursday as the lunch periods approached. Although an avalanche of e-mails and reports had already been perused or completed, and several recalcitrant students for bad behavior had to spend time in the front office area doodling with crayons, there was only a month of school left. The usual plethora of minor problems regarding students and faculty still arose. Yet most had been successfully solved, including early interviews for the annual five to seven Teachers or faculty members retiring, resigning, or transferring. Mrs. Guadalajara was optimistic, barring minor skirmishes and mishaps, that the year could be concluded without major incident.

There was, however, one more hurdle of significance that day. The school needed an additional shelter in place and lockdown to fulfill annual emergency preparation requirements. She was reluctant to call another drill, given the disruptive reality of the drunken parent episode earlier. However, the nature of any Principal's job meant myriad impediments, disappointments, and even occasional feelings of futility. Disruptions and a labyrinthine course to steer were all part of any school administrator's diurnal and annual responsibilities.

She decided to call the shelter in place that afternoon. Mornings were the best time for kids to learn. There was always a settling in period after any of the drills, and keeping kids focused during afternoons always remained a challenge much like the last few minutes of a competitive ball game.

Between 12:55 and 1:55 p.m. Mr. C was hosting Ms. Cortez's fourth-grade group in his domain. For the most part they were good readers, and the core group of four to six that helped with the book fairs, also revolved in and out of ferrying the book cart throughout the Library to put returned books away. A solid core of these fourth graders seemed to have a sense of communal responsibility many of the fifth graders lacked, and he seldom had to raise his voice or leg it back into the Library to admonish students over talking or loitering with intent of avoiding reading. They were solid students, they tested well, and seemed to possess a reasonably disciplined approach to education giving many faculty members hope for their fifth-grade journey the following year. Mr. C looked forward to being able to log in some new books as they quietly read at tables or were selected for e-book readings at one of six computers.

It was a week during which he was reading aloud from paper rather than electronic books to each class. For fourth grade he had read the first two chapters of one of Louis Sachar's *Wayside School* books. When he completed his reading, using different exaggerated voices for the oddball characters, he got a round of applause.

Minutes later he was calling names from the class roster for the computers. Doing so brought one of the most surprising elements of the new electronic world. While many students hoped to go to one of the Library's six Apple desk screens, they wished to do so to find the easiest course of action. They weren't allowed to go to the Coronado Library home site's offering of educational game sites, because upon some of those destinations mindless non-educational games could be found. Reading of paper or electronic books was the focus. The Librarian had to pay attention, however. Skilled students could switch back and forth between a reading site and a game or video site almost instantaneously. Surprisingly, most who could read preferred paper books to electronic. Yet even on the sites offering the largest arrays of contemporary books, like Epic, could be found books and videos during which students built LEGO-type constructions or painted, or did science experiments, enabling kids to be entertained without actively reading. In contemporary times, visual learning was becoming more and more predominant. Reading abstract sentences, even with artfully rendered illustrations, was becoming less popular or even obsolete. Mr. C constantly had to monitor the computers behind his desk, and any distraction to the Librarian from the main room created opportunities for chatting, dallying, and predictable furtive tomfoolery. Because he mandated those going to computers stay focused on e-book reading, most of the students in fourth and fifth grades turned the opportunity down.

The whole penultimate afternoon hour went smoothly, however. Mr. C only had to raise his voice once because someone he had already warned had crawled under a table. Mrs. Cortez's fourth grade noisily lined up and disappeared out of the cavern of two languages.

The final period of the previous week's Thursday had been a free one for the Librarian. He had confined himself to weeding old books off the shelves and placing these relics for free giveaway on a cart outside the Library door. Because the cart and its ancient and/or distressed contents weren't being depleted fast enough, Mr. C had decided upon logging in new books from cartons he had received and put on shelves in the storeroom. However, on this Thursday, Ms. Sevilla's fifth-grade students, the class that in the previous two weeks had missed their usual Library hour due to a field trip to *El Rancho de las Golondrinas* living history museum and testing, were scheduled for the final hour.

Because Ms. Sevilla's class was the only one of three fifth grades in which the students were English-only speakers, the class was comprised of almost 30. They arrived like a mob attending a Broncos game, dropping book bags on the floor behind the Smart Screen and unprepared for the silence required in a Library. Getting them all situated at tables was always a challenge, simply due to strength in numbers. Normally Mr. C had help, however. Because of his paraprofessional status, regulations mandated a certified Teacher or another paraprofessional be present. Ms. Sevilla normally sat at a Library table and did class preparatory work. On this Thursday, however, she had an appointment with Principal Guadalajara and would be gone for most of the hour.

"Your attention. Your attention, please," came Principal Guadalajara's voice over the intercom. "This is a shelter in place. I repeat: this is a shelter in place."

Most of the kids began to get up and slide chairs under the table or log off their computers.

"O. K. kids, just keep doing whatever you're doing," said Mr. C, as he stood up at his desk. "It just means we stay in place and carry on with whatever activity we are currently doing. There will be no trips to the bathroom during the drill. If anyone is desperate, we do have a portable toilet that can be used in the storeroom."

The Librarian was aware the school needed one more set of drills for the year, having been informed at a bi-weekly staff meeting. Although in almost every instance the drills were simply that: drills, he began to wonder if they would also have a lockdown, and if so, how long the whole process would take. There was little time for concern that the drill could involve a real situation. The drunken parent incident seemed to have resulted in the school's one real-life episode of possible danger. Two in one year were highly unlikely. In the same era, however, other schools throughout the country had endured serious episodes of violence. Mass shootings were almost commonplace, with virtually any educational district thought to be immune then finding unexpected disasters. Yet it was the last hour of the day, and after administrators conducted their usual stroll throughout the school, Mr. C was confident the day would end without any serious disruption.

"The shelter in place has now become a lockdown," came Mrs. Guadalajara's voice over the intercom. Even though her voice revealed nothing unusual Mr. C. quickly enlisted student aid in drawing all the venetian blinds, covering the front and exit doors with black paper, and getting all the kids to sit quietly in the back corner underneath their favorite dinosaur and animal books.

Again, the whole process was familiar, both to the students and faculty. Principal Guadalajara was forced to put her meeting with Ms. Sevilla on hold during the lockdown. While the fifth-grade Teacher was not allowed to return to the Library or her classroom, she assured the Principal she had plenty she could do on her laptop while sequestered in the front office. Almost every student, even having transferred from other schools, had been through these drills each year, and little more had been said regarding the previous incident in the Coronado Library. It was the end of the day, the kids were tired of learning, and the lockdown drill created an opportunity for down time and whispering while sitting in the back of the Library.

Meanwhile, Ms. Guadalajara and Ms. Sandoval began their routine odyssey throughout the hallways. The pair ambled throughout the school checking doors for being locked, falsely knocking on doors to see if anyone erroneously answered or opened up to possible dangerous intruders. No one bit. No one opened a door or answered entreaties from a small Kindergartener the Principals had enlisted to beg admittance.

When they had completed their rounds, Ms. Guadalajara and

Sandoval found the two secretaries sitting in a dimly lit conference room. Mrs. Guadalajara told the secretaries to relax, that she would shortly announce the end of the lockdown.

The Principal was just walking to the phone/intercom, when one of the front desk phones began to ring. Secretary Maria Vargas asked Ms. Guadalajara if she should answer it. Principal Penelope had a strange premonition that the call should be answered, and signaled Miss Vargas accordingly. Seconds later the secretary held her hand over the phone's mouthpiece.

"It's the police," she said, raising her eyebrows regarding the purpose of the call and holding the phone up.

"This is Mrs. Guadalajara," the Principal spoke into the phone.

"This is Lieutenant Nestor Ortiz of the Santa Fe Police," came a voice on the other end of the line. "We just got a call from a boy informing us that his brother may have taken his gun to Coronado Elementary School."

"Oh," answered Principal Guadalajara apprehensively. "Can you tell me the student's name?"

"The person calling said his name was Courtney Ray. He said his brother Odysseus Ray is in fifth grade at Coronado Elementary, and..."

Mrs. Guadalajara barely heard the rest of what Lieutenant Ortiz said. Her heartbeat was well over a hundred as she slumped down in a secretarial chair. *This can't be happening!* Of all the students in the school, Odysseus was the most likely to do something crazy like bring a gun to school. She immediately glanced down at a list of classroom numbers, picked up a desk phone, then put it back down when she realized the Teacher was in the conference room. She quickly moved to the conference room to speak to Ms. Sevilla.

"Is Odysseus with your class in the Library?" Principal Guadalajara asked while enduring a bombardment of desultory thoughts.

"Yes, why?"

"The police have just phoned and have reported his brother Courtney called and told them Odysseus may have taken his gun to school."

Ms. Sevilla remained the bulwark of a Teacher reacting quickly to any quandary. "I'll go down there," she said, beginning to climb out of the rolling chair.

"You can't. A lockdown is in place for everyone but Victoria and me. And it would be too dangerous. The police are on their way," added Principal Guadalajara, slumping down in a chair. "We have to think this through..."

~ THIRTY-EIGHT ~

The fifth graders in the back of the darkened Library were begin-ning to squirm. They had been sitting quietly with their legs crossed for almost twenty minutes. Whispering was overtaking more and more as the students and the Librarian began to wonder about the delay in ending the lockdown. The good news was that there was only a half hour of school left. The bad news was it was uncomforta-ble for ten-year-old's to sit still for any extended periods other than through a riveting fictional film or video presentation.

Mr. C began to have his concerns. The only other bout of a seri-ous lockdown he had endured had come while substitute teaching at another school years ago. Apparently, a man angry with his wife had a gun and was threatening to kill anyone he saw in his neigh-borhood—right across from that school. At that time students had hovered under desks for two hours before finally being released.

Now he began to wonder if a similar peril of some sort were unfolding. With several unfavorable scenarios passing through his mind, he noticed a student in the corner rise to his feet. As Mr. C began to walk over there, he recognized Odysseus.

"Everyone needs to stay in the corner unless they need to use the emergency toilet in the storeroom," the Librarian warned.

Odysseus, ignoring Mr. C, started walking. "I need to get something from my backpack...a book," he said as if he had contrived an excuse on the spot.

"No exceptions! Odysseus," Mr. C whispered loudly.

"Sorry," said the fifth grader as if he wasn't really. "I have to get it."

Ten minutes earlier, less than a mile away, Lieutenant Ortiz had been briefing the armored members of six squad cars.

"I know this Courtney Ray," he quickly told them. "I think he's trying to get membership in the *Agua Fria Carnívoros* and thought it would be cool to be given a machine pistol. His brother's only a ten-year-old. But given what's happened in other city schools we need to be fully prepared in case brother Odysseus decides to use it." He looked at his watch. "Five minutes have already elapsed since the informant's call and our report to Coronado School that a possible incident might be in progress. Headquarters, our squad cars, and Coronado administrators will stay in radio or command post contact until we are within 50 yards of the school Library. Everyone at the target location, including the Coronado office staff, is in lock-down. I've given you the layouts. The six S.W.A.T. team members led by Lieutenant McGarrity will approach the back exit door and six of us the main front doors. That's it for now. Let's get going."

There was no panic, yet, anywhere in Coronado Elementary School. There were classrooms silently observing nervous vigils, hopeful that another real-life event inside or outside of the school was not unfolding. Fourth-grade Teacher Mrs. Cortez had consistently dealt with nine-year-old's thinking the whole Thursday afternoon scenario a lark. Third-grade Teacher Amanda Montecielo had to dig out her five-gallon paint barrel porta-loo from a cabinet to enable two other girls to hold up a spare bulletin board in front of a student relieving herself in the corner. Counselor Genoveva Juarez was uncomfortable locked in her small utility room stacked with boxes and supplies everywhere. She wondered if indeed visiting Counselor Emerald Star remained sequestered with Christian

De Leon in the Library office all this time. Art Teacher Melissa Moody considered how her daily commute to and from Rio Rancho might expand to more than an hour should the lockdown continue beyond 3:00.

Odysseus Ray felt a rising sense of power as he ignored the instructions from Mr. C. *He's better than most of the Teachers I've had. Yet all of them are in for a surprise,* he thought as he arrived at the pile of jackets and backpacks near the front door. *No one can stop me now.* Like all potential life takers, the fifth grader had a point of no return. Without the weapon yet in his hands, that point had not been reached.

Six squad cars turned off flashing lights and continued siren silence as they wheeled into the expansive Coronado parking lot. The likely outcome would probably be taking a ten-year-old into custody without incident. If they were lucky. Lieutenant Ortiz and the eleven officers disembarking outside Coronado's small gym had seen every type of tragic disturbance on the planet: death from car crashes or gunshots; irate married couples shouting as if no one else was within miles; suspects running through neighborhoods intent upon escape; small plane crashes having destroyed stucco houses; whole neighborhoods in a windy inferno. Yet the unpredictable nature of any call for help, assistance, or escape from perils of almost any nature made every day and every incident distinct and remarkable.

The twelve had communicated extensively over radios on the short drive down to the school located on Las Vegas Road. Before departing, they had scrutinized the layout of the school Library. Past instruction warned them to be wary: even the most harmless individual, with a weapon, particularly an automatic weapon, could be extremely dangerous. One mistake and fatalities could occur. Delay could cause fatalities, as well. From television shows the public had some idea of the perilous nature of encounters, no two of which were ever the same. Yet the average citizen lacked a realistic concept of just how volatile such situations could become. The typical viewer or reader thought school shootings during which three to twenty students, or more, were wounded or killed to be anomalies. And they were right. But for most law enforcement officers such disastrous occurrences were merely variations of the human condition, differing only by the ages of victims and perpetrators.

McGarrity motioned to his six S.W.A.T. team members to fan out and circle the backside of the Library adjacent to the gym. By cell phone, Ortiz and the eleven other officers had informed the school of their arrival. Now, barring emergency necessity, radio and phone contact would remain silent.

On the front side of the school, sixty feet from the Library, the hall door was held open by a stone. Six police officers led by Lieutenant Ortiz slipped inside the hall silently. Maintenance man Ronaldo Estevez, the man having propped the door open, was motioned to walk quickly back toward his storage room refuge. The officers entering the long front hall had black leather boots with rubberized bottoms. Maintenance had also turned off all the hall lights near the Library. Enough sun circumvented the edges of the many windows blocked by shades, however, that the six in file would still have been visible had any possible perpetrator chosen to peek through Library interior window venetian blinds.

Watches had all been synchronized prior to the short drives from various locations to the school. Ortiz and his men stopped in the hallway just around the corner from the Library's locked wood and now opaque windows-covered front doors. Approximately two minutes remained before simultaneous entry of twelve armored officers through the front and back exit doors. It had been decided, if no shooting had begun, that surprise would be their best strategy to avoid or limit possible student injuries and/or deaths.

In the front office, the five women, including fifth-grade Teacher

Sevilla, sat silently at tables in the conference room. The small glass panel in the door was covered with black paper, as were the two locked entrance doors to the office atrium. Principal Guadalajara prayed that Odysseus Ray could be caught unexpectedly before he used the reported automatic pistol. Ms. Sevilla considered the option of demanding to make a trip to the Library. The police might take too long to arrive. She knew Odysseus' behavior well. She thought she might avoid any violence if she could just talk to him. Secretary Maria Vargas kept running visual imagery of shootings like Columbine and Sandy Hook through her head. She wondered just how such tragedies might have been avoided. When such incidents unfolded, what exactly might have saved some or all the lives? Did Odysseus have his brother's pistol?

He did. In fact, as he walked toward the jumble of backpacks near the front of the Coronado Library, Odysseus knew Mr. C would be futilely following. *Such a misguided man intent upon books in a world of electronic information; such a foolish man for having embarrassed me on so many occasions.* Ten-year-old Ray considered how he was finally going to get his revenge. Not complete revenge, as his 5K Fitness Run nemesis Antonio Lopez might avoid extinction much quicker than all the paper books of the world, as well as some of those now still sitting or standing in this ridiculous cavern of millions of words. If Odysseus Ray could think of one thing that was the biggest waste of his time, it was reading. Millions of abstract words, sentences, and whole paper containers taking up space for so few people able to read and understand them. No one cared about reading when the internet, *Mindcraft, Fortnite,* texting, twittering, videos, high-definition films and videos, and the incredible world of sounds through Apple watches, headsets, headphones, iPads, iPhones, tablets, had evolved. The fifth grader was almost overwhelmed by endless screen-visible information overtaking the far more simplistic and glacial communication made with words on endless and time-consuming paper pages.

When he arrived at his backpack, Odysseus hesitated just briefly. Reaching inside the bag meant others as well as he himself might lose their lives. Yet not doing so meant a life of perceived impotence and boredom. It meant no revenge upon all those having mistreated him. All these kids trapped like rats for most of each interminable year. Tormented by Teachers and smarter and quicker students. Yet the contents of his backpack would become the great equalizer. Not only would he wreak havoc upon his own class and Teacher, but as Odysseus Ray unzipped the top of his backpack, he simultaneously contemplated the thrill of randomly selecting targets along the hallway and then in the front office itself. He had four clips in his backpack and enough ammunition to shoot up unanticipated distressing surroundings and annoying persons.

When he pulled out the pistol, he could barely see it. Yet in the dimly lit aisle just beyond the two black metal vertical stands displaying the books he would no longer be forced to peruse, Mr. C could be seen rapidly approaching.

"Stay back!" the armed fifth grader now yelled, brandishing the automatic weapon.

The Librarian came to an abrupt halt. He could now see the pistol. His worst fears suddenly were being realized. Odysseus Ray really did have a gun. A real incident of violence could be unfolding. He couldn't go, throw, or get his kids to safety. The fifth grader really was pointing a gun at him. Before Mr. C could say anything or take any action, however, Odysseus looked upward and raised the machine pistol.

It was amazing this is actually happening, thought Mr. C. The rapid fire had a weird sound of exploding propellant and buzzing noise of a muted dentist's drill. Several plastic posters of famous authors and people were riddled with holes before dropping to the floor. Kids in the back were screaming. Sparks flew from the metal unlit fluorescent light banks from which the posters had been suspended. "Stop it!" someone yelled, quickly bringing Mr. C back to the reality of every second counting.

"Odysseus, give me the weapon," the Librarian tried to calmly command, sticking out his open left hand. With his right hand he leaned on his cane, hoping something he said might snap the fifth grader out of his insanity.

Poor devil, thought Odysseus before he briefly pinched the trigger and one of several bullets hit the Librarian in the lower leg.

"Ahh," Mr. C suppressed his pain, pulling a chair out and painfully lowered himself into it.

The crashing of glass from both one front door window and the exit door pane shattered simultaneously, a hand reaching through each broken pane to turn the doorknob.

Odysseus turned and sprayed the front doors, the hand disappearing to the other side.

One of the six backing away from the front doors had on a headset and she immediately broke silence to speak to S.W.A.T. team commander McGarrity. "He's at the front of the room, firing to prevent entry. Librarian wounded up front. Kids in back. Suggest using shelves as cover to advance down aisles extending from the exit door to the front desk."

Inside the Library office, when she first heard shots, Emerald Star had tried to get Christian De Leon to hunker down under a counter opposite the desk. With the lights off and the door locked, she desperately hoped whoever was doing the shooting wouldn't bother entering their unintended refuge. She knew Christian's fifth-grade class members were probably sitting down at the other end of the Library.

Christian, however, felt a strange sense of his own power. Oddly, it came from his ability to read. Each week, as he had found more and more vocabulary meanings and complex sentence structures readable, his fear of the world and classroom participation dissipated more and more. He no longer feared raising his hand in class or being bullied on the playground. Intellectual improvements had resulted in physical confidence, as well.

For a moment he began to contemplate what they had been told if such an incident began to unfold. Go, throw, or fight. From the automatic weapon fire, he knew there was little chance of escaping from the Library. He could break the office window and maybe his Counselor and he could escape by climbing to freedom. But if the shooter heard the crash of breaking glass, he might quickly break into the Library office and shoot them even as they escaped.

No, suddenly it came to him: if the shooter was unaware anyone was in the office, maybe Christian could crawl out in the dim surroundings and hit the shooter with something. In his hand, he still held a Harry Potter book he had been partially successful reading to Ms. Star. As he gazed down upon the heavy tome, it came to him as if wizardry magic: maybe he could use the book as a weapon. If he just sat under the counter, many kids might die; if he tried to sneak out of the office, it would at least give him a chance to prevent unknown needless injuries and deaths.

"Where are you going?" said Emerald Star whispered, ducking down farther as she heard a volley of three more shots.

Christian ignored her. He had already quietly opened the door and on his hands and knees had begun crawling out toward the rear of the crescent moon front desk.

Meanwhile Odysseus edged to the back corner of that same front desk to avoid anyone possibly firing through the front doors. He wanted to go to the back of the Library and take out some of his class un-favorites. He could hear some kids crying quietly out of sight to the rear of the Library, from the corner where the dinosaur, insect, mammals, and predators' sections were. Shooting at the front doors had kept whoever was outside from coming in. But someone had broken through the back door. It was now open, sunlight briefly illuminating a small area at the back of the Library before the door was quickly shut again and the light extinguished. The ten-year-old saw a couple of figures in black and dark helmets duck behind a row of shelves. *Well, at least if they get me, I'll take a few with me,* he thought.

Just before the crashing of door windows, Mr. C sat bleeding and sagging upon an oak table chair. *This could be it. More mindless shootings by someone so young he never should have had access to a weapon in the first place. More kids would be needlessly killed.* He felt old enough his injury and possible death were of no importance to him. He would die of something soon, anyway. But the kids in the back corner were too young to lose their potential futures of non-violent adventure and exciting experiences. Most of those students hovering were painfully aware of the real-world scenario unfolding around them. They remained unaware, however, of the amazing vicarious worlds also surrounding them like paper skeletons slowly disintegrating in Roman catacombs.

As the boy of a hundred glasses half empty, however, Odysseus was reacting as many estranged shooters before him in other parts of the country had: the dual torments of futility and hopelessness; feelings of inadequacy in most things attempted; disenchantment with a home life valuing and sharing few of his own hopes and aspirations; notions of redemption through the power of destruction; and when impotence in his own destiny had seemed manifest, thoughts of sudden importance. What he really needed to change was simply to grow older.

"Shoot me," the Librarian groaned. "But don't shoot anyone else. They're not the cause of your misery."

A minute earlier, after the hail of gunfire disturbed and injured an enormous vestigial repository of great silent distinction, before armored officers had broken through door windows, when lives were in jeopardy and in danger of being concluded early, and subsequent, to that point beyond which only destruction, disappointment, and more widespread misery occurs, kids were tragically experiencing the terror of what other schoolchildren had suffered. Budding readers sat fearful in the back of the room along with myriad paper dinosaurs also facing possible extinction. The De Vargas twins held each other and sobbed while considering Odysseus Ray might choose them as two of his next targets. Caliban Chimayo thought of the many times he had heard Odysseus talk of revenge and retribution with no follow-up. Now the shooter's normally intolerant *amigo* was really scared, wondering if his classmate would consider him enough of a friend to exclude him from being shot. Matilda Blackstone held Carolina Montoya's hand. As two of the only African Americans in Coronado, they both wondered if Odysseus would ignore any race or gender prejudices while shooting classmates when he reached them. Others were holding their ears with heads between their knees, wondering if this is how the last few moments of their lives were to be spent.

Indeed, most of Ms. Sevilla's fifth graders were only ten years old. Each tried to avoid contemplating that the horrors of school shootings could really be happening at Coronado. Yet each feared they couldn't go, couldn't throw, and couldn't fight. They felt the end had unexpectedly arrived like a ghoul from within, while many would perish like all the weak and wretched of the Earth.

At the other end of the room, Odysseus briefly glanced down at his pistol. *This is the End*, by the nineteenth century's Jim Morrison suddenly came to mind. Soon, even if he didn't survive, the inmates of Coronado would have paid the penalty of ignoring, berating, disciplining, or penalizing him. When now facing the boy they had ridiculed, they might no longer consider him one of those never quite good enough to make the cut. He checked his back pocket into which he had stuffed two more clips. It was time.

Seconds later the shooter saw a bent-over figure creeping in the center aisle. Odysseus fired a noisy staccato of bullets shredding Rosemary Cleary and Roald Dahl books partially concealed along the aisle's rolling shelves. But the man ducked between portable oak shelves and remained invisible.

"Stop it! Odysseus, Stop it!" yelled a girl in the back.

Odysseus recognized the voice. *It's that Carolina Montoya*, he thought. *She'll be one of the first to go when I get back there. She always thinks she knows more than anyone else.*

Around the corner of the rear end of the front desk Christian De Leon was on his hands and knees. He was contemplating whether he should attempt to jump up and tackle his classmate. The smell of burnt powder from the rapid fire arrived like the smoke from burning forest fires.

Simultaneously, however, the front oak doors splintered open with more shattering glass and a loud crash. Several officers had duck-walked the heavy cart of free books as a battering ram through the doors. Odysseus was just about to send another volley at the arriving cart and semi-concealed officers when his legs were jerked out from under him. A Harry Potter book whacked him on the back on his blond head.

"Get the gun!" Christian yelled. Silently a S.W.A.T. member in all black hunkered up behind him, putting a reassuring hand on his shoulder. At the same time two other officers arrived at the sprawling fifth grader. One grabbed the gun. The other put his foot on Odysseus' back as the shooter dazedly tried to get up.

"Hold still, son! Don't move or it may be your last!" He removed handcuffs from his belt and reached down and cuffed each wrist together behind Odysseus' back.

"You're hurting me!" the captive yelled.

"Not as much as you will be hurt if you don't hold still and remain quiet!"

Lieutenant Ortiz and Sergeant Helena Contreras lifted the cuffed boy to his feet. Ortiz removed his two-way radio from his belt.

"Headquarters and Coronado front office come in," he said with full voice into the device. "This is Lieutenant Ortiz breaking radio silence."

"HQ here," came one voice loud and clear. "Coronado front office here," said Principal Guadalajara's voice.

"We have suspect Odysseus Ray disarmed and in custody. We need HQ to send an ambulance: the Librarian has a leg wound that doesn't appear to be life threatening. There are believed to be no other casualties. We will bring the suspect to the front office before he is remanded to custody. Suggest calling and alerting his parents."

When the call ended, quiet applause came from the back of the room of dinosaurs and their frightened observers.

~ THIRTY-NINE ~

Coronado Elementary School would never be the same. As a learning institution its reputation was now permanently damaged and irreparable. Soon its name would probably be changed. There would be no school for students that Friday and the following Monday and Tuesday, as a respite to the students, faculty, and community. Additional security would be installed. An armed guard would be placed in the front office. Parents and guardians would consider removing their children to other schools; but then would realize copycatting meant any other school might prove even more dangerous. Staff meetings were held with various police and security instructors regarding future policies. None was aware of Odysseus Ray's immediate destination, nor what his future might bring.

On the Tuesday following the incident, the staff was summoned to reconvene for meetings. Mr. C was informed he could remove the yellow-and-black crime scene tape from across his front doors. After opening the loosely closed shattered oak-and-glass remains, he intentionally ignored the cart with glass shards sprinkled over the top shelf books as well as more covering the carpet and linoleum tile.

At his desk he opened a *State Capital Tattler* he had pulled from a machine near Starbucks. A front-page story headline read: **Student Gunfire Reaches Capital City School**. After the date and location

Mr. C began to read what only a few students in his school were capable of fully understanding:

> The City Different thought it was just that: different from other cities in other parts of the country in which there had been school shootings. Yet yesterday in the penultimate hour at the south side's Coronado Elementary School, gunfire resonated in the school Library. The gunman was a 10-year-old, an apparently disenchanted fifth grader who somehow brought his high school brother's automatic pistol to school in his backpack and began what fortunately turned out to be short-lived revenge.
>
> After shooting Librarian Christopher Connelly, who tried to intercede, before police arrival through both front and back doors, the suspect had his legs jerked out from under him by fellow student and celebrated hero Christian De Leon. Capital City Police and S.W.A.T. team members immediately grabbed the boy's weapon and subdued him. (full story on page four).

Mr. C refolded the tabloid newspaper and put it on a large plastic bin under his desk. His head was spinning, but he walked over to the book-and-glass-laden cart and stood there preoccupied. All his efforts had been for naught. School security was a myth.

Camera surveillance, guards, police drive-bys, front-office scanning devices, and vigilant Teachers hadn't avoided the inevitable. Even if the school had had metal detectors in place, there were too many outside entrance doors held open by stones, others used by cafeteria or playground staff and students, backpacks, or jackets for concealment, I.T. and other contractors coming and going at all hours, all meaning too many ways of avoiding the detectors.

He stood there looking down at the shattered glass on the carpeting and tile. It had really happened. Fortunately, his leg wound had been superficial. No students or faculty had been wounded or killed. Yet even with all the education and affluence in the world, there would always be those angry students, relatives or outsiders who felt shooting others brought at least fleeting redemption.

Was it all worth it? He wondered. Were those spending their lives trying to induce third-millennium students to read wasting their time? Would paper books and language itself be replaced by myriad audio-visual information in a constant barrage from devices, televisions, radios, screens, and other picture and sound bombardments? Was the silent world of imagination comparable to the horse gazing at faster horseless carriages whizzing by? Was the art of communication through words about to face the same extinction that life faced when an asteroid hit the planet millions of years ago?

Would parents finally say 'We've had enough?' and withdraw their kids from public and private schools for safety reasons? It appeared there was no hope in removing several hundred million guns from the public's hands: no possibility of federal and State legislators banning automatic weapons. It was American's right to bear arms and shoot at will. Even given schoolchildren being slaughtered by the hundreds. It would never stop.

Then why were ten-year-old's reaching such points of desperation? Why would someone like Odysseus Ray, with financial advantages millions of other kids lacked, go off the rails and now face an ominous future? Had the importance of close-knit families been supplanted by a hatred of antediluvian values?

Mr. C went and sat down behind his desk. But his heart was no longer in it. Getting kids to believe in abstract words requiring imagination and no illustrations might be disappearing like glaciers in global warming. What for kids in the nineteenth and twentieth centuries had been stereotypical cowboys and Indians and crusader fights were now warlike video games and superhero battles. Violence, even in many contact sports, was reaching a stage of deification. Fewer and fewer now wished to endure the trials and tribulations of teaching school. The three-class system was devolving into the two-class system with rich and poor.

Mr. C logged onto his Apple computer and discovered the usual avalanche of e-mails. He began to open them. The first was one of hundreds of entreaties to buy books from publishing houses. *At least they are trying*, he thought. Then he reached down and opened a cardboard box of new books he had received. His spirits lifted as he placed a stack of hardbacks and paperbacks with colorful covers on his desk to begin logging them in. *Well*, he thought to himself. *There are those miniature appreciative Kindergarteners who tell me they love the Library and come up and hug me. Maybe I'll give it another year...*

OTHER WORKS
by
P. J. (Paul) Christman

Santa Monica Dead Palms
Nothing More, Nothing Less
Skins of Lightning
The Madwoman of El Malpais
Black Christmas Pudding (Play)
Sour Apples (Play)
The Purple Runner

Printed in the USA
CPSIA information can be obtained
at www.ICGtesting.com
LVHW010541300324
775934LV00037B/261